WHILE THEY DIED

A MEMOIR

Robert Patterson

Book Design by: Cole + Company, Boise, Idaho

ISBN 0-9668369-0-1

Published by Patterson Press
Emmett, Idaho

Printed in the United States of America by

CHJ Publishing
1103 West Main
Middleton, Idaho 83644
(208) 585-2602

The title *WHILE THEY DIED* is an account of crooked politics, graft and corruption, black market, and poor military judgement that was being exercised in Vietnam while young American and Allied Soldiers were dying in vain. With the utmost respect to the American Flag, my Country, and the American people, I must define this war as "THE GREAT AMERICAN FIASCO." This was the War with no purpose.

This book is dedicated to
my two wonderful daughters
and my three fine sons:
Sue----Paula----Scott----Pren----Kelly
And to their loving families.

Special thanks to Paula Murphy
for her support and patience through the years
while waiting for the book to be completed.

Special thanks to Sharon Mackey
who so expertly edited the work.

Special thanks to Roger Cole
for his creative design.

Special thanks to Cort Conley
for his positive and encouraging comments.

Prologue

This is a true story about two years in Vietnam. It was a fiasco that haunts me even after thirty years. I had some good times, and I had some bad times. I saw young American soldiers die without purpose, and I witnessed the slaughter of the enemy. And I fell in love with Susie, my Vietnamese companion. It begins like this..............

The divorce was final February 9, 1967, and this was, ironically, the same date as my sixteenth wedding anniversary. It had been the past November when Georgina and I separated, and it was now mid-April. Five months without my family was devastating.

MY GOD! I had fathered five loving children: There was Susanna, who had just turned fifteen, a beautiful young lady, and thirteen year old Paulina, so sweet and genuine. Scooter was twelve, who looked to his dad for guidance, and to take him fishing and pheasant and duck hunting. Robert Pren would be eleven June 1, deserving more attention, and needing more love than the others. Little Kelly was seven, and a lovable lad. He was no trouble to anyone, and just wanted to be part of the family. My children deserved the best, and they were depending on their dad to be a good provider.

I had been a dedicated junior executive at Boise-Cascade Corporation with its numerous lumber, plywood and chipboard mills, and wholesale and retail outlets.

My relationship had been terminated with the conglomerate giant nearly two years earlier, and I was financially strapped. The only income for my family was what Georgina was making as a waitress.

Companies were impressed with my resume, but were reluctant to hire. My age of thirty-nine years and my reputation with problem drinking were serious obstacles. The chance of finding a job at a decent starting salary in the Boise area was grim.

Overseas employment in the construction field was an option, and had to be seriously considered. I had extensive experience in the wood products industry, and I would be useful in warehousing, purchasing, and expediting materials. Perhaps my only alternative would be to leave the country and start a new life.

The Vietnam War was at its height, and American companies were flocking to Southeast Asia with lucrative government contracts worth billions of dollars. Morrison-Knudsen (M-K), headquartered in Boise, was a major component of this venture.

Vietnam would have financial opportunities, and the risks in that war-ravaged country would force companies like M-K to pay top wages. I was desperate and my family needed help!

North and South Vietnam had been at war for several years, and the United States had become politically and militarily involved. North Vietnam, a communist country, was trying to reunite with South Vietnam, a democracy. The United States was assisting the South with hope it would remain a free nation.

When Boise-Cascade and I dissolved our relationship, Mr. Jim Hayes, general manager of the wholesale and retail divisions, said if I ever needed assistance to contact him. His exact words: "My door is always open."

I contacted the executive, and was immediately invited for a conference. We had enjoyed a good relationship in the past as fellow employees, and I wasn't aware of any animosities that might have developed.

Hayes rose, shook my hand, and settled back in his plush leather chair behind a sprawling walnut desk. "Bob Patterson! I understand that you're a man of leisure. What can I do for you?"

"Jim, would you pull some strings for me? I'd like to work for Morrison-Knudsen in Vietnam."

"Why Vietnam? There's a war going on over there, and you have kids to support. You might not come back!"

"Sir, overseas jobs pay good money, and I'm willing to face the perils of war to support my family. Let me explain the situation."

"O.K. Bob, I'll hear you out."

I sighed deeply, hesitating to gather my thoughts. I began explaining how a joint venture of major construction companies has been formed in Vietnam called RMK-BRJ. It was operating under the sponsorship of Morrison-Knudsen Corporation, and included as participants Raymond International, Brown and Root, Inc., and J.A. Jones Construction Company.

These giant companies had converged as a military support group for the United States Government. They pooled their resources, and were constructing a complex system of military airfields, communication facilities, off loading docks, ammunition depots, and other installations and services within Vietnam. Construction sites stretched from the mountainous north-coast of Da Nang, through the central highlands to the southern delta region of the Mekong River.

RMK started this far reaching operation in January 1962 under a $22,000,000 contract awarded by the U.S. Navy Bureau of Yards and Docks. Additional contracts had multiplied the amount to billions of U.S. taxpayer's dollars.

The venture did not include Brown and Root and J.A. Jones Construction Companies in 1962. BRJ became a participant in 1965, after the assassination of John F. Kennedy, and the swearing in of Texan Lyndon B. Johnson as President of the United States.

President Kennedy had planned to de-escalate the Vietnam War, but Johnson escalated the conflict almost immediately after Kennedy's death by encouraging the military to commit more American troops to the troubled region. Since Brown and Root was headquartered in Houston, Texas it was reasonable to assume that this was a political ploy to include the Texas company in the overall profit picture.

There were over two hundred U.S. companies in Vietnam, and

each company was working on a "cost-plus basis." There was no competitive bidding for contracts in the Vietnam operation, which translated into simple words: "THE MORE YOU SPEND—THE MORE YOU MAKE!"

I expressed to Hayes that I was a native of Idaho, and Morrison-Knudsen's name had been familiar all my life. They were reputable and experts in the construction field, and it would be a privilege to work for them.

Hayes realized I was serious about my venture, and that I was aware of the risks. My knowledge of activities in Vietnam impressed him, and my salesmanship paid off. He promised to check into the matter.

Being hired stateside eliminated the risk of seeking employment in a strange land, and the company would pay my expenses to my destination.

I anxiously waited for three weeks, and finally received an answer that my application had been denied. I felt dejected and abandoned. The situation was serious, and it boiled down to the basics for my family. Trying to be employed by a company in the States for a foreign assignment was futile. My only alternative was to plan my own destiny, and go to Southeast Asia on my own volition. After all, I'd done it before.

My first real test into the unknown was in the early 1950s when I ventured to the Territory of Alaska. It was a thirty-one hundred mile trek over the Alcan Highway to Fairbanks in January with two hundred dollars and no job prospects. I arrived at my destination to find five thousand people out of work. I was broke, and it was fifty below zero. Out of kindness an old sourdough Alaskan hired me to work in his hardware store to keep me from starving.

My wife Georgina and my daughter Susanna joined me at Fairbanks, and for nearly three years shared the good times and the hazards of the frozen North. My family grew rapidly, mainly due to the long winter nights, and no television! Paulina and Scooter joined the crew in that order.

I took the family outside to Idaho in June 1955, and worked in the local sawmill until January 1956. Having trouble adjusting to local conditions I returned to Fairbanks, and signed a one-year contract as an administrative assistant with Puget Sound And Drake Construction Company. PS&D had U.S. Government contracts and was headquartered at Fairbanks and Point Barrow.

The Alaska venture ended upon completion of my contract building radar sites along the Arctic Coast in the shadow of the North Pole.

Map of Saigon, Vietnam.

Chapter One

I desperately needed money for my venture to Vietnam, and my mother was my only source for financial support. This was a difficult situation, and probably the hardest decision in my entire life. The family had laid our beloved father to rest only two weeks before.

I dreaded asking for a loan, and then telling my mother I was going to Vietnam. She needed me at home, not running off on some wild adventure, but I had no choice.

Mom reluctantly gave me fifteen hundred dollars. It wasn't the amount, it's that she had lost one son in World War II, and dreaded the thought of losing another.

"Son, I won't deny you the loan," she said, "but you should reconsider. Georgina can't manage five children under any circumstances, and they need your love and supervision."

I emphatically shook my head. "Mom, I can't begin to make enough to survive by myself, let alone support the kids. I am behind on child support now, and before long the Ada County prosecutor will put me in his debtor's prison. The child support is set so high that I can't live in America. I'm sorry, but I have no choice. It's leave the country or go to jail." My mom cried, and hugged me with all her might. But it was final.

Travel plans had to be carefully prepared, and all details precisely worked out. I didn't have ample finances, so time was of the essence, and I couldn't afford costly mistakes. I needed to talk to someone who had worked in Vietnam, and the T-K tavern was a good place to start. I knew the owner, and it was a hangout for construction workers.

The word was spread, and after two days I met Tom Grey at the T-K. He had been with Raymond-Morrison-Knudsen (RMK) in Vietnam for six months, but poor health forced him to waive his contract, and return to the States.

Tom and I found a table at the rear of the tavern, and I ordered a large pitcher of beer. He explained that it was necessary to purchase a round trip plane ticket. I wouldn't get through U.S. or Vietnamese customs with only a one-way ticket. The two Governments didn't want American civilians wandering around Saigon broke on their butts and no jobs. There was enough black marketeering in the country without a pack of potential con artists setting up shop and causing havoc. There was a war being fought in Southeast Asia.

I hadn't figured on a round trip ticket. An immediate outlay of eleven hundred dollars would leave me four hundred. A passport was fifteen dollars, and another hundred for my medical shots and clothes.

Grey informed me that I could only get a seven day visitor's visa at the Saigon airport. In other words, I had five working days to be employed, Monday through Friday. If I didn't have an employer within the seven day period my visa would expire, and I'd have to leave the country.

I would arrange my schedule with the travel agency to arrive in Saigon on Sunday. This would give me five working days to sign a contract with an American company.

Grey told me that after I had cleared through Vietnamese customs at the Saigon Airport I should take a taxi to Tu Do Street. From there I was would create my own destiny. Grey shook my hand and wished me the best of luck.

Grey had emphasized that Tu Do street was Saigon's main drag, and Americans frequented this area more than any other. I could ask questions, and help find my way to a bar or hotel. Everyone in Vietnam knew Tu Do.

I immediately left for my mother's place in Cascade to make necessary preparations. Cascade was located seventy-five miles north of Boise in a long valley that stretched for fifty miles.

It was early Spring, and the rugged peaks were still covered with deep snow. The Payette River was a rushing torrent, and its tributaries were splashing down the mountainsides in the midst of the Spring runoff. The lush valley was turning green, and the bluebirds and robins were beginning to nest. The grass would soon be belly deep to cattle grazing in the meadows.

The quietude was great, as it allowed me to bang out some letters on Mom's old manual Royal Typewriter, and we could reminisce about my growing-up days. It would likely be awhile before we could be intimate with each other again.

I drafted a resume and a letter "To whom it may concern" to explain why I wanted to be in Vietnam. I would also need "letters of introduction."

I journeyed to Boise to obtain letters from Boise-Cascade people. I contacted Jim Hayes and Jim Frear for help, and both responded favorably. I was confident that my superiors were aware that my contributions to Boise-Cascade Corporation through the years were significant.

I returned to Mom's green paradise late in the afternoon on April 21st, and began packing my suitcase. I would wear my light blue, single-breasted suit on the trip. It looked businesslike, and was light weight and comfortable.

I had just completed my packing when Mom gently knocked on the door. She handed me my dad's 32-20 Colt Police Positive Special revolver, along with forty rounds of ammunition. The revolver fit snugly in a weather-beaten leather holster.

Dad had purchased the handgun back in the early thirties, and it was in amazingly superb condition. The hammer and trigger and the cylinder functioned with precision. I had fired it before, and it was accurate up to thirty yards. The six inch barrel made it a good defensive weapon.

"Son, take the gun with you," she said, "your Dad would want you to have it." I hugged her, but I couldn't find words. We both wiped tears, and she left the room. Mom was so small and fragile, and I shuddered to think of her spending long winter nights alone. The below zero degree temperatures and deep snow weren't pleasant for anyone, especially a seventy year old woman. She was a pioneer, and a seasoned veteran, being born at Alpha, a small village ten miles south of Cascade. But age wasn't in her favor.

I realized it was impossible to hide the firearm. I slipped it back into the holster, and placed it on top of my clothes. If U.S. or Vietnamese customs opened my suitcase they would confiscate the weapon and my passport. It was a chance that had to be taken, but I wasn't going to a country at war without a firearm.

Mom and I silently got into her car the next morning and drove to an aunt's house thirty-five miles from Boise. My estimated time of departure was early the next afternoon.

I arose the next morning, and realized this was the day to stay calm. I was mentally prepared to accept the challenge.

After I had showered, shaved, and dressed in my blue suit, I knew there was no turning back. My mom casually commented with a quick laugh that I didn't have to go to Vietnam. "Son, everything will work out at home. Come and stay with me until you can find a job. You are brave, but so foolish. I lost one son in World War II. I couldn't stand losing another. I beg you not to go."

"Please. It's hard enough to leave you and my family. I'll write soon. Don't worry."

Mom and my aunt drove me to Boise. I thanked both for their hospitality, and gave each my deepest love. Mom was a tough pioneer, and had weathered many storms.

Georgina, my ex-wife, and Paulina, my youngest daughter, were the only volunteers to drive me to the Boise airport. The other four children just wanted to say good-bye. It was hugs, kisses, and tears.

The good-byes at the airport were emotional. Thank God United Airlines announced last call for boarding the aircraft. I had said my good-byes to my loved ones in years past, while working in the Far North, but this was different. I felt like I was plummeting into sheer darkness.

I took a window seat on the Boeing 727, and anxiously waited for the departure to San Francisco International. A large, pale-faced gentleman took the seat next to mine. He was dressed in a dark gray, pin-striped suit, and a heavily starched white shirt with french cuffs. The cuffs were fastened by gold cuff links centered with small diamonds. His expensive dark blue tie sported a precisely centered diamond pin. He nodded politely, settled back, took a deep sigh and relaxed. He was a frequent traveler.

After being airborne for several minutes my friend asked if I cared for a drink. I ordered a Bourbon and water, and he asked for scotch and soda, and his accent and mannerism proved his English ancestry.

Our conversation was intimate, discussing our very personal and private pasts. His name was Connelly, and his home was on the outskirts of London. I enjoyed our visit and momentarily forgot my forthcoming mission.

It was absolutely amazing how our lives had paralleled each other's, and how effortless it was for us to relate. His wife had divorced him five years previously, and he had five children at home in England. He was now a successful factory sales representative, and traveled extensively throughout the U.S., Europe, the Middle East and Orient.

Connelly could relate wholly to my present circumstances; divorced, apparently still in love, and with five loving children. He asked my destination.

"I'm going to Saigon, Vietnam, and hope to become employed. I've never been out of the U.S., except Alaska."

"My word Bob, you're going to the sex capitol of the world!"

We laughed, and ordered one last drink together. Just one more for the road. We had truly become exceptionally good, special friends in a way that lasts a long time. I hoped our paths might cross again.

The United Airlines captain called over the intercom, and advised to fasten seat belts. My breathing quickened and my heart thumped rapidly in my throat as the aircraft approached San Francisco International airport.

While They Died

Pan American Airlines was my first priority at San Francisco International, as they would be my keeper until I reached my destination at Saigon. My luggage was checked through after getting an O.K. from U.S. custom officials, and thank God they didn't ask to open my suitcase and expose the revolver.

I wasn't familiar with Pan Am's famous champagne flight to Hawaii, so I was delighted when the flight attendant announced that beverage would be served free of charge on the entire flight. I thanked her at least eight times for the sparkling wine. It would be dusk when the plane reached the Islands.

I wasn't disappointed with the view of the Pacific Ocean. At thirty-three thousand feet I continually explored the horizon, and I sensed the vastness of endless blue space. I was anxious to go beyond.

We approached Honolulu and the captain informed the passengers the aircraft was circling over Diamond Head. Moments later we touched down.

As I descended down the steps of the Boeing 727 a hot blast of humid air slapped me in the face, and I could feel the effects of the champagne. I enjoyed the warm breeze as I strolled toward the terminal. It was still April which meant cold weather in Idaho.

It seemed like forever before we started boarding the plane for Guam, via Wake Island. Manila was the final stop before departing for Vietnam; obviously this flight was the milk run to the orient.

I located my seat, fastened my seat belt and burrowed in. Across the aisle on my left was a fifteen year old boy; I greeted him warmly and shook his hand. The kid's name was Jimmy Thompson, and had been staying with an uncle in San Francisco. His dad had been employed with RMK for eighteen months, and his mother had been in Vietnam for four months. His dad would meet him at the Saigon airport. What luck! I felt confident I could get information to steer me in the right direction.

Since we were traveling east the plane literally caught up with the sun, and this was one bright day. Daylight would prevail all the way to our destination.

I studied the people on the plane, talked with many, and asked their destinations. Most were Asians going to Vietnam, Thailand, and Hong Kong. There were several Indians aboard wearing turbans and native dress. Much to my surprise all were from Saigon, had lived there for many years, and owned businesses.

The stop at Guam was short lived, but I had time to stretch my legs and marvel at a real South Sea Island. I discovered that packaged liquor could be purchased in the terminal for two dollars a fifth. Even though Guam was a possession of the United States, liquor carried no local or federal tax. It was a reminder of how Americans were paying exorbitant taxes back home. I bought a couple of fifths of bourbon for future reference.

Guam residents were courteous and hospitable, and their broad smiles exposed perfect white teeth. It wouldn't be difficult to fall in love with these happy and caring people.

The closer we approached Southeast Asia the more I could feel the dense humidity and the penetrating heat. It was a healthy atmosphere, and the air was fresh and clean.

Once again we were high above the vast Pacific Ocean. Time passed, and the passengers were obviously content. The quiet was interrupted when the captain announced the Pan Am 707 was approaching the Philippine coastline.

Beautiful islands were surrounded by deep blue water and endless white sandy beaches. Huge waves tumbled over the top of the water, and the massive green velvet jungle stretched far beyond what the eye could see.

Soon we were in sight of the Manila airstrip. After a long, gliding approach we came to a gradual stop. I headed for the bar in the terminal for fortification, while the aircraft was being re-fueled. Jimmy Thompson, my adopted friend, said he would pass the time by just watching people inside the terminal.

He and I had something in common. I didn't want to lose sight of Jimmy, nor did he want to lose sight of me. Saigon was two and a half hours flying time from Manila, and I certainly wanted to meet his parents. A few minutes with the Thompsons would be comforting, and potentially profitable.

The Pan Am Boeing 707 roared down the runway, and my heart pounded inside my chest, and my mouth was dry as cotton. My gut knotted as the aircraft suddenly climbed into an endless blue sky.

The landing gear retracted into the wing, and the smoking light came on. I ordered a soft drink and settled back in my seat. Two and a half hours flying time and I would begin two years of an unforgettable experience. It would be filled with happiness and sadness, love and bitterness, and adventure.

Jimmy was pre-occupied talking to a young lady and quite unconcerned. This was an education for this young man, learning about a different society, and how to cope with every day life in a foreign land. He and I would learn how the Vietnamese survived in a country that has had been ruled by outsiders for centuries.

The Chinese had ruled Vietnam for five hundred years. The French ruled them for eighty years, persecuted them, bled the people of their possessions, and denigrated them as the lowest form of life. The Americans would free them and educate them, and introduce them to democracy. I, too, had much to learn about the Vietnamese people, and war, and death.

Time went quickly. The plane dipped its right wing, and gradually aimed its nose towards the runway for the final approach to the Saigon airport.

Saigon was a sprawling city of three million people, and activity at the busy airport was bustling. I was hot and tired, my knees were weak, and I would soon test my courage at the customs counter.

Jimmy and I walked together, and as we entered the terminal his eyes lit up and he started grinning. His dad was standing on the other side of customs waving to him. We found our suitcases, and I knew the time had come to face the inevitable. I hoped that I could appear totally nonchalant, and hoped that customs wouldn't open my suitcase.

White uniformed custom officials were strategically located at three separate lines to receive passengers for inspection. There was a long table in front of each Vietnamese official, which allowed an inspector to deal with each passenger and check personal effects as they approached. Police armed with automatic weapons were stationed at various locations within the terminal and at all exits.

Our line consisted of all Americans, and two other lines were mixed with Europeans, Australians, Asians and Indians. Passenger's luggage was being opened and searched at random.

A white uniformed Vietnamese inspector opened Jimmy's suitcase and a toilet kit he was hand-carrying. He vigorously rummaged through everything, and then directed him to another official seated at the end of the table.

My heart raced, and there was a hollow feeling in the pit of my stomach. It was the feeling I got in high school, just before the start of a very important basketball game.

The Vietnamese inspector, who had a remarkable resemblance to Peter Lorre, slowly looked me up and down. He eye-balled my suitcase and looked straight through me, but made no attempt to open my luggage. With a slight gesture of his head I was directed towards the man who stamped the visas for approval.

This official inspected my shot record, took my passport in hand and examined it thoroughly. He stamped the passport with a seven day visitor's permit, and I was on my way. I looked up and thanked God.

Jimmy and his dad were waiting in the main lobby of the terminal, and he had told his dad of my predicament. His dad shook my hand firmly. "Bob, I'm Hank. It's nice knowing you, and thanks for seeing to my son all the way from San Francisco."

Hank, Jimmy and I walked outside to the street where taxis and lambrettas were waiting for passengers. The lambretta was a new experience. It was about eight feet long over all, was supported by three wheels, and steered by handle bars the size of a large motorcycle. It was equipped with benches on both sides in the back, and it's top was attached to slatted side boards. The motor resembled a 1940 model Maytag washing machine, and a thick smoke screen of oil was escaping from the exhaust. They were economical, and less expensive than taxis.

Yellow topped and blue bodied taxis parked at the curb resembled the Volkswagen Beetle. They were of the nineteen forties vintage, and some were the worse for wear. God only knows what held them together. At least, both lambrettas and taxis were clean inside and out.

Hank motioned for us to get into the back of a lambretta, and he said something in Vietnamese. The driver started the motor of the vehicle that sounded like a sick lawn mower, and we went bump-a-tee-bump down the dusty street.

Traffic was heavy with small foreign cars darting in and out beeping their horns like crazy. There were dozens of people on bicycles traveling near the curbs. American military vehicles were inching their way. Army jeeps, huge six by six GI trucks, three quarter ton weapon carriers, pick-up trucks, and hundreds of Honda motorcycles crept along in unison. It was amazing how the traffic could flow at all, especially with numerous vehicles entering the mainstream and miraculously blending in.

People were everywhere! Most were dressed in short sleeve shirts, casual pants and thongs on their feet. The bulk of the women wore plain grey tops and black shiny pants. Some of the younger women were wearing tight fitting skirts, and some wore their native dress. Young men wore form fitting pants, and cuffs were drawn tightly around the ankles. Every young woman my eyes encountered absolutely fascinated me. Their figures were flawless from the tops of their heads to the tips of their toes.

It was twenty minutes before our lambretta driver pulled into a narrow street. Hank paid the man, and the three of us walked down a narrow path, weaving in and out of shabby looking buildings. Hank's house resembled hundreds of others, and I was amazed how he located it.

As we entered into the living room a woman pecked Hank on the cheek, and then turned her attention to Jimmy. Tears of joy ran down her face, and it appeared she might hug him to death.

"Bob, this is Shirley, my wife of twenty-two years."

"Nice meeting you Shirley."

"Honey, Bob took care of Jimmy on the trip over here. He needs a downtown hotel until he can find a job. You get around more than me. Any ideas?"

Shirley raised her eyebrows in surprise. "Bob, you mean to say that you are in Saigon without a job or sponsor?"

"I tried to get on with RMK back in the States with no avail. I have just divorced, so with five kids, it's essential for me to get on a payroll."

"How much cash do you have," she asked, curiously.

"I declared thirty U.S. dollars at Vietnamese customs, and they gave me the equivalent in piasters."

"My God man," Hank asked, "is that all you have?"

"I've got a hundred dollar bill in the heel of my shoe."

"You best change the money on the black market," Shirley advised, without hesitation. "A hundred dollars in U.S. green would have a good exchange rate. You can probably get two hundred-thirty." Hank stopped her.

"Bob needs a place to stay tonight and start looking for a job tomorrow. There isn't time to teach him the ropes about changing money on the black market. He'll learn soon enough."

"Bob, we'll get you a taxi to downtown Saigon," Hank said, encouraging. "I'll tell the driver to stop on Tu Do Street at the Continental Palace. It is more expensive than other hotels, but you'll be safe."

"Relax Bob," Shirley said softly, squeezing my arm. "Just try not to appear like a newcomer to Southeast Asia. Don't tell anyone it's your first trip into the country.

"Look Bob," Hank said, reassuringly, "we're not trying to frighten you, but if you aren't alert, somebody will steal everything you own. Stealing is a way of life in Vietnam."

"Sounds a lot like the good ol' U.S.A.," I said.

Jimmy and I bid each other farewell. His eyes were wet, and my hug proved my affection for him.

Hank and Shirley hailed a taxi. Hank shook my hand, and Shirley gave me a reassuring hug. "Good luck and take care. Maybe we'll see you again." I felt forever indebted.

While They Died

Chapter Three

The taxi driver came to a sudden halt in front of the Continental Hotel, and I hesitantly stepped to the curb. He sat my suitcase on the sidewalk, nodded politely, and was gone.

Weariness had taken its toll on my mind and body. It had been fifty-two hours from the time I boarded the plane at the Boise Airport until it touched down in Saigon. I hadn't slept soundly and was feeling anxiety. The thought of a hot shower and a cold beer sounded like sweet music.

I stood on the sidewalk with my suitcase in hand, and looked at the Continental in complete awe. Facing the huge structure revealed a wide, open entrance. Attached to the left side of the structure was an open-air bar and restaurant which was supported by large marble columns. Snow white linen cloths covered round tables.

With suitcase in hand I walked to the registration desk. I was greeted by a Vietnamese clerk neatly dressed in black trousers, a starched white shirt, a black bow tie, and wearing a black blazer. I asked how much for a room. In a thick French accent he replied that rooms were twenty-five dollars in U.S. military script (MPC notes), or three thousand piasters. But he had no vacancies. I was relieved because I just couldn't afford it.

I walked to the street, and set the suitcase down. I was amazed at the throng of people on the streets. It was late afternoon, and it was humid. I stood in the shadows of a setting sun, and wondered what time it was back home, and what the kids might be doing. I remembered my return plane ticket, and seriously considered running for home.

Suddenly out of the nowhere a small Asian man approached. He bowed politely, and picked up my suitcase. He put it on his shoulder, waved to me, and walked toward Tu Do Street. I didn't know whether he was stealing my suitcase or wanted me to follow. Every few steps he stopped, turned around, and waved. I weaved in and out of people on the densely crowded sidewalk never losing sight; the intense heat made it almost unbearable. My God, I was exhausted.

My newly found friend walked across Tu Do street. He made a left turn, walked two blocks, and made a right turn. I followed close behind. He stopped. The little man pointed to a sign above him that read "Royal Hotel." He walked through the single wood door, sat my suitcase down in front of the desk, and rang a bell to summon the manager.

The manager entered the room, fetched several bills from under the counter, and handed the money to my suitcase bearer. The man grinned from ear to ear, stuffed the money into his pocket, and bowed out gracefully. I realized that's how people were encouraged to stay at the Royal Hotel. Perhaps unorthodox, but I was impressed with their free enterprise system.

Benny, the manager, was a short, plump and happy little man, who was bubbling over with friendliness and kindness. I knew immediately that I trusted him. There was no doubt in my mind. I signed the register, and he asked for twelve hundred piasters. This was less than half the price as the Continental.

With suitcase in hand I followed Benny up the stairs to the second floor. We walked down a narrow hallway, and he paused to unlock the door. I took the key and entered, and the little man politely bowed and left.

It was nice to be alone. I lay on the bed, and looked around the room. Directly above, a ceiling fan wobbled clumsily as it slowly turned. There was a small desk with a table lamp, but there was no telephone or pictures hanging on the walls. I stood, and walked into the bathroom. Not bad. There was a wash basin with hot and cold water, a mirror above the basin, and a shower. This was adequate, and under the circumstance I was completely satisfied.

I sat back on the bed, and observed several small lizards clinging to the walls. They seemed to be planted there. One moved towards an insect faster than the eye could see, devoured it, and remained motionless. I wanted to shower.

The cool water was soothing, but the shower floor soon filled with water. I noticed enormous cockroaches swimming around, evidently enjoying themselves, and I sincerely hoped they were happy, because I was in heaven.

A complete change of clothes was in order. I opened the suitcase, and stared at my revolver. I slipped into clean duds, placed the gun under the mattress, shrugged my shoulders, and hoped for the best.

It was dusk, and the streets were less crowded. I didn't want to stray far for fear of getting lost. I walked to the corner of Tu Do, and found a restaurant. I wanted a good stiff belt of booze, but my better judgement said no. All I needed was to get smashed, and probably get rolled.

A waitress brought water and greeted me in French, and handed me a menu written in French. I pointed to the plate of a man seated at the next table, and nodded my head. Soon I was eating what I think was pork stew and french bread.

I ordered coffee, and reviewed my success over the past eight thousand miles. Oh my God! I suddenly realized the restaurant was empty. I paid the tab and hurriedly walked to the street.

Damn! The street was deserted and strangely silent. Not one living soul or vehicle in sight. Suddenly I spotted two white-uniformed policemen on the far side of Tu Do street, and realized they were focused on my movement.

It was 2030 hours (military time) and pitch black, and I wasted little time returning to the hotel. A petrifying shock wave traveled through my body. A gigantic accordion-type gate was pulled together and secured with a heavy chain and padlock. How was I going to get inside the hotel?

The gate was at least ten feet high, and made of thick solid iron vertical bars. Horizontal bars were secured between each section of the gate, and pointed spears were mounted on the top, obviously discouraging intruders from attempting to climb up and over.

A dim light burned above the registration desk. No one in sight, so I whistled loudly in hopes of attracting attention. It was absolutely futile. God, it was quiet, and I dreaded the thought of spending the night in the street. I frantically shook the gate again and again. I looked upwards and without hesitation started climbing. I was about two feet from the top when I looked downward. Benny had come to my rescue. "You don't know eight o'clock curfew?" he said, laughing and waving his arms. "You go bed now. Choi oi!"

Tomorrow was the big challenge. Five days to find a job or return to America in total defeat. My mind flashed back thousands of miles to where my home had been just hours ago.

I fumbled through my suitcase, and located a writing pad and pen. I expressed my love and affection to my family, and it was simple enough to describe my emotions, but I could not conceal my loneliness.

Satisfaction was attained after several pages of heartfelt words. I folded the letter, and slipped it into an envelope. I couldn't describe the pain, and it crossed my mind to go home, but sleep triumphed.

It was 0700 hours when the sun entered through the window. I jumped out of bed, not hesitating to face my challenge. After showering I donned my favorite blue suit. I looked businesslike. I charged down the stairs, and greeted Benny. The coolness of the morning air was refreshing, as I headed for the French restaurant.

I enjoyed a good breakfast, and drank several cups of delicious coffee. I sat at the table watching people bustle up and down Tu Do street, and even in war time it was apparent that life goes on. The local citizens appeared unconcerned; perhaps they had faith about their future democratic society, if and when it might come.

I reluctantly walked back to the hotel, pondering what to do first. I needed to meet people and ask questions about how and where to find a job.

I tried to appear casual as I approached the desk where Benny was tending to daily business. He knew I had just come into the country, and in his coyness, was waiting for me. Smiling cheerfully, he pointed in the direction of the bar in an adjoining room.

It was early and business was slow. I cautiously sauntered towards two men in their early thirties sitting at the bar, each sipping an American beer.

"Are you Bob?"

I answered with a nod.

"Benny told us you checked into the Royal last night, and you're probably looking for a job. Am I on course?"

"You're on course, and so is Benny." All three laughed, which broke the ice. "Could use some advice about where to start looking for work."

One was American and the other Australian, and each had been in Vietnam for two and half years. They were employed by Alaska Barge, and had just completed contracts. Both were returning to their respective homes for a much needed vacation. They had been rewarded handsomely as wages were far better in Vietnam than in most countries, including the U.S.

The two seasoned veterans had been discussing my predicament. They agreed I should to go to the United States Consulate and get a list of American contractors with contracts in Vietnam. When I returned to the Royal they would make suggestions about which companies would be the most receptive to hiring me. Wages would be a factor, as they varied widely among contractors.

I expressed my thanks, and went back into the hotel lobby to talk with Benny.

"Everything O.K. Bob?"

"Thanks for your help. I am grateful to you. Where is the U.S. Consulate Benny? How do I get there?"

"I go get cyclo. I have driver friend. He will take you where you want to go. He no hit you on head, and take money. No Sweat." The little man chuckled.

There are two types of cyclo-taxis in Vietnam. Both were three wheeled vehicles with the passenger seat located on the front-end. One cyclo pedaled like a bicycle, and the other was motor-driven.

Benny said that most cyclo drivers wore wooden shoes. Sometimes they suddenly turned into an alley, removed a shoe, quickly attacked and stole their customer's valuables.

He left and quickly returned with my transportation. I had the letter to mail, so he told the cyclo driver to stop at the buu din, and not to lose sight of me under any circumstances.

Cautiously, I climbed into the bucket on the front of the cyclo, and the driver pedaled towards Tu Do street. The pavement gradually inclined for several blocks before leveling off. My trustworthy driver's face showed signs of strain, but his legs appeared amazingly strong, and I wondered how many daily trips he made up the hill.

We approached the buu din, and papa san stopped. It looked like any post office in the States, only it wasn't the most modern facility.

A clerk looked at the letter, asked for two hundred piasters, and handed me several large stamps. They were huge, but I managed to leave the address exposed on the envelope. I was sure the folks back home were anxiously waiting for news.

My cyclo driver was waiting, and he continued grinding away until we reached the consulate. He pulled along side the curb and stopped.

A small sign read "United States Consulate." I wasn't too impressed with the appearance of the building. It was old and badly needed paint.

Located next to the Consulate was the handsome U.S. Embassy building. The new structure had just recently been occupied by U.S. Ambassador Ellsworth Bunker and his 250 man staff. RMK-BRJ, the general contractor, had every right to be proud of excellent workmanship in the construction of this project.

The Embassy occupied a three acre compound along Thong Nhut Boulevard. Six stories high, 208 feet long and 49 feet wide, it had 240 rooms for offices, lobbies, conferences and communication facilities. Among its many features was a roof-top helicopter pad, a convenience that eliminated a time-consuming trip through congested Saigon traffic to Tan Son Nhut Airport.

The new Embassy stood well off the street and was surrounded by an eight-foot wall of reinforced concrete. Its upper stories were protected, as well as enhanced, by a facade of precast concrete

Robert Patterson

latticework, and all windows were of plexiglass. It also had its own water and power supply.

I walked to the entrance of the Embassy where a plaque had been placed to explain the history of the construction and dedication.

The new building was dedicated by Ambassador Bunker to "that noble band of Americans," both military and civilian, "who have served their nation in Vietnam." The new Embassy's dedicatory plaque was inscribed "EMBASSY OF THE UNITED STATES OF AMERICA - Built in time of war - Dedicated to the cause of peace - In memory of those who have served their nation in Vietnam - Ellsworth Bunker - Ambassador"

"This building," said Ambassador Bunker, "stands as a symbol of our commitment to the Vietnamese people. Nearly a million fighting men and more than 10,000 civilians have served the United States in Vietnam since 1954. These are very special Americans who justly deserve to be remembered."

This elaborate structure cost the U.S. taxpayer millions! Furthermore, it was inscribed "built in time of war." War was never declared by the U.S. Congress.

My driver sat motionless on his cyclo as I approached the Consulate. I ambled up to a long counter, and waited. A young, neatly dressed Vietnamese receptionist advanced and asked if she could be of service?

"Do you have a list of U.S. contractors working in Vietnam?"

She politely nodded, and left the room.

The time dragged, as I anxiously waited. Presently the young lady reappeared carrying a document comprised of several pages. I thanked her, and walked to the street.

My driver still remained stoically silent, as I paused to scan my prize. I couldn't believe this! There were multiple pages of contractors. The list numbered 231 companies in alphabetical order complete with addresses. My morale shot up a thousand points on the survival scale.

I boarded the cyclo, and the driver eagerly headed toward the Royal. It was downhill all the way to Tu Do Street and the hotel. I glanced back at the driver, and he showed positive signs of relief.

I went directly to the bar where the American and Australian were waiting. They were casually drinking beer and waiting for my return from the Consulate.

The Australian saluted. "Hi Yank. You strike pay-dirt?"

My two new acquaintances thumbed through the list of names with their eyes growing wider and wider. Their heads nodded with approval, as they checked off names of contractors.

The two seasoned veterans were amazed that the extended list contained not only Saigon street addresses, but it also indicated what U.S. Government agency they were affiliated. There was U.S. Army, Navy and Air Force. USAID, of course, that was the U.S. taxpayer's giveaway program. A lot of companies were associated with OICC, which stood for *Operation's Intelligence Command and Control.* Nobody will ever know what the U.S. Government was hiding with such a sophisticated name.

The American said there was no doubt Alaska Barge & Transport was the best company, and that they paid top dollar. The list continued with Air America. But it was CIA. I would probably be manning a machine gun on one of the CIA's gunships stationed in Thailand that were raising havoc in Vietnam and Cambodia.

My new friends checked off Pacific Architects & Engineers, Page Communications Engineering Inc., Philco Ford Corporation, Pope Evans & Robbins International, Ltd., RMK-BRJ, Sealand Services Inc., Ralph M. Parsons Co., Trans Asia Engineering Assoc., Inc., and Vinnel Corporation.[1]

"This should keep you busy for a while," the Australian said, smiling. "Give 'em hell, Yank!"

The American stood and firmly grasp my hand. "Bob, you got guts. Think positive and keep your eyes open!"

The morning was nearly gone, and my friends suggested that I wait until 1300 hours before taking a taxi to Alaska Barge's office. Their offices would be closed at noon for lunch. Since I didn't speak Vietnamese, it was suggested I write the street address on paper, or on the palm of my hand. Show it to the taxi driver and he would understand. Furthermore, Alaska Barge's office was located in the Gia Dinh precinct. It was on the outskirts of Saigon and a thirty minute ride.

[1] Appendix-List of U.S. Contractors in Vietnam.

The veterans gave me some last minute advice. "Be alert at all times, use common sense, be patient, and remember that nobody in Saigon is in a hurry to do anything."

I had some time to kill before venturing to Gia Dinh, and I needed to cash my U.S. hundred dollar greenback. The meager cash I declared at the Saigon airport was gone. Benny gave me directions to the Bank of America.

The bank was within walking distance of the hotel, and luckily I didn't get lost. I approached a Vietnamese teller and handed him the hundred dollar greenback. I asked for the equivalent of eighty dollars in piasters, and twenty dollars in U.S. military script.

I was suppose to have declared all American currency at the airport's Vietnamese customs. The teller looked at the "C" note, and immediately called an American. He informed me I could get into serious trouble by having U.S. greenbacks in my possession. I explained how I had just arrived in the country, and really didn't know any better.

The American looked around to see if we were being watched, then quickly slipped the piasters and MPC notes into my hand. He pointed to the door, raised his eye brows, and I was out of there.

It was past 1300 hours, and I was anxious to go to Alaska Barge's office. I wrote 24-A Chi Lang, Gia Dinh on paper, and hailed a taxi. The driver glanced at the address, made a U-turn in the middle of the street, and sped up Hai ba Trung Street toward my objective. Every time another car started to infringe on the driver's domain, or if a pedestrian walked into the lane of traffic, the driver honked the horn, and honked and honked. I was beginning to understand. This town was one crazy circus.

It was 1400 hours when the taxi stopped at Alaska Barge. I paid the driver three hundred piasters and walked inside the office. The place was humming with busy people.

A middle aged American wearing suntans and a short sleeved shirt ambled by. "Sir, excuse me. Can you direct me to the personnel manager?"

"Stand by one. Waa, show this guy to Harrison's office." He gave me a thumbs-up, and disappeared.

3

The small Vietnamese receptionist obliged. "Come please. Mr Harrison maybe see you. O.K.?" I followed her down the hall to a room and she gestured for me to sit.

The American behind the desk was smothered with papers. He looked up. "What's your business?"

"My name's Bob Patterson, and am looking for a job."

He leaned over the desk and shook my hand. "I'm John Harrison, and we're not hiring. Who you working for?"

"Sir, I just got in from the States yesterday, and you're the first company I've contacted. I have a resume, letters of introduction, and would appreciate if you would look at my work history."

Harrison appeared dubious as I handed over my documents. "Just got here yesterday? I haven't seen anyone come from the States without a job. You're not pulling my leg?"

"No sir, I need work. Here's my passport, and as you can see, it is stamped April 24, 1967. Please, at least, look at my credentials. I understand that you're a good company to work for."

John looked at my papers quite carefully. "You have experience in warehousing, and I see that you have worked on construction projects in Alaska. We have a hard time finding good men that are willing to work, and have know-how. So many Americans we hire are overseas bums, or international bums, if you prefer. A lot of them have been beating around the Orient since World War II. They're cut-throats; they can't be trusted, and they are lazy. But don't get me wrong, we do have a few damn good men."

Harrison continued to thumb through a large stack of papers, and wearily shook he head. "Look Bob. If you'll come back next week, I can put you to work. I have explicit orders from the project manager not to hire. We're firing several bad apples this week. It's kind of a general house cleaning, but I can honestly use you."

Self control was important, but the job was slipping out of my grasp. "Dammit sir. My visa expires this coming Saturday, and they will run my butt out of the country. I've got to find a sponsor pronto."

Harrison was trying to help me, and I realized he had his orders. "I am sorry, Patterson. If you don't find anything, and can stay in the country until next week, I will personally get you on with Alaska

Barge."

"I simply don't have the cash to leave the country, come back next week, and get another seven day visa," I said, dejectedly. "I better keep looking. Thanks."

Harrison shook my hand. "Damn Patterson, this is a tough break. Best of luck."

I hailed a taxi and within the hour was safely standing at the Hotel's desk. Benny could tell that I hadn't succeeded, and suggested I go to the bar.

The beer was satisfying, and I ordered a refill. After weighing my present situation, I was satisfied with the day. I had a list of contractors, and had learned how to get around Saigon. Tomorrow won't be wasted time. Mapping out my itinerary would be simple enough.

After a tasty bowl of Chinese noddle soup I went directly to my room. I took a quick, refreshing shower with my friendly cockroaches, and bid my cherished little gecko lizards a pleasant good night. I checked the revolver under the mattress, and thanked God for getting me through another day.

Benny greeted me with his very special good morning, and waited for my first question of the day. I took the contractor's list out of my plastic folder and pointed to Pacific Architects & Engineers, 135 Nguyen Hue. "How do I get to this street?"

"Nguyen Hue is tee-tee from hotel, no go same same Tu Do. You go other way."

I thanked my friend and walked to the sidewalk. I took a left and discovered the first street was Nguyen Hue. I sauntered along to number 135. PA&E was stenciled on the door.

I knocked and entered a large room. A middle aged man was sitting at a drafting table obviously engrossed in his work. He slowly turned, and curiously peered over the top of horn-rimmed glasses.

"Excuse me sir. My name is Bob Patterson, and I'm looking for Pacific Architects and Engineers."

While They Died

"**I**'m Larry Miller, and there are two Pacific Architects & Engineers in Saigon. This is a small company that I started nine years ago. You want the PA&E located in Phu Nhuan Precinct. It's in the vicinity of Tan Son Nhut Air Base. You go Hai ba Trung to Vo di Nguy, and right to Nguyen Hue street. It's on the outskirts of the city and across the road from the only golf course in Vietnam."

"Mr. Miller, may I share a few moments with you?"

"Sure Bob, what's on your mind?"

"Last Sunday was my first day in the country. I'm looking for a job, so any help is most welcome. You've been here for nine years?"

"Yes, this has been my home since '58. My wife and I divorced that year, and I needed a diversion. I have a degree in civil engineering, and after extensive research discovered Southeast Asia was in dire need of people with my credentials. I'm not wealthy, but I'm comfortable and content. Material things aren't a priority."

The engineer offered me a chair and continued his story. "I've found unequivocal serenity. I didn't think this kind of euphoria existed on earth. I attribute most of my happiness to my lovely Vietnamese wife who is blessed with indisputable integrity, decency and self respect.

"This is quite personal, but I'll tell you something that I've never divulged to anyone. Believe me, and I'm not bragging. Dianne was twenty seven years old when I married her, and she was still a 'cherry girl'. I mean, one who still has her virginity. This should tell you something." He gazed out the window and slowly shook his head.

Larry Miller wanted to expound, and I was willing to listen. "Bob, my beloved Vietnam is a disaster. When I arrived in Saigon it was quiet and peaceful. The city wasn't overflowing with people. Nine years ago bicycles were the main mode of transportation, but today it's exploded with cars and trucks and motorcycles.

"My God! Today's Saigon is a nightmare. Both the communists and the allied forces are gearing up for something. The big show is looming on the horizon.

"Bars and nightclubs are on every corner of the city, and prostitution is commonplace. Many of our young women have been forced to become whores. Their husbands have been killed in the war and most have children to support. These are warm and decent people, and it's unfortunate and very sad."

"Larry, you mentioned overflowing with people. I don't understand?"

"Bob, refugees are literally pouring into Saigon from outlying villages. The American and ARVN troops, that is, the Army of the Republic of Vietnam, and other allied troops have raised havoc all around Saigon. They're killing women and children and old men and burning their villages. The people are frightened. The peasants have little alternative but to take refuge in the larger cities. The Saigon people take entire families into their homes, and share their food and shelter. Can you imagine ten to fifteen men, women and children living in a four hundred square foot room?

"The Vietnamese people adjust to adverse conditions much easier than you and me. They have been fighting wars for centuries. The Chinese ruled Vietnam for five hundred years, and the French dominated and persecuted them for another eighty years. But they are survivors."

I informed Larry that I had smuggled a Colt revolver into Saigon. "Bob, you're a survivor, too. I'll put it in my safe if you'd like. I've never had anything stolen."

"I'll see how the job search goes. Thanks, Larry."

Miller was angry. "Beginning with Nguyen Cao Ky, Vietnam's prime minister to top military brass, government officials have become totally corrupt. Our massive local police force is overflowing with dishonesty and treachery. We refer to the police as the 'white mice'. Money is their only objective, and it will buy anything in Vietnam."

"Bob, I am leaving Saigon. I can't tolerate the frustrations and adversities created by politics, war and communism. I'm moving my family to Singapore. It is a small country, but the people are well disciplined. The city is clean. It has a low crime rate, firearms are totally forbidden, and it is drug free. Their president has integrity, and he cares for his people."

Larry handed me a map of Saigon. "Take this, it might help." He shook my hand. "Good-bye Bob, and best of luck."

I really enjoyed the time with Miller, but I had to focus on PA&E. I hurried to the street, and hailed a taxi. In an expert way I wrote on paper - Phu Nhuan - 135 Nuygen Hue. The taxi driver looked at the address.

The taxi went up Hai ba Trung Street. We turned on Vo di Nguy Street to where Nguyen Hue intersected. There was a roadblock at the entrance to Nguyen Hue Street. The golf course and PA&E's office were off limits to unauthorized personnel.

I paid the taxi driver. It was hot, and I was fortunate that the road was lined with giant Philippine Mahogany trees that rendered welcomed shade.

By the time I arrived at the entrance to PA&E's office I was carrying my coat under my arm, my shirt was saturated, and sweat was pouring down my face.

I stopped to cool off under some trees and watched a foursome with envy as they prepared to tee-off on number one hole at the golf course. It looked like paradise, and I envied the privileged few that were enjoying themselves.

I took a deep breath, and strolled into Pacific Architect & Engineer's office. It was an ancient wood structure, but the main office looked well laid out. Most of the employees I could see were Asian.

I walked to the receptionist's desk, and asked a petite young lady to see the personnel manager.

"Please sit. Mr. Brunnel very busy man. May take long time."

The day was still young, so I waited on a bench with another man. This was an opportunity to start a conversation and learn about PA&E. This guy was deeply tanned, about my age, and was neatly dressed in a short sleeve white shirt and suntans.

"Hello sir. Do you work for PA&E?"

"Yeah, I've been with PA&E nine months. I work at their material storage warehouse in Cholon, and I'm here to see the paymaster to get a draw. It's against company policy to write personal checks and cash them downtown Saigon. I guess they are trying to stop money changing on the black market."

"I don't know anything about changing money. I just arrived in Saigon on Sunday. I'm trying to get a job. Tell me about PA&E."

"Oh, PA&E has been around since the Korean War. Several ex-army people, along with some U.S. Government civilian workers, got their heads together and started a support group. They convinced the military that they had more expertise in warehousing, maintenance, and shipping and receiving. This freed military personnel to focus on dealing with ordnance and other military supplies."

This guy was loaded with information, so I kept pumping him. I got him stopped long enough to ask his name.

"Henry Wilkins."

"Bob's my name. It's a pleasure."

"You see the secretaries working in the office? Most are Koreans." He pointed to one. "See her facial features differ somewhat from that of a Vietnamese. They are physically stouter, although they are about the same height."

Henry paused to light a cigarette. "The Korean women control this company. They might lead you to believe their husbands call the shots. No way. Korean women make the major decisions, and they control the cash. Koreans are tough people. They can be gentle, or they can be mean as hell. Absolutely ruthless."

Wilkins explained how large PA&E had grown through the years with contracts in Vietnam, Okinawa, Hawaii, and other Pacific Islands.

The charming little secretary came forward. "You come now. Mr. Brunnel see you in office."

She walked down the hallway very erect. My eyes were fixed on her cute little buns and her well shaped legs. She stopped at an office door and gently knocked. A deep, commanding voice on the other side directed me to enter.

The name plate on the metal army desk was inscribed Jasper Brunnel, Personnel Manager. The tall man stood upright, and put his hand out. "Brunnel here. What can I do for you?"

"I'm Bob Patterson, fresh in from the States Mr. Brunnel. It is my understanding that your company deals in warehousing, maintenance, and other support activities for the military. My resume is current, and I have letters of introduction from past employers concerning my experience." I hesitated to catch my breath.

"Sir, Please forgive me if I seem to be over aggressive, but I feel confident that my background will be an asset to your cause in Vietnam. My practical knowledge will be beneficial, and——." I was abruptly interrupted by the personnel manager.

"Hold on, Patterson! You don't want to see me. Our superintendent in charge of inside storage and open storage warehousing makes the decisions to hire. Here, I'll write an inter-office memo to Tom Kraig. He may be interested in hiring you. You seem to be determined and God knows you're willing. We need experienced people."

It was 1045 hours, and time was in my favor. Brunnel scribbled an introduction on a memo pad. "Go to our warehouse at the old rice mill in Cholon. That's where Kraig's office is located."

"How do I get there, Sir? Is Cholon another city in Vietnam?"

"Wait a minute, Bob, and I'll see if our courier is still here." He picked up his telephone and dialed an inter-office line. "Has Kim left for Cholon?" He waited a minute, and then nodded. "Hold that wild Korean, because I've got a passenger for him."

He hung up the phone. "Kim is just leaving for Cholon, and he'll be there for some time. Ask Kraig to have him wait for you. It'll save you money for a taxi, and God knows that you would never find your way back."

Kim was a wiry little man about five-foot-two, and probably weighed a hundred-ten pounds soaking wet. He grinned broadly. "You go Cholon to see Kraig? He good man. He do for you, if you be good man to him."

I warily crawled into the front seat of the jeep with Kim. I immediately realized why Brunnel called him a wild Korean. We took off like we'd been shot out of a cannon. My feet left the floorboards, my head snapped backward, and I frantically grabbed hold of the jeep's frame. This guy went hell-bent out to the main drag, took a right and swerved in and out of traffic. He beeped and beeped the horn as people scrambled for their lives. I thought there's no way I'd live to see another day.

We went down Hai ba Trung Street, through downtown Saigon, and then linked with Tran hung Dao. This was a wide street, and heavily traveled. Kim glanced at me, and then started laughing. No doubt there was extreme fear in my eyes, and he was enjoying every minute of it.

The crazy little bastard didn't slow down, but I can say he was one helluva driver. At any rate we were still intact as we entered the Cholon precinct. Kim gestured with his hand. "This where many Chinese people live. This called Chinese sector, and they come from China. They not same Vietnamese."

For future reference I was trying to observe where we were going, but all the buildings looked the same. All the people looked alike too.

Kim turned off Tran hung Dao onto Nuygen Bieu, crossed over a Canal, and followed a winding dirt road along side a slough. Hundreds of boats bobbed up and down like corks in the water...and there were small shacks squeezed together along the waterfront.

These shabby little houses extended out over the water on pilings made of bamboo shoots. They didn't look sturdy, but they appeared to have been standing for many years.

The stench of human waste was prevalent, which made me appreciate the few unpolluted streams that still existed back home. The big American corporate conglomerates that were responsible for contamination in the U.S. should be forced to tour this part of the world.

We skidded to a halt in front of PA&E's warehouses, and I was amazed that my body was still intact. It was incredible that this bizarre little man had survived so long.

The two story building that housed the U.S. Government material was in poor condition, but so was every other structure in the immediate area. Each level was occupied with shelves and bins filled with hardware and items that I couldn't identify.

I slowly sauntered to an office in the rear, observing everything possible that may help land a job.

"You Bob Patterson from big office?" a receptionist asked.

"Yes, that's me."

She immediately took me to Kraig's hideout. This had to be an indication they were interested in my background. I thanked the little Korean, and she bowed politely.

Kraig's office was neat and well organized, and he was clean shaven and well dressed. I concluded he was probably ex-military. He stood erect as I walked into the room and we shook hands.

"I'm Tom Kraig, and this is my assistant, Bill Wilson."

"Sir, I'm Bob Patterson. Nice to meet you." I nodded toward the other man. "Mr. Wilson, how do you do?" Kraig motioned for me to sit down.

"Mr. Patterson, Mr. Brunnel called and gave me a brief rundown on your background. May I look at your credentials?"

I sat erect in my chair, remembering my training as a cadet at a leading military school back in the 1940's. Kraig took my documents, leaned back in his chair, and intently read every single word.

There was a picture on his desk of he and a woman, no doubt his wife, and three children. He was wearing a U.S. Navy uniform with chief petty officer insignia on the sleeve.

After reading my papers, Kraig thumbed through each page again. He turned toward his assistant, who was sitting at another desk. "Mr. Wilson, read this resume. Mr. Patterson may have the qualifications we're looking for."

Wilson reminded me of a weasel, with an unusually long neck and small beady eyes. He had the quick smile, and sported a hairline mustache. He reminded me of a used car salesman back in the States.

Wilson leaned back in his chair, and was trying to mimic his boss with no success. After thoroughly examining my resume he leaned forward. "Mr Patterson, just what kind of a job would you like to have with Pacific Architects and Engineers?"

"Mr. Wilson, it looks to me like you've got a pretty good job, I'd like to have yours." I glanced out of the corner of my eye towards Kraig. He was smiling.

The superintendent scribbled "approved for hire" on an inter-office form and sealed it in an envelope. All three rose and we shook hands.

"Welcome aboard Mr. Patterson. Return to our main office, and after you've finished processing report back to me. You are our new inventory and adjustment supervisor. I wish you luck."

My eyes and Wilson's never met, and I completely ignored the man. I don't know why, but I didn't trust the guy.

Kim was sitting in the jeep poised like a jockey ready to leave the starting gate. "Kim, give her hell!" We laughed all the way to PA&E's general office.

I thanked Kim for the hair-raising experience, and forged ahead to Brunnel's office. I was stopped short by a sweet little Korean personnel guard. "You wait! I tell you when to go. Mr Brunnel very busy."

The day had progressed rapidly, and I wanted to be reassured that I had a job. I couldn't afford to make mistakes, so I quietly and patiently waited. A cold beer crossed my mind.

The Korean secretary led me to Brunnel's office, and abruptly turned and left. I was feeling cocky, but over-confidence could be devastating.

I handed the "for hire" slip to Brunnel. He looked at it, and nodded his approval. "Patterson, it's getting late in the day. Here is an application form. Fill it out, and be in this office at promptly 0800 hours tomorrow. You will take a physical examination and be given a brief orientation. If things go satisfactorily you will sign a contract late tomorrow or Thursday morning. Now get out of here. I've got work to do!" He was smiling.

I extended my hand in appreciation. "Thank you, Sir. Thank you very much."

There was no reason why I couldn't pass a physical exam, even with excessive fat hanging over my belt.

I relaxed in the back seat of the taxi on the way to the Royal Hotel. I rushed to the hotel desk. "Benny, we did it! I go back tomorrow, and sign papers to get job."

Benny grinned from ear to ear and rubbed his fingers and thumb together. "Bob, you make boo coo money. You send money home to baby sans?"

"Yes Benny. Thank you."

I headed for the bar, and asked for an American beer. The bartender shook his head. "No have American beer. Maybe tomorrow. I give you bomi bom beer. It made in Vietnam, and number one beer."

I nodded my approval, and he put a bottle on the bar. I examined it closely, and it appeared to be all right. It had a "33" on the label, signifying the brand name. I was hot and dry, and I eagerly took a good healthy swallow.

The stuff was absolutely unfit for human consumption. I couldn't describe the taste, but beer is beer. I gulped it down in record time. It was potent, and I felt nauseated.

I went to my favorite restaurant, had a bowl of Chinese soup, and wearily returned to my room. Stress had taken its toll, and sleep was the only remedy. I didn't shower with my cockroaches or even check my firearm under the mattress. It was oblivion within seconds.

Benny awakened me at 0530 hours. I was tired, but this was my big day with PA&E. I hailed a taxi within the hour. Traffic was light, and the ancient taxi cruised up Hai ba Trung Street towards Phu Nhuan precinct. It stopped at the off limits sign on Nuygen Hue, and in the cool morning I briskly walked up the road to PA&E's office. It was an hour before PA&E would open.

The Saigon Country Club was a two story, concrete building of French architectural design, and it looked expensive. But by American standards prices were quite reasonable. I walked into the restaurant and took a table by a large picture window, and ordered a breakfast roll and coffee.

I had a perfect view of number one fairway where a foursome was preparing to tee off. Each player in the group had his own Vietnamese women as a caddy. They had to be hardy little people to walk this course all day in unbearable heat, and carry a bag full of clubs on their shoulder. There were no motor-driven golf carts.

The bill for my breakfast was more than I expected, and my bankroll was nearly gone. It was time for PA&E to enter the picture.

The PA&E receptionist pleasantly greeted me. "Good morning, Mr. Patterson. You come with me please. Mr. Brunnel wait for you." The tall business-like man smiled. He didn't utter a word, but studied my application quite thoroughly. Finally he nodded his approval.

"Patterson, your application is quite satisfactory. Go to room 200 down the hall, and Doctor Bryson will give you a physical exam. After completing that, go to the Seventh-Day Adventist Hospital for a chest x-ray. I'll write down the address - 777 Vo Tanh. Its only about ten minutes from here."

Doctor Bryson asked me the usual questions. He listened to my heart, checked the blood pressure, and tapped my knee with his hammer. He looked at my shot record for discrepancies, and we talked casually for a moment. He informed me it was important to hand-carry my x-ray film from the hospital. This would complete my examination provided the picture was satisfactory.

There were several taxis parked at the off limit sign. I showed a driver the address. I really wasn't paying much attention, but finally realized we had been gone thirty minutes. I was lost.

The driver kept going on and on. I shoved the address in front of his face. "Where the hell are we?"

This guy didn't flinch. "Stop. Stop. Damn it. Stop!" I jumped out and slammed the door. I thought maybe he had in mind to roll me. He could be Vietcong. Robbing me would have been the greatest disappointment of his life.

It was noon when another taxi finally delivered me to the Adventist Hospital. A sign read, "Closed Wednesday afternoon." The door was locked. Waiting until tomorrow for a chest x-ray was ridiculous. Think man!

I walked up Vo Tanh Street. At 1300 hours I got a taxi and went directly to the golf course. I laid on the grass and reminisced about the many years I had enjoyed playing the game.

At 1400 hours I walked to PA&E's office. To save precious time I avoided the secretary, and went directly to Doctor Bryson's office.

I lied to the doctor by telling him that the hospital was busy, and they would deliver the x-rays the next day.

He knew I was lying and doing a poor job of it. He signed the necessary papers. "Patterson, I like my job. Please forget we ever met."

Brunnel took my medical papers and stapled them to some others. "Patterson, sign this contract, so I can put you on the payroll." I took a deep sigh of relief.

Brunnel explained company policy. "You have a choice to either live at PA&E quarters where we furnish board and room, or you can live on the economy. Understand?"

"Yes sir, and I will go the economy route for the time being."

"We use the honor system. There are no time clocks. No personal checks cashed in Vietnam —Period. When you need an advance on your salary, you must report to the paymaster. If we find out that you have written a check in country, you will be immediately discharged. Do I make myself clear?"

"Yes sir."

"You can draw four hundred dollars per month. Here is a map showing you how to get to the rice mill in Cholon. Mr. Kraig will be expecting you tomorrow morning at 0800 hours. Any questions?"

"Yes, Mr Brunnel, could you please direct me to the paymaster?" He rose very slowly from his chair, and motioned for me to follow.

I approached the man behind the cage. "Sir, I would like a two hundred dollar draw on my wages." The personnel manager ordered the man to give me the advance. Brunnel had a hard time being the tough guy. He had a heart as large as a watermelon. I thanked him.

Signing a contract on the fourth day was most gratifying, and I could hardly wait to spread the news. I was overjoyed.

I rushed into the hotel, and Benny was at the registration desk. "Bob, you do O.K. When you go work?" I just grinned, and my eyes filled with tears of joy.

"Tomorrow morning at 0800 hours, Benny. Don't let me oversleep." I went directly to my room and wrote a letter to the family.

Georgina and the kids will be joyous. I didn't explain in detail about my job search, nor did I show my delight. I didn't want to disappoint them about cash flow, or about our future. Too much could happen in a war zone, and I didn't have time to keep up with current conditions in Vietnam. It was rumored that the U.S. might commit more troops to push the communists out of the South.

I finished the letter, and placed it inside an envelope with the unused portion of my plane ticket. The ticket was worth five hundred-forty dollars.

The PA&E paymaster had explained to me about income tax withholdings. My only deduction would be social security. The IRS ruled that any person continually employed outside the US for a total of five hundred ten days paid taxes on everything over twenty thousand dollars. It was called the "five-ten" exemption. It seemed like forever.

Chapter Five

It was Friday morning and Benny pounded on my door. "Bob! Must go work. Get up now. Must go work! De de mau! De mau len!"

"O.K. I get up. Thanks, Benny."

The cockroaches and I took a shower together, and I rushed about shaving. I slipped on a white shirt and suntans, bid the lizards a cheery good-bye, and headed for the restaurant.

I finished breakfast at 0700 hours, as I wanted to be at the rice mill early. People were hustling around, and shops were already open for the day's business. The Vietnamese were early risers, but closed their shops at mid-day to take a long siesta to rest and escape the heat. The shops usually remained open until after dark. Taxis were plentiful this time of day.

A taxi driver studied the map of the rice mill location that Brunnel had given me. He nodded approvingly, turned off Tu Do street onto Le Loi, and soon we were humming down Tran hung Dao. It was a busy morning with heavy traffic, and going was slow. But it was definitely more comfortable to ride with this driver than with Kim, the crazy Korean.

Soon after entering the Cholon sector of Saigon the taxi took a left on Nguyen Bieu street and traveled a short distance. The small car stopped dead. The driver shook his head, and shrugged with his

4

shoulders indicating he wasn't sure of the direction. I unfolded Brunnell's map, and sure enough, this was where the trail ended. I had no idea of which way to go.

"I don't know," I said, "I only know rice mill. Do you understand?" He sat motionless. "Go Tu Do Street."

After paying the man I trudged back to the Royal. Benny looked surprised. "No can find PA&E rice mill?" he asked." My friend studied the map thoroughly. "Maybe you go back to PA&E office. Say you no can find."

"No way Benny. It would be embarrassing to ask Brunnel how to find the rice mill. I'll try again in a couple of hours."

The map was shown to two more taxi drivers, and each time they abruptly stopped at the same place as the first man. Each time I returned to the hotel, and each time Benny wholeheartedly sympathized with me.

It was late in the day and I was dejected. "Benny, I wait until tomorrow." I smiled wearily , and went up the stairs to my room.

I wasn't too concerned about my revolver, because Benny had taken protective charge over me, so I didn't look under the mattress. I opened my suitcase, and stared at the two fifths of Black Velvet I had purchased at Guam. I unscrewed the top from one bottle, and took a long blast. It was hotter than hell going down, and no fresh water to drink. It was sheer torture. Suffer you son-of-a bitch. Why couldn't you have been more observing? You could be working rather than suffering from self-pity.

After several stiff belts I began feeling like Sampson. The heat caused the alcohol to rapidly penetrate my blood stream. I was drunk, and I didn't give a damn. To hell with it all.

I walked through the lobby to the bar, and ordered a beer to put out the fire in my belly. I sat there unsociable like, realizing I had to get a handle on the situation. I couldn't screw up now.

The bomi bom beer tasted lousy, and from past experience I was aware of my condition. I went to the restaurant and had Chinese soup. I went back to the room, and had one huge belt of Black Velvet. My eyes desperately tried to focus on a lizard sitting on the chest of drawers in the dimly lit room. I fell back on the bed and slipped into never never land.

It was before 0600 hours Saturday morning, and Benny pounded on my door. "Get up, Bob! You go find rice mill. Maybe you lose job. You go. De de Mau!"

"O.K. O.K. I'm up!"

After completing my morning ritual I thought it best to continue my search for the rice mill. It meant my only source of income, and I had mailed my return plane ticket to the folks back home.

Once again the map to the rice mill was handed to a taxi driver, and once again I returned to Tu Do Street. Twice more I tried my luck with no avail. Benny asked several people, including Americans, if anyone had heard about the PA&E warehouse at the old rice mill. But everyone only shook their heads. It was futile.

Tomorrow was Sunday, and PA&E's offices would be closed. I may as well make a fresh start Monday morning. By chance I might talk to someone tomorrow who can help. If absolutely necessary I'll swallow my pride and go to the main office on Monday.

Walking might help cure my ills, and besides, getting oriented in Saigon would be a major challenge. It was early in the afternoon, and I needed to occupy my idle time.

By mid-afternoon it proved to be stiflingly hot and the humidity was high. There was no wind, and there was stillness in the city. Everyone paced themselves when exposed to the ever present and tortuous heat.

I wandered aimlessly, and soon realized I was lost again, but I couldn't be far from Tu Do. Suddenly I realized I was walking along side a caucasian male going about my stride. "Sir, are we pretty close to Tu Do Street?"

"You're headed exactly in that direction. I'm headed that way. Care to join me?" I quickened my pace to stay even.

"Thanks. I appreciate it."

"Where you staying?"

"I have a room at the Royal Hotel for now. I've only been in Saigon since last Sunday."

"Oh? You appear like you've been in country for some time."

"Thanks. I didn't want to look too conspicuous. I've been cautioned to keep alert. My name's Bob Patterson, straight from Idaho. It's damn good to talk to an American."

This guy was taller than me, weighed about one-eighty, and was about my age. He was well tanned with sandy colored hair and blue eyes, and carried himself like a man with confidence. He'd been around.

"I'm Sax Ruppe, and I'm Canadian. My home is in Calgary. I've been working up north of here at Cam Ranh Bay for RMK-BRJ, and I just changed companies. It's good to be back in Saigon. Maybe I'll have a little night life. Cam Ranh is all right for scenery, but my sex life has suffered considerably. Have you had a chance to see Saigon's sparkling glitter?" I turned and smiled.

We continued walking toward the Royal. "Sax, I'm a little frustrated about myself. I arrived here six days ago, landed a job with a company called PA&E, and now I can't find the damned warehouse where I'm suppose to be working. Helluva situation. I could have been fired by now!"

This guy went into hysterics. He laughed so hard tears were rolling down his cheeks. "Bob, are you suppose to be working at the rice mill in Cholon?"

"Y-Y-Yeah." My face was red as hell.

"That's where I started to work last Monday." Ruppe was still laughing.

"I've been trying to find the mill for two days, and you work there?"

Sax wiped the tears from his eyes. "Bob, follow me. I think you need a drink."

He had a stride like a miler, and I tried to keep up. We turned into a bar called the Casino, and each straddled a stool.

"The Royal Hotel is in the next block," Sax said, "in case we become separated you don't have far to your room."

The Casino appeared to be O.K. It had an "L" shaped bar and there were several tables. ARVN and American soldiers and white and Asian civilians were sitting at the bar. Mixed couples were seated at tables, and several young Vietnamese women were milling about; it was crowded.

The bartender spoke to my newly found friend. "Where you been

Ruppe?"

Sax yelled over the noise. "I've been up north at Cam Ranh. Give us each a whiskey-coke."

"Where's Cam Ranh?" I asked, "and what is RMK-BRJ doing up there? And what did you do for the company?"

My friend moved his stool closer to mine so he could be heard over the clamor in the barroom. "Bob, Cam Ranh is a natural harbor on the Vietnam coastline some 200 miles northeast of Saigon. It was a small fishing village until 1965, when it became the site of an American air base and seaport to serve military operations in the central portion of South Vietnam."

"Cam Ranh Bay will never be the same. In just over sixty days a new airstrip was constructed of metal planking, better known as psp matting, to accommodate jet fighters. Just before I left we completed another 10,000 foot runway paved with concrete along with a 10,000 foot taxiway and an aircraft parking apron."

Sax ordered two more whiskey-cokes. "I helped construct dozens of warehouses and barracks, and other groups were building facilities for a major logistical depot, plus dredging a deep harbor. Brown and Root and J.A. Jones construction Companies have joined the RMK venture, and are operating a full-scale effort. Believe me, RMK-BRJ is an enormous enterprise!"

Ruppe frowned with concern as he gulped down his drink. "Bob, I'll give you an idea of material requirements shipped in from the States. RMK-BRJ has received over 150,000,000 board feet of lumber, 750,000 sheets of plywood, more than 3600 prefabricated buildings of 40 x 100-foot average size, almost 11,000,000 pounds of nails and 98,000,000 pounds of asphalt. To these can be added such other items as 850 pickup trucks, 800 flatbeds trucks and more than 200 tractors. And remember Bob, RMK-BRJ is only one company in Vietnam. Try to imagine material requirements for many other companies operating in the country. It'll blow your mind."

Ruppe sighed. "It's an enormous project, and it's costing the U.S. taxpayers billions of dollars. I hope the American Government knows what the hell they're doing."

"Hell, Sax, I picked up a list at the American consulate of 231

U.S. contractors operating in Vietnam, and it includes what military departments they work for, and their Saigon addresses. That helped get me my job."

"You're bullshitin' me. My God, 231 companies?"

"Yeah. I'll show it to you. I'm starting to get the big picture about America's involvement in Vietnam."

"Yeah, Bob, maybe this war is more about economics rather than stopping Communism."

After several drinks I was completely relaxed and enjoying myself for the first time since being in country. It was beginning to feel like old home week.

An Asian sitting next to me was pretty well oiled, and I asked Sax if he was Vietnamese. "No, he's larger than most Vietnamese. He's Korean. The U.S. Government and general contractors hire a lot of Koreans. Also, the Republic of Korea (ROK) has a large number of fighting troops in Vietnam."

Sax said the Koreans, plus civilians from other countries working in Vietnam, were referred to as third nationals. The Vietnamese were local nationals. Third nationals hired to work in country were well paid in U.S. taxpayer's greenbacks. They made about half the income of an American, but here this was big bucks. When they returned to their respective homelands these men and women would be financially well off.

The drunken Korean sitting on my right kept leaning into me. He nudged me hard, and I damn near fell off my stool. I gently pushed him away. The son-of-a-bitch elbowed me hard in the ribs causing me to flinch, and in complete arrogance he looked me straight in the eye and grinned.

"You American bastard. Maybe you like I use karate. You like that?"

Ruppe slowly shook his head. "Be careful. These assholes can be mean as hell."

I smiled weakly. "I don't want any trouble with this guy."

I wasn't in the best fighting condition, and I tried to ignore the Korean. The only advantage would be for me to hit him first. Sax and I tried to carry on a conversation, when the arrogant bastard elbowed me again. It hurt like hell, and I was mad.

The American bar owner was watching. He didn't want trouble, so he told the Korean to leave. This guy slowly got off the stool, and then ripped my shirt, causing me to lose my balance. I caught myself by grabbing hold of a table where several people were sitting. In turn, their drinks were spilled, and they jumped to their feet.

The music stopped, and everyone in the room focused on the unexpected disturbance. "You come American. We go outside," the Korean said, slurring his words in drunken stupor. "I do American bastard with karate."

There were no options. My hands were shaking, and my knees were weak. I was sick to my stomach and wanted to vomit. My mind flashed back to my younger days, when I worked in the lumber mills. There was no harder physical work than sawmilling. We worked hard during the day, and drank and fought hard into the night. That was clean fun. This is different. If I didn't play this bastard's hand I was sure I'd lose my credibility with Sax.

The Korean beckoned for me to follow as he staggered toward the door. Just as he walked through the entrance I hit the son-of-a-bitch in the back of the head with a tightly clinched fist. He literally left his feet, stumbled over the sidewalk, and plowed into the cobbled street. He lay motionless, and for a moment I felt sorry.

I walked back into the bar and faintly smiled at Sax. "All's fair in love and war."

Sax laughed heartily. "Bartender, give my friend and me another whiskey-coke." He grasped my hand vigorously that sealed a strong bond. This was a bond of trust and everlasting friendship.

Young Vietnamese women clad in the bare necessities approached and pressed up against us. I watched Sax handle the situation. A girl snuggled close and asked, "You buy me Saigon tea? You nice man. You buy me Saigon tea, and I sit with you. O.K.?"

"I no buy you tea tonight, friend and I talk. Tomorrow I buy you tea. De de Mau." He completely ignored the exotic little creature.

He said the women worked for the Casino Bar. The Saigon tea was diluted coke, and each small glass purchased by a customer entitles the tea girl to a commission. It was survival. Some girls had families to support, while others were prostitutes. But some looked for a husband or a man who wanted a "live in" girl friend.

The war had taken a tremendous toll on young Vietnamese men, and large numbers had been killed in the war or were missing in action. As for young women, single and married, prostitution was a part of every day life, and it paid for necessities. The war has changed the life-style of these good people.

Ruppe and I drank several more whiskey-cokes, and neither was feeling any pain. We weren't drunk, but just pleasingly plastered. My friend reminisced about his past.

"I am a native Canadian, raised on a ranch on the out-skirts of Calgary, and am real proud of my heritage. I was eighteen when I enlisted in the Royal Canadian Air Force, and was stationed in England. I received my wings as a bombardier, and flew missions over France and Germany. I returned to Calgary after World War II, and worked on the ranch for several years. I married a nice gal and moved to California, where I became a successful building contractor. Financially, I wasn't hurting, until my wife and I divorced. I lost damned near everything, and took up drinking full time. I drank until all I had left was a pocket watch and kidney trouble. I've had some good years, and I've had some bad years."

He hesitated long enough to drain a glass of whiskey. "I hired out of RMK's San Francisco office for this tour, and I just completed an eighteen month contract. PA&E's pay scale is much higher than RMK's, so that's the reason I'm here."

Curfew time was approaching rapidly, and I told Sax about my experience the first night in Saigon, when the Royal was locked up tight as hell. He roared with drunken laugher, and then we staggered to the hotel. He said his hotel was only a half block away, and he would see me at 0900 hours sharp in the morning.

Sunday morning arrived, and my head was thumping from the over consumption of alcohol. My friend was right on time. "Let's go to the USO," he said, "it's not far from here. We can get American food that's been flown in from the States. How does Bacon, eggs, and hash browns sound?"

"Great! I'm hung over, and my hand hurts from that Korean's hard head." We both chuckled.

After devouring breakfast and several cups of coffee we went out into the fresh morning air and sunshine, and walked slowly toward the Saigon River. Sunday was just like any weekend in the States. Few shops were open, sidewalks weren't crowded and traffic was light. I liked what I had seen of Saigon.

"Don't be concerned about last night and the Korean in the bar," Sax said, "he was plastered. Most Koreans are nice guys. They're here for the same reason as the American—money. War isn't important—it's secondary."

I was satisfied that Sax Ruppe and Bob Patterson had a lot in common. Both had a code of ethics, and each had a good sense of humor. It had been an enjoyable Sunday, and Saigon was truly an amazing and unique city.

It was a dark Monday morning, and Sax was standing in front of the hotel. We exchanged greetings, and briskly walked to PA&E's shuttle bus. We found seats, and settled back for the thirty minute ride to the rice mill. I was hungry, but I needed to lose weight. Two notches had been taken in my belt, and I felt mentally and physically sound.

Upon arrival at the rice mill I went directly to Kraig's office. He looked surprised to see me. "Thought maybe you weren't going to show, Mr. Patterson."

"Mr. Kraig, I'm really sorry for not reporting to you last week. I honestly couldn't find the place."

"Mr. Patterson, you're not the first person that couldn't find the rice mill. I'll admit that map Mr. Brunnel gave to you is skimpy." Kraig chuckled, and all seemed to be forgiven.

Leaning against the wall was a husky, balding man in his mid twenties. He was a six footer with blue eyes and huge hands. His biceps were larger than normal, and his neck and sloping shoulder seem to be molded into one mass. This guy would tip the scales at two-twenty-five.

Kraig introduced us. "Mr. Patterson, this is Lou Brown. He is your immediate superior, so you two get acquainted."

Brown sauntered toward me and extended his hand. "Mr. Patterson, welcome to PA&E. Mr. Kraig talked of your extensive knowledge of products, and your experience with inventory control and warehousing. Our job is to receive, warehouse, and distribute hundreds of millions of dollar worth of expensive materials, and we must be accountable for these materials. Mr. Patterson, follow me. I want you to meet another superior."

We walked up a flight of stairs to the second floor. One large room was filled with desks, typewriters, and filing cabinets. Young Asian men and women were occupied with their particular duties, and I was surprised at the large number of employees.

We went into a small isolated office where a middle aged man was working. "Mr. Alba, meet Mr. Patterson. He will replace you while you're on vacation."

The little man stood, and excitedly shook my hand. He was mannerly and spoke excellent English. "Mr. Patterson, I have waited a long time for some one to relieve me. Can we start right away?"

"Mr. Alba, he's all yours." Brown confronted me straight on. "Mr. Patterson, remember I'm your boss." He left abruptly.

Mr. Alba spoke direct. "Mr. Patterson, be cautious around Mr. Brown. He is like the Russian KGB. Everything that he hears or sees is forwarded to Kraig. He can't be trusted, and furthermore, he isn't too bright. He's an ex- pro heavyweight boxer, and was a contender for the championship before retiring." I thanked Mr. Alba, and assured him our conversation was confidential.

"Mr. Alba, before we get started, may I ask your background with PA&E?"

"Mr. Patterson, that is a good question. You want to know who you're dealing with. I am Filipino, born and raised in Manila and a citizen of the Republic of the Philippines. I am a graduate of the University of Manila in business administration, and have worked as an accountant for fifteen years. PA&E accepted my application for employment in 1955, and sent me to Okinawa. I was elevated to inventory and adjustment supervisor two years ago and was immediately transferred to Saigon."

Alba explained my duties as I&A supervisor. PA&E's goal was to keep a perpetual inventory of all materials on hand. This involved accurate record keeping of receiving, warehousing, and issuing of material to the job site.

"We have advanced our technology into computerized data processing," Alba said, "and it's a little complicated unless you've had proper training in that particular field. But it speeds up the process and helps eliminate error." He looked at me skeptically. "Am I making myself clear Mr. Patterson?"

"I don't know data processing. Inventory card system is my only experience. Everything is done by hand. Computers sound complicated, but I can only do my best."

"Mr. Patterson, the major problem we have in our system is pilferage. Perhaps that isn't the appropriate word. Pilferage means stealing in small amounts. The little guy's theft is minor, but our losses are massive."

"Give me an example of heavy losses." Alba was a serious guy, and concerned about his job. He hesitated.

"I haven't been in Vietnam long, but this is a war zone."

The Filipino frowned. "Sometimes we lose truck loads of material, and other times we not only lose the material, but also the truck and the driver. We never see them again. The drivers must be VC, but how can one tell?"

Alba was a comedian, and didn't know it. I laughed, but I could see the serious side. Somebody had to be responsible for losses, and that means "somebody" could be Bob Patterson. I didn't like signing my name to any document, particularly in Vietnam. History has proven that when the U.S. Government has problems its radar zeros in on a scapegoat. Bob better be damned careful! Leavenworth, Kansas would be a dreary place to spend the rest of his life.

All I wanted was a simple job with no complications. It was frustrating, but I promised Alba I'd be productive. It was difficult for me to absorb this new data processing system.

Six days passed and both were discouraged with my progress. Alba worked feverishly, and disregarded my lack of experience with computers. He was anxious to visit his family in Manila, and his home was only two and a half hours flying time from Saigon. Thank God the week came to an end.

While They Died

Saturday evening when I arrived at the Royal Hotel, Benny stopped me before I went to my room. My friend looked troubled. "Bob, you stay at hotel long time and no have girl friend. Maybe you sick? I find for you and no cost money. I do for you. O.K?"

"I go to Casino tonight, and maybe I find girl friend. Thank you."

Sax and I didn't have dinner as planned, but beamed in on the Casino Bar. The curfew wasn't a cause for alarm tonight. Benny had advised me a friend would wait for my return.

The Bar was humming, and the patrons were having a good time. We managed to get bar stools, and ordered whiskey-cokes.

The American owner had thought of everything for entertainment. Couples were dancing to American music, and American brand beer and liquor was readily available. Saigon tea girls were everywhere.

Two tea girls eased up to the bar, one settled in on Sax's left, and one crowded in close to my right. I quickly surveyed the one that had undoubtedly moved in to conduct business.

My expert observation quickly concluded she was at least a number nine on a scale of ten. Her make-up was perfectly applied, and her shining black hair was fashioned in an up-sweep. Her breasts were small compared to the average American, and her eyes were more narrowed than the average local Vietnamese. She wore a tight black dress with shoulder straps, and the hemline came just above the knees. Her black sparkling eyes were her main attraction, and her smile warmed my heart.

"You American GI?" she asked.

"No, I'm an American civilian."

"You work Saigon?"

"Yes. I work in Cholon."

"May Susie sit with you?

"Sure, Susie. You can sit with me."

"Maybe you buy me Saigon tea?"

"O.K. I buy tea."

"If you no buy tea, American bartender tell me to go away." She gave me a Hollywood look of sadness.

"Bartender! Give me whiskey-coke and one Saigon tea."

"Your name is Susie, and you work in bar?"

"Yes, I work to bar. I have two baby san and must work. What your name?"

"My name is Bob. Susie, what does your husband do?"

"My husband die in war. Vietcong kill long time." There was a long silence.

My first impression gave Susie high marks. She had class. Her English was relatively good, although I asked her to repeat several times. I wanted to know more about her.

Sax was moving along with his Saigon tea girl and vise versa. He had his arm around her waist, and both were laughing. She was taller than Susie, her hair was shoulder length, and her eyes were round. She looked younger, and her figure was also a number nine on the scale of ten. Her tight black dress revealed a perfect body.

Time passed quickly, and it was late, and Susie took my hand. "Bob, I must go home to my baby san. Curfew come soon, and police take me to jail." I didn't want her to go. But this was Saigon and this was war.

"Susie, I no work tomorrow. Can I come to the Casino, and maybe we talk, and I buy you Saigon tea?"

"Yes. Please you come tomorrow." She squeezed my hand, and

motioned to her friend. They vanished into the night.

Sax and I had one whiskey-coke for the road. Both were preoccupied for some time. "Bob, what do you think of Vietnamese women?"

"Susie is a remarkable little lady. I like her, and I'll see her tomorrow."

Sax confirmed his liking for Asian women. "This girl is O.K. I've had Asians, and she rates number one in my book. Her name is Lon, and she's only twenty-two years old. That somewhat bothers me. But what the hell, this is war." We both laughed.

We left the Casino feeling euphoric. The drinks had something to do with our enthusiasm, but there was more going on than either cared to discuss. We made plans to meet at the French restaurant for breakfast at 0800 hours. It was after curfew and I walked briskly, staying close to the buildings to be less conspicuous.

An old papa san was waiting for me at the Royal, and he immediately opened the iron gate. I gave him two hundred piasters in appreciation.

After a hearty breakfast at my favorite French restaurant, Sax asked how much I had been paying for my room.

"The hotel's rate is eleven hundred piasters. Why?"

He shook his head. "I pay sixteen hundred. There's a place not far from here. It's the Tourist Hotel at 53 Hong thap Tu Street. There are security guards on duty twenty four hours, and two-bed rooms are available for only three hundred piasters per day. It has a restaurant on the main floor. What do you think?"

"Let's go. I'm nearly broke."

I was impressed with Hong thap Tu. Tall mahogany trees lined both sides of the street, and the area was clean, and the buildings were well maintained. The taxi stopped out front of the Tourist. It was peaceful.

Two armed security guards eyed us thoroughly, as we entered through the gate that attached to a foot thick concrete wall. A wide brick sidewalk stretched from the entrance to steps leading up to the hotel's large double doors. Neatly groomed grass and shrubs covered the grounds, and there was a sun deck off the patio.

We recognized several people standing out front that were PA&E employees from the rice mill. "Sax, maybe this is old home week."

We walked into the hotel and approached the desk. The clerk greeted us cheerfully, and we were asked to sign the register.

The clerk asked if we were working, and Sax assured him that we were employed by PA&E. He said that was good. The hotel had a monthly agreement with PA&E. He gave us each a key. The elevator was occupied so we walked up the stairs.

I approached room 304, and unlocked the door. There was a young American laying on one bed, and he motioned toward the other. I glanced around the room. There were no lizards clinging to the walls, but I was confident that cockroaches would be hiding in the shadows.

Mark, my new roommate, had dropped out of college. It appeared this guy was suffering from apathy, and wasn't sure of life in general. He had been employed by the U.S. Government, had quit his job, was running out of funds, and would probably go home. He had a sarcastic attitude about the war.

"Maybe you're lucky you're not in uniform," I said, disgustedly. "How'd you like being in the U.S. cavalry or infantry? You wouldn't be laying on your ass in bed between clean sheets at the Tourist. You'd probably be laying in a muddy Vietnamese rice paddy."

The kid confessed his dad was a big time Los Angeles lawyer, and had enough pull to keep him out of the U.S. draft system. The kid was spoiled rotten and I didn't like him!

Sax patiently waited for me in the lobby. I told him about the spoiled roommate with peach fuzz. He laughed. "It takes all kinds."

We took a taxi to our respective hotels. We would move our personal effects to the Tourist and rendezvous at the Casino Bar.

I packed my clothes in the suitcase, and reached under the mattress for my trusty 32-20 Colt. I wondered how many people working at the Royal knew about the gun. I'm sure Benny instructed the employees not to touch.

It was difficult to tell Benny why and where I was moving. He gracefully accepted my departure, and asked me to visit him.

It was afternoon when I strolled into the Casino. The place was almost empty, and I could hear girls talking in another room. No doubt they were applying their war paint, and preparing to ambush the patrons. I ordered a cold American beer, and chuckled to myself about Saigon tea.

Sax came in and ordered a beer. He had moved his belongings, and was settled at the Tourist. Evidently, someone told Lon and Susie we were at the bar. They walked up and sat down beside us. These two were experts of the trade.

Sax took Lon by the hand, and they walked to a table in the corner of the room. I took Susie's hand and held it firmly. She smiled, and moved closer to my side.

"Bartender, I buy American beer and Saigon tea for Susie." This was like the movies, and I was trying to be subtle.

"Susie, do you just work at bar? Don't you do anything else?"

Her head snapped up. "I not whore." I sighed with relief, not that it would have made any difference. I was content to sit with her and sip beer.

"Bob, I tell you something about Susie." I squeezed her hand.

"I was baby san in Hanoi. I live there sixteen years. My mama san, she Vietnamese, and my papa san was Japanese soldier. My family come to Saigon long time, and I marry Vietnamese soldier who I say die in war. I have two baby san. I have girl name of Tuyet, mean snow, and boy name Hai. I live with American before, and my boy has round eyes same same American. No lie to Bob. O.K?" Her eyes were wet, and I was moved.

This sincere and remarkable lady was speaking with complete honesty. "Susie tell you anything. I sing and I dance long time many places in Vietnam. Boo coo people watch me, and sometimes I sing and dance for Vietnamese soldiers. I make them happy. Sometimes I go Vung Tau, sometimes to Nha Trang, and Thu Duc. Everyplace I go. You understand?"

"Yes, Susie, I understand."

"Everybody know my name is Zoom when I sing and dance. I am twenty eight, and I am old. Now I sing and dance little bit. Not like before."

"Bob, you have wife and baby san?"

I told Susie of my marriage and divorce and about my five children.

Her eyes were searching deep into mine, hoping what I said was true. I had another beer and ordered another Saigon tea.

The place was beginning to fill, and talk was loud. Susie wanted to impress me. "Bob, I sing to you song. I sing American song. You come close to me. I sing to your ear."

Patiently I waited, and in a very low voice she began. She sang "Summertime" in English. It was beautiful, and it made me think of home, and I had tears, and she looked at me. She knew that my heart was deeply touched, and she knew that I had warmth for her. I wanted to have her.

It was late, and I'd had enough beer. Work tomorrow, and I needed food. I told Susie I would see her soon, and she squeezed my hand with approval. We bid the girls farewell.

My Canadian friend and I were each preoccupied for some time. On the way to the Tourist Hotel I remarked that maybe we should get an apartment and set up housekeeping.

Sax looked at me and grinned. "Lon and I talked about it."

We had dinner in the hotel dinning room, and then went to our rooms. My roommate Mark informed me of an extra service extended by the Tourist Hotel management. Four house boys were stationed on each of the five floors. Two boys were placed at each end of the corridor. Their responsibilities consisted of supplying the rooms with toilet paper, soap and supervising the cleaning and bed making.

In addition, the house boys kept a close eye on intruders that might have a tendency to steal. Stealing was survival in Vietnam, as I was learning. One very important service was supplying hotel guests with members of the opposite sex. This service was available twenty four hours a day, and rates were very reasonable. It was an example of their free enterprise system.

The following morning Sax and I had breakfast with other PA&E personnel in the dining room, and we all left the hotel about the same time. It was a three block walk to the shuttle bus stop. That was more convenient than living at the Royal, but I missed Benny's smile.

Mr. Alba greeted me a cheery good morning, and the wheels of progress started turning. Learning computers was boring. I had an abundance of product knowledge, but their system of inventory control was complex. Alba was disappointed and becoming impatient, because he was anxious to go on vacation. I was longing to see one black-eyed Susie.

I had been asked to have lunch with several others at a U.S. military police mess hall. At noon five of us climbed into a PA&E jeep and were off. The American behind the wheel knew the terrain, and he maneuvered in and out between old houses over a bumpy dirt road. We reached our destination and the jeep rolled to a stop. We piled out and hurried toward the army mess.

The military police compound consisted of older buildings rented from Vietnamese private citizens. The mess hall was hidden among them, and it was filled to capacity with GIs. This took me back to my army days of the 1940s. It hadn't changed, and we stood in line with metal trays and utensils like everyone else. We moved along as K.P.s slapped food on the trays.

I topped off a decent chow with GI pie and coffee, and a cashier at the door accepted thirty-five MPCs for services rendered. I walked outside into a blast of a torturous muggy heat.

The other PA&E people had left the mess hall, so I had difficulty finding my way. The jeep was gone! I couldn't believe that I had been left behind. It's understandable; the other employees weren't aware of my presence, so they evidently assumed everyone was in the jeep when it left. Furthermore, this was my first day for lunch at the army mess hall. I wasn't part of the regular group, and wouldn't be missed.

Lost again! Now what? Who can I trust in an area that is totally foreign? In Saigon proper I could hail a taxi, but not out here on the waterfront where houses were supported on stilts.

People were staring, and they probably wondered why this nut was aimlessly walking about. I was angry with myself for not paying attention. Why was I always getting screwed up?

I stumbled along the dusty road, and I wasn't sure, but left seemed the logical direction. Traffic was heavy with people who were busy buying and selling goods.

After walking for thirty minutes I was beginning to feel hopeless. Suddenly a jeep out of nowhere came skidding to a halt, as its wheels threw dirt in all directions. It was Mangie, a young, blond-haired, blue eyed, throwback from the ape family. He was laughing, and at the same time trying to apologize for leaving me behind.

"You lost? Everybody had been working for about fifteen minutes at the rice mill when someone said, 'Oh shit, we forgot Patterson!' Here I am to the rescue, and away we go!" Mangie was crazy. He was young, long haired and crazy. I wondered where these young kids got the idea to wear that damned long hair.

Thursday evening after finishing dinner at the Tourist Sax and I decided to walk to the Casino for a beer. We casually talked about the girls.

"I have been thinking all week that maybe the four of us could get together."

"Why the hell don't you get on with it Patterson? I know what you're trying to say. Let's ask Lon and Susie if they want to get an apartment."

"They're damn good people. Both are extremely street wise, and they can be good companions. The war will probably intensify, and we can all help one another."

Ruppe informed me these little ladies weren't free. Susie had two children, and the going rate for support was about one hundred-fifty dollars a month in U.S. green. She had to have someone take care of her baby san, and her daughter was of school age. Schooling was expensive in Vietnam. Furthermore, we would have to pay a maid, and provide her board and room. Splitting the expenses seemed reasonable for the maid service.

We approached the girls about the idea, and neither Susie nor Lon hesitated when asked to find a place to live. They started chattering excitedly in Vietnamese while Sax and I sat contentedly at the bar sipping beer.

Susie and Lon had accomplished their goals. This meant they no longer had to work at the bar, and both girls were overjoyed. They promised to contact us when an apartment was found.

When I arrived at the rice mill Friday morning Lou Brown was in Mr. Alba's office. I greeted them, and started sorting through stacks of inventory cards. Brown was there for a reason.

"Mr. Patterson, after a lengthy discussion with Mr. Alba, it has been decided to transfer you to PA&E's open storage warehousing facility at Long Binh. Mr. Alba's secretary, Miss Kim Che, will be your replacement. She has been in our employment for several years, and is quite capable. Monday morning I will personally drive you to Long Binh. It's an hour drive, and I will explain your new duties. Any questions, Mr. Patterson?"

"No Sir"! This was music to my ears.

Brown left abruptly, and Alba started to apologize. "Mr. Patterson, I hope you don't feel badly toward me. I am only doing what I think best. I am truly sorry."

"Mr. Alba, you made a good decision. I wasn't very receptive, and I'm sorry to cause delay of your most deserved vacation. Please forgive me." Alba and I shook hands without animosity.

Saturday passed quickly. The shuttle bus stopped at its designated point on Hong thap Tu, and all PA&E rice mill employees stepped off.

My friend Ruppe didn't know I was being transferred to Long Binh, and I didn't know where in the hell it was located. At dinner that night I was sitting with Mangie, Sax, and Wilkins, and I popped the question. "Where is Long Binh?"

They all looked surprised. "Bob, are you gong to Long Binh?" Wilkins asked.

Mangie interrupted. "We're all going to Long Binh next week. I got the word from Brown. I've heard working conditions are lousy. It's hotter than hell and dusty in the dry season, and hot and muddy in the wet season. The Vietcong are close by, and take pot shots. Sometimes they set booby traps, that can cost you a hand or leg, or maybe your life. We'll be putting in seven-elevens.

"Bob, that means we'll be working eleven hour shifts seven days a week. You can figure two hours travel time on a shuttle bus. We're looking at an approximate sixteen hour day." Mangie seemed well informed.

"We won't have an American bus driver," Mangie said. "There's a work agreement between the two Governments that all vehicles would be operated by Vietnamese. We all know what it's like riding with a crazy oriental."

I didn't tell my friends I would be riding with Brown to Long Binh Monday morning. The conversation ended when some guy walked in the room.

"Are Ruppe or Patterson in the hotel?" We both stood and identified ourselves. He raised his eyebrows and smiled. "Couple of good looking ladies across the street asking about you."

Sax and I walked out past the security guards. Susie and Lon were standing across the street waiting patiently. Each was dressed in a white silk ao dai (native dress), and smiled radiantly as we approached.

"Bob, I find apartment," Susie said. "You come, and I show to you. You say O.K. and we stay. You say no O.K. and we look more." Sax nodded his approval.

Susie took me by the hand, and hailed a taxi. "We go to Chinese Sector in Cholon. Number one place to live. O.K. Bob?" She looked into my eyes.

"O.K. I'm with you."

In twenty minutes we turned off Tran hung Dao, and it was getting dark when I paid the driver. Susie led the way down a dimly lit side street, and we entered through a narrow doorway. She knocked on an inside door, and much to my surprise an American appeared.

He was clad only in soiled shorts and thongs. He was grimy and unshaven, and seemed unconcerned. "What's on your mind buddy?"

"You have place to live?" Susie asked, politely, "we come to see."

He pointed upward. There was a steep narrow stairway leading up through a three foot square hole to the second floor.

We climbed up through the hole and peered around. This was strange indeed. The room had a single light hanging from the ceiling. There was a bed with sheets and one chair. A wash basin and a toilet were in one corner with a partition in front of the toilet for privacy, and there was a clean towel hanging next to the wash basin.

Susie slowly came close to me, and she put her arms around my neck. Her full lips gently kissed mine, and her white ao dai trailed to the floor. My hands gently removed her black lace brassiere and panties, and in the dimly lit room I could see the silhouette of the small trim figure. Her eyes never left mine as she gently lay back on the bed. I modestly slipped off my clothes and lay beside her. Our breathing quickened and we embraced. She seduced me.

There was no doubt this lovely little lady had buried her deepest affections deep, very deep into my heart. The affair was stirring, and it was satisfaction in its entirety.

"Bob, now we go look to apartment. O.K.?" We climbed down the ladder and walked out to the street. Our taxi sped along the dark street of the Chinese sector of Saigon, and it halted at the entrance to De Tram Street.

De Tram was narrow and poorly lit. It could be somewhat troublesome because of the darkness and it's length. I didn't like walking into a threatening unknown.

Susie walked cautiously with me following close behind. It was late and the street was vacant, except for older men and women sitting on steps in front of doorways, taking advantage of the cool evening air. I could feel their eyes following our every move.

Deep into De Tram street Susie turned into an apartment building. We felt our way up a narrow stairway to the second floor. She knocked, and an attractive, middle aged Vietnamese woman appeared. She had been waiting, and handed Susie a key. We thanked her and walked to the third floor, where Susie opened the door to our new apartment. At least, it was new to us.

The place was small, but adequate. Susie looked at me questioningly, and I put my arm around her. "Susie, if you like, and Lon and Sax like, then I like." She smiled, and reached up and kissed me with approval. Housekeeping was in the making.

Sunday morning Sax and I checked out of the Tourist Hotel. With suitcases in hand we walked down De Tram Street to the apartment building, where the two flights of stairs to our burrow tested our physical fitness.

We went inside, and Lon informed Sax that their bed was in front, and Susie and I would occupy the bedroom. Sax and I snooped around and discovered the girls had everything in place. The beds were made, and there were pots and pans and utensils. Plates, cups, and glasses were visible. The two ex-Saigon tea girls were rather efficient with the entire maneuver; it was unique and comfortable, but a little cramped.

One last surprise. Waiting outside was our maid, and I'm sure she had been there waiting the final approval by the masters of the house. Susie brought her into our humble home.

"This is Baby San. She twenty year old, and still cherry girl. Her home is My Lai, and is long way from Saigon. I tell her mama san I take care of her. Baby San work hard, and do good for us. She no speak American."

Baby San was short like the majority of Vietnamese peasants, and she was stoutly built like a tank. She was dressed in a simple grey blouse and shiny black pants.

Each of us seemed content with our new living arrangements. The two girls left the room to prepare for bed, and Sax and I had a couple of drinks. All settled in for the night.

Monday morning Lou Brown was waiting for me. He motioned to get in his new 1967 Chevrolet pickup truck. There was no greeting. He informed me that employees at his level could drive their own assigned vehicles, and they weren't required to have designated Vietnamese drivers. This didn't surprise me; he was trying to prove his authority with a subordinate.

Brown was a good driver, and it was obvious he knew the short-cuts to Route 1, the main highway. This North-South thoroughfare started at Saigon, and went all the way to Hanoi, and beyond. It was the most traveled highway in Vietnam, and undoubtedly the most treacherous highway in the world.

It was a supply route for the South Vietnamese military, and also the main route for the North Vietnamese troops above the DMZ. It was supposedly a two lane highway with a designated outside lane for two and three wheeled vehicles.

At times the highway became a four lane nightmare when military heavy equipment was moving. GI six by six trucks went hell bent. The young American drivers really didn't much give a damn, and if the situation presented itself, they'd take off down the middle of the road. To hell with the white stripe separating the two lanes. The young American GIs wanted to go back to the World. Fuck the war!

Ton and a half flatbed trucks, buses, jeeps, three quarter ton weapon carriers, and every other wheeled thing was going like crazy along Route 1. Occasional enemy small arms fire could be heard, which caused accidents and general chaos. The fatality rate was high on Route 1.

The Chevy pickup glided along the highway at forty miles an hour, and I was happy that Brown was a defensive driver. He began telling me about PA&E's locations and my duties at Long Binh.

"Mr. Patterson, I hope you will be happier and more productive out here in the jungle than you have been at the rice mill. You're still inventory and adjustment supervisor, and your three crews will routinely conduct inventories of materials and make adjustments for shortages. It is unusual when our inventories show no shortages. It's amazing how things disappear out here."

"PA&E has three storage facilities designated as Area 206, Area 207, and Area 208. Your office is located at 208. The others are smaller than 208, with one American in charge of each. Labor crews are much smaller in these areas."

We left the main highway, and traveled three miles on a dirt road to Area 208. There were checkpoints along the way manned by military police. Each carried an M-16 rifle.

Brown parked the pickup, and we entered the building together. I was impressed and surprised at these newly constructed buildings that housed the office employees. There were other buildings three hundred yards to the east: a motor pool, tire shop, and mechanic's shop.

The PA&E office work force included inventory supervisors, open storage supervisors, security police, assistant supervisors, and several secretaries. Brown also had an office at 208. This surprised me. His desk was located where he had a clear view of my desk. This could be a coincidence, and then again, maybe I was getting paranoid.

Brown walked directly into the office and took a chair behind his desk. I stood facing him like a small tin soldier. He motioned to a Korean seated next to my desk, who limped noticeably as he came forward.

"Mr. Patterson this is Mr. Kim Choung Un, your most able assistant. Kim came from Korea six months ago, and has been ramroding our inventory crews at all three areas."

Kim gripped my hand. He was all of five feet tall, and maybe weighed one hundred ten pounds. He was probably a karate expert, too.

"Kim, it's a pleasure, and your experience and cooperation will be appreciated. I'm fortunate to have you as an associate."

"Lou, I should be boss," the Korean said, abruptly, "I be here long time, and I know inventory."

"Kim, Mr. Patterson has much knowledge with materials and inventory control. You will work for him. Do you understand?" It was settled, and I appreciated Brown for his assist. The Korean was arrogant, but I respected him for stating his grievance.

Kim and I pulled his small desk next to mine, and we preceded to get acquainted. He was thirty-eight years old with a wife and two baby san back in Seoul. He had been a lieutenant in the ROK Army during the Korean War, was seriously wounded, and lost the use of his leg. He was given a medical discharge from the service, but times had been hard for his family. He had friends that worked for PA&E in Korea, and he had managed to get hired.

"I make eight hundred U.S. green dollars every month, and I send home," he said. I detected bitterness about the North Koreans, and how he had been mistreated by his own government as a disabled veteran.

There were many nationalities working for the American Government in Vietnam, and making big bucks. Just to mention a few third national countries: Republic of the Philippines, South Korea, Thailand, Laos, Cambodia, Australia, India, and Canada. Once again, it proved the generosity of the American taxpayer.

Brown didn't ask me to ride back to Saigon with him after work. It was 1930 hours, and Americans and Vietnamese office workers began boarding the shuttle bus for the trip back to Saigon. Sax and the other transfers from the rice mill climbed onto the bus. They were dirty and tired.

The day's work began at 0700 hours with an hour lunch break, and it ended at 1900 hours. Seven days a week and no overtime pay. This was going to be most interesting.

Sax and I were lucky. The shuttle bus was routed to stop at the Tourist Hotel, and then proceed to downtown Saigon where other employees lived. After winding through the main drag, it finally found its way to Tran hung Dao, stopping across from De Tram Street, then preceding on through the Cholon sector.

There was a bar on the corner where the bus stopped, and Sax and I went for drinks. It was called Fanettes, and was dark and loud like most bars in Saigon. It was smaller than the Casino Bar, but stocked with American alcoholic beverages and an ample number of Saigon tea girls.

We had a couple of cognacs, then headed out the door and crossed the street. "De Tram is a damn scary street to walk down alone," Sax said. "Look at the punks hanging around. They're better known as cowboys in Saigon. Don't turn your back on them. They'll kick the hell out of you and steal everything you've got. Bob, be careful when you're alone."

Sax carried a small duffle bag that contained a U.S. Army 45 cal. semi-automatic, and he advised me to get a firearm. I thought when I wrote home next time I would have Georgina pick up a 25 cal. automatic that I could carry in my pocket. The 32-20 was too large to conceal on my person.

Each apartment had a balcony, and Sax and I could see the girls standing there, waiting for our arrival. Both were dressed in their native ao dai dresses. Lon's dress was all white, while Susie's was white with red roses, and each dress was made of Thai silk. It was truly a warm welcome home.

The apartment was full of surprises. Sax and I had a whiskey-coke sitting on the table, along with fresh crab meat, french bread, and rice. Not bad. While we ate, the girls were busy heating water for our baths.

Sax took his shower first. He emerged in about ten minutes wearing a large white silk robe, and wore an expression of contentment. Very soon I was to discover why.

Little Susie called to me. "Bob, come take shower. Have American soap and boo coo hot water." Baby San was giggling like a school girl, and Susie seemed elated about life in general.

The bathroom was larger than one would expect for such a small apartment. The shower had average pressure, and a nice even flow. The shower base was big enough to keep the water from running all over the place, but the water was cold. There was a large vat that caught rain water, and stored it in case of need. Susie had heated water in a deep oval tub, that she and Baby San had carried into the shower.

I went into the shower, and Susie undressed me. When I was bare, she completely undressed. I stood under the shower, and she poured hot water over my head, and soaped me from top to bottom until I was squeaky clean. She slapped my butt and sent me on my way. There was a large white, terry cloth robe hanging on a nail outside the shower, and new thongs.

After Susie finished showering she came into the bedroom. The only sound was a ceiling fan turning slowly above the bed. The fan was cooling and helped keep the mosquitos away.

My newly found love stripped as I had done, and cuddled up close to me. She was truly a sweet and lovely lady, and I had discovered a new, wonderful world with warm and caring people.

Chapter Seven

When I rolled out of bed Baby San was scrubbing the kitchen floor. My God, it was only 0445 hours. Susie and Lon kissed Sax and me good-bye and wished us good luck. They wanted to be at the local market early to buy fresh produce, but this was a daily routine. Time means nothing when people are happy helping one another.

We walked down the stairs to the dark street, and after a long wait a motor-driven cyclo stopped at the curb. We pointed down Tran hung Doa toward Hai ba Trung Street. The driver stopped at the Newhouse Hotel.

This eight-story building had been rented from the Vietnamese to house American civilian workers, and it also served as a bachelor officers quarters for the U.S. military. There was an American restaurant on the top floor.

Sax and I approached the only elevator. A sign read, "Do not overload - Maximum capacity 750 kilo."

We got on the contraption, and it slowly moved upward to the eighth floor. It literally quivered to a stop, and I slid open the accordion type door.

We stepped out onto an open walkway with a horrifying shock. There was a four foot high wall separating us from the street eight stories below. This was a helluva thrill at this time of the day. At least, I had brains enough not to look down. Sax did look down. He let out a holler and flattened himself up against the wall of the building. "Shit! What in the hell's the matter with me," he said. I wasn't going to laugh, it would have been a sure death.

Young Korean waitresses served an excellent breakfast. The menu consisted of bacon and eggs, toast, and tomato juice. Milk was also available. Great way to start any day. The elevator incident had *nearly* been forgotten.

It was past 0615 hours, when we headed for Long Binh, and already the notorious Route 1 was humming with traffic. Papa San floorboarded the gas peddle, which was good. We didn't make a good target for VC snipers, but we were vulnerable to being wiped out by a GI six by six truck.

Some of Papa San's passengers were asleep, but you can rest assured, I was sitting in a stiff, upright position. My eyes were glued to the highway, and when the bus passed on the left, I could see trucks bearing down from the other direction. I closed my eyes and clenched my fists. It was a white knuckle trip all the way to the job site.

I was sitting in the front seat just opposite Papa San, and I watched him. He faced straight ahead, and was aware of the dangers. He was an excellent driver, and quite conscientious for everyone's safety. I respected him, but I knew I'd never get used to Route 1.

We were right on schedule. It was 0655. Everyone piled out of the bus, went into the Area 208 office, and all Americans signed the register to indicate their presence for work.

Kim handled most of the paper work, while I watched. We had lunch at an army mess hall, and then Kim and I took a jeep assigned to the inventory group for a tour of Areas 206 and 207.

We drove about a mile to Area 207. This area was flat terrain like 208, that made it simple to warehouse. I was dumbfounded at the mountains of building materials warehoused in various staging areas. There was row after row of lumber, barbed wire, corrugated galvanized roofing, psp landing mat used to build air strips, thousands of drums of asphalt, and hundreds of thousands of other items.

The American taxpayers wouldn't believe this conglomeration. It was unadulterated government waste, and the American corporations and crooked politicians were making huge profits. We were an outside storage area in a war zone, not a giant-sized hardware and building supply store in the middle of a jungle. I discovered hundreds of conex boxes that contained electric stoves, washers and dryers, sinks, hot water heaters, and plumbing fixtures. There were stacks of well casings, various sizes of galvanized pipe, and millions of dollars in large electical components. The list goes on and on, and much of the material would never be used to fight a war. The local Vietnamese people would enjoy these gifts long after the American military and civilians had departed.

Joe Horton, the area supervisor, approached as we were in the process of inventorying some galvanized roofing. He was husky, round shouldered, and remarkably strong. He was a man who understood brute strength, and the strain on his tanned and weathered face indicated considerable physical labor in his fifty plus years. His large hand clasped mine, and definitely confirmed his great strength.

Kim and I got into the jeep, and headed for Area 206. I waved farewell to Horton, and told him I'd be back soon. We would become good friends.

We drove back out to Route 1, took a left, and covered the three miles to Area 206 in short order. This site was similar to Area 207, but it was smaller, and the terrain was rolling hills.

Maxie Rubbin, the area supervisor, stepped out of a small shack and smiled broadly. It was quite apparent this guy was a character. He said something to me in French, and patted Kim on the head as if he were a young boy. We introduced ourselves, and shook hands.

"You're our inventory wizard?" Rubbin asked. "Welcome, my friend, and lots of luck in your new venture."

"That bad, huh?"

"You'll get along, so don't worry."

It would be quitting time when we got back to Area 208. I asked Kim what he thought about inventory and adjustment. "Patterson I like you, and if you smart get out of inventory. Get Brown to put you into open storage supervisor like Maxie, Sax, and Mangie. You like better, and no have trouble for losses. Brown still your boss, but you only see him in open storage. No sweat."

Kim was right. Of course, I was aware he wanted this job and to be Brown's boy. I didn't like signing for lost material. The prospect of being a U.S. Government scapegoat and the federal penitentiary at Leavenworth bothered me.

The next three days were spent inventorying galvanized corrugated roofing, as there seemed to be a definite shortage. I used all three crews to work the three areas. The information was tabulated, and sent to Kraig's office in Cholon. The same day Kraig got me on the radio, and I was told that my inventories were inaccurate. I had indicated a shortage of thirty nine hundred sheets, and the shit hit the fan. Kraig told me to inventory again.

I'd had enough for one day. I told Kim I wished to get a haircut and a shave; I was starting to look like Mangie.

It was still early afternoon, so Kim and I jumped into the jeep. He wandered down a hill, and through the jungle for a few minutes. We approached a village in a valley of several thousand inhabitants. I looked back up the hill, and Long Binh could barely be seen three miles away.

"Bob, now you in Honai," Kim said, "I come here sometimes, and drink bomi bom beer and get haircut. Sometimes I get con gai (girl friend) and boo coo bum-e-lum (make much love)."

"Kim, you're very cunning. What about Vietcong? Maybe they cut your throat."

"No sweat. We pay barber boo coo money. Why bite hand that feed you?"

"Excellent deduction, my friend."

We entered the barber shop, and the old papa san bowed. Kim made him understand that I was a friend. The happy little man leaned the chair back. He steamed and lathered my face, stropped the straight razor several times, and preceded to scrape away. The razor glided across my throat giving me a chill, while Kim sat smiling. A young girl wearing a white smock sat in a chair to my left, and began manicuring my nails.

Strange world to think these people were just like the people back home in America. It was quite obvious that they were trying to be friends.

The haircut was accomplished with scissors and hand operated clippers. The entire grooming took about forty five minutes, and then the papa san massaged my neck and shoulders in a most professional manner. I gave the barber two hundred piasters. "Bob, you give papa san boo coo money, and he make you King of Honai."

As we left in the jeep, the old barber and his manicurist waved good bye. They might be Vietcong, but today they are just human beings. Perhaps someday my fellow Americans will kill them.

Two days rolled by, and shortly after I arrived for work Kraig called on the radio from the general office in Saigon. "Mr. Patterson, my office in Cholon has informed me that your galvanized roofing inventories are still incorrect. It appears that with three crews taking inventory, that you couldn't possibly show a loss of thirty nine hundred sheets. Do you have an answer?"

"Mr. Kraig, the only way to prove the shortage is for you to come to Long Binh, and I shall enlighten you. I realize you are busy, but if you want satisfaction, please come."

The following morning Kraig walked into our office at exactly 0900 hours. He went into Brown's office for several minutes, then motioned for me to step outside with him.

"Mr. Patterson, did you have something to show to me about the metal roofing? It's a long haul out here, so it best be good."

Kim and I motioned for Kraig to get into the jeep. I told him to drive to the area where we could see Honai. All three got out of the jeep, and I pointed toward the village.

"Mr. Kraig there's your galvanized roofing!" Every hut in Honai Village had a new galvanized roof. We climbed back into the jeep, and Kim headed back to Area 208.

"Mr. Patterson, this is a job well done. You can rest assured your word won't be disputed again. I'll inform Mr. Brown before I leave for Saigon." Kraig and I had just forged a good understanding.

The happy hour on Saturday night at Fanettes bar was boiling over with activity, as American GIs and ARVN soldiers, several Australians, and Saigon tea girls were living it up. We had to stand, but were recognized by the bartender, and soon Sax was sipping on a whiskey-coke, and I had cognac in hand.

A striking and most alluring tea girl moved in close to my side, and in a low seductive voice she asked, "Bob buy me drink."

I promptly ordered one Saigon tea. "Who are you, and how do you know my name?"

She smiled. "My name Le Lynn, and I see you every day with Sax. I have house on De Tram Street, and I start to work Fanette's Bar one week. O.K.?" She was obviously well oiled.

The bartender served her cognac instead of tea. It was unusual for Vietnamese women to drink hard liquor, but I didn't question. There were many eyes following the curves of this time bomb. Susie would kill me for sure if I ever thought bum-e-lum.

Le Lynn pushed up hard against me, and it was noticeable. Susie might have friends in the bar, and it would hurt her. I bought Le Lynn one more cognac. We clicked glasses, and her lips touched mine. "Chin Chin to you Bob." She was drunk, but my God, what an exotic and radiant drunk she was.

Sax and I bid Le Lynn farewell, and started for the apartment where Lon and Susie were patiently waiting. We kept a close eye on the cowboys loitering in the shadows of De Tram Street. We always walked rapidly with our arms swinging, and our eyes straight ahead. Some day these thugs were going to cause trouble; I could feel it.

The two girls greeted us with open arms at the apartment, and were bubbling over with happiness as they prepared drinks. After three drinks Susie made me stop. "Bob, no more drink. You get drunk, and maybe no can work tomorrow. You take shower, and chop chop. I have good Chinese soup for you."

As we ate Susie and Lon excitedly told us about a VC woman who had shot and killed an American captain early in the day. I had read in the papers about her before I left the States.

"Susie, do they call her the Tiger Lady, and does she ride her Honda up to American officers, shoot them, and quickly disappear into the crowd?"

"That you know is good, because you must be careful. I am afraid for you. Tiger Lady is bad bad Vietcong."

I informed Susie not to worry, because the Tiger Lady was interested in killing American military officers, not civilians. I also told her I was writing home. I needed some boots, and I would have my family send a small hand gun, something I could carry in my pocket.

"Susie, GIs will get the Tiger Lady. No Sweat."

"Bob, go to bed now, must work tomorrow, and make boo coo money." She was content with my reassurance that I was a civilian, and not as apt to have trouble with the Vietcong as American military personnel.

At work Sunday morning there was a coolness between Brown and me. I wasn't trying to buck him in any way, but sometimes he used poor judgement, and lacked common sense. I was using constructive criticism; trying to help him organize outside warehousing. I was fifteen years his senior, and I was experienced in the field. He was young, and boxing had been his only profession. How did he come into this job? Maybe PA&E wanted a tough guy to intimidate people. It was obvious that the black market was widespread. I thought of the huge material shortages. Was Brown dealing heavily in the market?

Sometimes the material, truck and driver all disappeared into thin air and were never found. There must be Americans involved. Too much expensive material was unaccounted for.

Perhaps I am too thorough in my job. I had always worked hard, and tried to do my level best. I needed this job, and the pay was above average. Tomorrow I would talk to Brown, and see what I could find out.

After work that night when the bus stopped, Sax walked alone to the apartment, and I stopped at Fanettes for a drink. I had some soul searching, and as much as I cared for Susie I wanted to see Le Lynn.

The Bar was nearly empty, so the female time bomb sat down beside me, and I ordered two cognacs. We didn't talk, but I think Le Lynn wanted my friendship. She had seen me with Susie, and for all I knew, they could be sisters.

After several drinks and two hours later, I walked across Tran hung Dao and entered De Tram Street. The cowboys eyed me, but they were still reluctant to make a move. I was vulnerable, and was damned relieved to get home.

Susie could see that I was plastered, and gave me the ol' silent treatment. She knew something was bugging me. I didn't eat, but had a huge blast of Black Velvet, showered and went to bed. Susie followed, but said nothing.

The following morning Sax and I went to the Newhouse as usual. We talked. He thought he had lost all his privacy. Lon owned a house. It might be best to go our separate ways, because living in cramped quarters could ruin a good friendship. Furthermore, Sax had always been independent. I could understand. I would talk to him later; I had too many other things on my mind, and besides I was hungover.

Soon after the bus arrived at Long Binh, I went into Brown's office, and immediately confronted the big man with my problems. "Lou, there seems to be some friction between us. What's the trouble?"

Brown leaned back in his chair. "Well, Mr. Patterson, it seems sometimes you are real anxious to get things done. Why don't you slow the pace, and let nature take its course? Sometimes we have to overlook things. You know what I mean, look the other way."

"Lou, I came to Vietnam to do a job, and I am well paid to do just that. Hell, we're just a bunch of Americans over here doing what has to be done. I feel responsible for the taxpayer's money. This sounds corny, but it's true."

"You just don't seem to see the big picture Mr. Patterson," Brown snapped, "you are immediately relieved of your duties. You're no longer inventory and adjustment supervisor. However, I do have another task for you. You are now an open storage supervisor. I'm assigning you an area far away from the office." Brown's eyes narrowed.

"Patterson, follow me and I shall enlighten you."

Brown took me to my newly assigned area. It was two miles to the location, and it was enormous. I would guess my storage section was at least two miles square, and it was loaded with goodies.

Storage pads were full of psp matting used for aircraft landing strips. There were thousands and thousands of drums of paving asphalt and stacks of steel bridging. Creosote treated poles and pilings ranging from twenty to ninety feet in length covered one large section. Pallets of barbed wire filled a pad. There was enough barbed wire to encircle the entire world. Stacks of well casings and stacks of galvanized pipe of various sizes were a tangled mess. The steel bridging was piled high and beginning to collect rust.

Thousands of pallets of cement were tagged "Do not use". It had been exposed to rain and was useless. Nothing was organized.

After completing the survey I confronted the supervisor. "Mr. Brown, this place is a disaster. If I can get some equipment and operators and some laborers I'll re-warehouse this fiasco. Give me two or three cranes and a half dozen rough terrain fork lifts. I can't do anything without equipment and bodies."

"You better make some room, because in a few days you'll begin receiving fifteen trucks an hour loaded with everything from psp landing mat to paving asphalt. You'll get your people and equipment."

Nothing was said as we returned to the office. It'll be better for me to be in open storage warehousing, I told myself, and I will have a challenge reorganizing the mess created by mismanagement. I boarded the bus for the trip to Saigon. It had been a grueling week. I'd kept my cool with Brown, and I was satisfied it was a job well done.

The old papa san driver awakened me at De Tram, and I stumbled off the bus. It was dark. Sax and Lon had gone to live in her house. I was alone, and I hesitated to walk into the dimly lit street. I had a couple belts of rot gut at Fanette's, and hurriedly walked down De Tram toward the apartment. I tried to ignore the cowboys standing in the shadows.

Susie and Baby San were standing on the balcony waiting patiently. Susie was wearing her favorite ao dai. She had added several red roses to the white native dress. It was always rewarding to see Susie's smiling face.

Baby San removed my shoes and slipped on my thongs. I poured three fingers of Black Velvet in a water glass and asked for water and ice."

I had three more shots of booze before Susie approached me. "Bob, now you take shower. When you get drunk you dinky dao. Please! Must work tomorrow."

She was right again. I pulled myself to a standing position, and made my way to the shower. I always enjoyed Susie's ritual in the shower, and I always came out squeaky clean.

After dinner Susie sat down in a chair beside me. "Honey, I tell you something. I go to market today and buy food. Cowboys follow me to De Tram. I go fast, but cowboys get me. They take everything, and they push me to the ground, and kick me. I am afraid."

"Susie, why would they hurt you?"

"Cowboys no good and they no work. Vietnam Army no want them. I live with American. Americans not liked by Vietnamese cowboys."

"Tomorrow night I will talk to cowboys, and if necessary we will move."

On the bus the next morning I made it a point to sit with Maxie Rubbin. He had lived and worked in the Orient for years, and was married to a Japanese girl. His wife was living in an apartment in Los Angeles, and they owned a house in Japan. Maxie and I could laugh together, and he made me feel confident when things weren't going right.

I mentioned Susie's incident with the cowboys on De Tram Street. "Bob, I know that section of Cholon, and it can get rough. Tonight after work I will come to your apartment, and we will talk. I also want to meet Susie. Don't worry."

My first day as an area supervisor went quite well, even better than I had expected. Brown gave me the manpower and necessary equipment to start reorganizing. I was confident.

Two experienced Korean crane operators were eagerly waiting, and apparently needed no coaching. Three Filipinos had been assigned; they were above average forklift operators, and three groups of laborers totaling one hundred fifty strong were standing by.

Only one Vietnamese was assigned as interpreter. He was also appointed as the storekeeper, and he instructed the laborers how to load and off-load materials. All my people were working in unison. How we communicated with this language barrier I'll never know.

Brown and Kraig drove slowly by once during the day. But they didn't stop. Evidently my work was satisfactory.

I stopped by the office after work, and Brown beckoned and asked me to visit. "Mr. Patterson, you seem to be making progress. The area needs a lot of attention. I have assigned carpenters to build a ten by fourteen foot building in your section. This will provide shelter and an office that can be locked for security reasons. I've arranged with an army supply sergeant to provide a footlocker for any personal valuables. Oh, incidentally, you have letters and a package."

"Thanks Lou, I must run and catch my bus." I was out of there. Things were moving along smoothly, and I didn't want to press my luck.

My adrenaline level was high, and I felt great. I sat down beside Sax on the bus, and opened a letter from Georgina and one from each of my two daughters. It was good hearing from them, and things seemed reasonably normal at home.

Georgina wrote small talk, and didn't say how the family was getting along in general. She asked nothing about how I was getting along, or about her job as a bookkeeper at a television repair shop. She did, at least, thank me for the money that I had sent home. Reconciliation appeared hopeless at this point, but I would mention the possibility to her in the future. The children certainly needed both parents.

Paulina's letter was lengthy, and she mentioned each brother and her sister. She talked about their progress at school, and said that she missed me. She wanted me to answer her letter soon, and to be sure to talk about the war. She was afraid for my safety.

Susanna wanted to know about the living conditions in Saigon, if I was getting enough to eat, and if I liked Vietnamese food. She missed me, and wanted me at home where I belonged. She casually mentioned that her mother had a boy friend; he worked in a bank in Pocatello, and called nearly every day.

The letters were warmly received. Georgina was single, and was free to do whatever. I, too, had a girl friend. But it hurt, and I missed her deeply.

The package contained a pair of Red Wing boots, and an expensive yellow sport shirt. Wrapped in carbon paper and onionskin paper was a 25 cal. Beretta semi-automatic and a box of ammunition. I had instructed Georgina to wrap the gun so it couldn't be x-rayed. It would have been confiscated if discovered by the Army Post Office (APO).

The Beretta was second hand, but looked to be in good condition.

Sax examined the gun. "Bob, this weapon isn't very big, but it could get you killed."

"Not at three feet." I replied. We both laughed, and Sax agreed.

I bypassed Fanette's Bar, as I wanted to meet with Maxie. Susie was waiting for me, and I told her about my friend, and that he would help.

Maxie came to the door, and I invited him in. Susie brought him a drink. "You must be Susie," he said. "Bob tells me you are number one girl friend."

Susie looked away. "Maxie, maybe Bob too good for me. He give me anything, and I try to be good for him. Maybe he drink boo coo whiskey, but O.K." Maxie approved of Susie, and we both assured her everything would be O.K.

My friend and I walked down the two flights of stairs to the street. Four cowboys were standing near by, and Maxie approached them. In fluent French he told them to follow and he would buy American beer.

We stopped at a sidewalk cafe where De Tram joined Co Bac Street. When we were seated, Maxie slowly reached under his shirt, and pulling out a 38 cal. S&W revolver. He smiled at the four cowboys, and gently laid it on the table.

He firmly advised the thugs never to bother Susie again. He ordered six beers, picked up the revolver and slipped it back into his pants. The cowboys bowed out gracefully, and Maxie assured me they wouldn't bother Susie again. They were only punks.

Maxie and I walked back to the apartment and had a drink together. Susie thanked him for coming to visit with us, and for helping us, and hoped he would return another day.

"Susie, take care of Bob. He and I think the same about this stinking war. This war make boo coo money for the rich American industrialist and crooked politician. They stuff money into their pockets."

Chapter Eight

Oने morning I asked Brown for the day off. I needed to get cash, and do some necessary shopping. He said my work seemed to be progressing satisfactorily, and gave his permission.

A fellow employee at Long Binh was an Italian named Joe Milletti. Once I was outside Brown's office Joe called me over to his desk. "I'm headed for Saigon. Want to join me? I am riding with PA&E's courier, and there's room for one more." I gratefully accepted.

"Bob, have you been to the Army PX and Commissary in Cholon or to the International House?"

"No, I haven't been sight-seeing in Saigon."

"Bob, this is good. You deserve a day to relax. We'll stop at the Cholon PX, and then have lunch at the International House. I explained I needed to get money, that my finances were exhausted. He said that could easily be arranged.

The courier honked his horn several times, and Milletti and I climbed aboard the jeep. The driver took off like a bolt of lightning, and we streaked down Route 1 in the storm of traffic. I was petrified with fear.

I suddenly realized it was Kim, the same crazy Korean that drove me to the rice mill for my interview with Kraig. It was bad enough riding with him in Saigon, but this was Route 1, the world's foremost death trap. I told Joe about my past experience riding with Kim, and he just sat there puffing on a huge cigar. Joe's expression confirmed his extreme fear.

The Italian was a little guy with a thin face, large, round eyes and an oversized nose. I thought he was going to devour the cigar, and I started laughing. I lost control of my emotions, tears rolled down my cheeks, and I couldn't get my breath. It wasn't just fear anymore; I was too scared to care.

Finally, Joe started laughing with me, and we both lost our fear of this crazy little bastard, driving like a maniac, leaning on the horn, and weaving in and out of traffic at fifty miles an hour. We just didn't give a damn.

Joe stopped the courier when we reached Gia Dinh, and we hailed a taxi. He gave an address to the driver, and we went several blocks before stopping in front of an expensive-looking villa. He knocked on the door, and a man cautiously peered out. "Marcel, this is Bob Patterson. He is a friend. No sweat."

Marcel was a very neatly dressed French National with a heavy accent. He was in his mid-twenties, dark complected, and quite handsome, with a radiant smile. "Come in. I will fix a drink. What is your choice, soft drink, whiskey, or cognac?"

"It's too early for a drink, and we don't have time, but thanks. Marcel, my friend Bob needs to change money. Can you help?"

The Frenchman asked where I lived, and I gave him my address on De Tram. "I will come tonight. Is this satisfactory?"

"Yes. Can I write a personal check? My Company frowns upon this, and I could lose my job."

"Do not worry. All personal checks are sent to Hong Kong for deposit. PA&E can't trace your check. I can get much better exchange rate for your money than you will get from your paymaster."

"Is PA&E short changing me?"

"The international exchange rate is one hundred twelve piasters for one dollar U.S. green. I will give you at least two hundred piasters for one dollar, and one hundred fifty in MPC notes. I will change three hundred dollars for your American check."

Milletti had done business with Marcel in the past, and had no problem writing a personal check. Marcel bowed out, and returned in ten minutes. He counted out the proper amount of piasters and MPCs to the Italian. Joe gave Marcel a check and nodded his approval of the transaction.

This was black market, and it was interesting. Marcel confirmed our meeting at my apartment on De Tram.

Joe hailed a taxi, and we beamed in on the Cholon P.X. and commissary. A military policeman checked our I.D. at the door and we went inside.

Joe told me Americans were limited to a maximum of twenty-five dollars in purchases per visit, but third nationals, such as Koreans and Filipinos were unlimited. He said the third nationals packed out merchandise by the arm loads, and sold on the black market. It was asinine, but the U.S. Government did strange things.

I purchased American toilet paper, bar and laundry soap, sanitary napkins for Susie, my monthly allotment of three fifths of Black Velvet, and four cartons of cigarettes. These items were either purchased at the commissary or bought on the black market for four times the cost. I wanted to purchase more, but had already spent my limit.

The Italian and I rendezvoused at the door, caught a taxi for a stop at my apartment, which was on the way to the International House. Susie was gone, but Baby San poked her head out of the kitchen. I left my PX purchases, and Joe and I headed for downtown Saigon.

In the taxi Joe told me about the International House, better known as the "I" House. It was membership only, and it took about six weeks to three months to be processed for a membership card. All walks of life were members, but little was actually known about the owners. Milletti didn't care who owned the club, as he was only interested in the excellent food and entertainment.

Upon our arrival Joe flashed his card, and we walked by several rows of slot machines into the dining room. We ordered American hamburgers with onions and dill pickles. It was delicious.

The "I" House was crowded with both men and women, and every conceivable nationality in the world was represented. I told Joe I would like to become a member.

We walked to the back of the club, down a hallway, and stopped at the manager's office. I filled out an application and Joe handed the man twenty-two dollars in MPCs. I was given a membership card. Joe told me that if an individual was given a card his application was strictly confidential. No one questioned a person about why he had an "I" card in his possession.

We left the building and the Italian said we had one more stop on Tran hung Dao. The driver stopped at a U.S. Army installation.

Joe shook hands with an army sergeant major who asked for my PA&E I.D. card. The sergeant inspected my card, and typed out a special I.D. card with my name. "Patterson, be careful, and don't lose this card. It will get you into any military installation in Vietnam. Understand?"

"Thanks, Sergeant, I'll take care."

"This card will get you into the Rex BOQ," Joe said. It's on Le Loi, just off Nguyen Hue. Susie will know where to go. I must go now. See you tomorrow." The little Italian disappeared in a maze of people.

Susie was home when I got to the apartment. She was elated about the purchases from the commissary and rewarded me with a kiss. It was late afternoon when I showed her my 25 cal. Beretta. "Susie, let's go find holster for my gun. Do you know where?"

"No sweat, Bob, we go Tu Do Street. Boo coo black market."

It was unbelievable. Sidewalks in downtown Saigon displayed black market merchandise everywhere. It wasn't hidden from view, and in places one had to walk in the street. The sidewalks were literally covered with everything from Kodak cameras to nineteen inch RCA TV sets. All American major brands of products were displayed, and there were items that couldn't be found in the Army P.X.

Susie and I looked around for some time, and I found a shoulder holster that was perfect for the Beretta. "Susie do you know Rex BOQ?" I asked.

"Yes, my American boy friend before take me there. Very nice place for to eat and drink. Have music and girls to sing and dance. We go?" I motioned for her to lead the way.

The Rex was a six story hotel that had been rented by the U.S.

Government to house American Officers, commonly known as Bachelor Officer's Quarters (BOQ). Upon entering I was asked for my I.D., we were admitted, and Susie and I walked to the elevator. She pushed the fifth floor button.

On the fifth floor was a shop displaying jewelry, expensive clothing such as sweaters, shoes, and tee shirts.

Just beyond the shop was a huge open room. There was a long bar, numerous cocktail tables and a band stand. To the left of the bar was a dining room, situated on the open air side. Barbecue grills were set up to accommodate people wishing to cook their own steaks, or other foods. I was impressed.

I took a table, and ordered beer, while Susie made a beeline for the shop. She returned to the table and smiled. "Bob, please come to see. I like, and maybe you buy for me?"

She had selected a short sleeved sweater. How could I resist? It was made from pure white angora rabbit hair, that proved Susie's excellent taste for the finer things in life. The sales lady put the sweater in a plastic bag, and we went home.

Soon after we arrived home Marcel knocked on the door. He entered cautiously, his eyes darted around the room, and then relaxed. "Bob I know you are Milletti's friend, but changing money is illegal, and it could cost me boo coo time in a Vietnamese prison."

"Marcel, don't worry. This whole damned war is a mess. I will write you a check on my bank in the U.S." He removed a large envelope from an attache case and counted out three hundred thousand piasters. He counted out two hundred MPCs and asked me to count them again.

I counted the money and confirmed everything was in order. We shook hands. "Bob, thank you for the business, and I trust we will meet again."

I gave the money to Susie for safe keeping. I knew it was in good hands. "Susie, we just made a profit of one hundred sixty three thousand piasters, and seventy five dollars in MPC notes." Her black sparkling eyes displayed her approval.

The following morning as I walked part way to our storage areas with Sax, I told him about changing money and getting an "I" House card. I hoped that some night he and Lon would have dinner with Susie and me.

The construction of my office was completed, and I was impressed with the professionalism of the Vietnamese workers. The building was ten by fourteen feet, and had the luxury of a wooden floor with four foot wooden side walls. It was enclosed above the siding with heavy wire. The door was equipped with a hasp and padlock, and the roof was covered with galvanized steel. It gave me a feeling of importance.

The footlocker given to me by the army was great. I had a place to store my letters, thermos, rain jacket, and other items. Some of the other area supervisors took advantage of the foot locker's security by storing cameras and several firearms.

I checked my people's performance at work; they were busy, and they knew their jobs. The Koreans were stacking drums of paving asphalt, and the Filipinos were warehousing psp matting. The laborers kept close watch over me, and wouldn't allow me to do anything physical.

The local national's wages averaged about twenty five thousand piasters per month. At the International exchange rate this was twenty plus dollars American green.

Third national's wages ranged from four to eight hundred U.S. green per month, and this was big money for them. We must remember it was U.S. taxpayer's dollars.

Everything at work was going quite well. Brown cruised my area, but normally he drove on. Sometimes he would suggest re-warehousing materials, and I would agree. However, I paid little attention because my area was becoming well organized and running smoothly.

My crews could receive thirty to forty trucks an hour, off-load them, and not fall behind. They could load thirty GI six-bys with materials in half a day, and Brown knew this efficiency kept the main office off his back. Other supervisors marveled at the progress in my area, and recognized how neatly the material was warehoused. They asked how I managed laborers and third nationals. My answer was simple. "You treat them like human beings, and they'll return the favor."

I was concerned about Susie. She was dealing with the cowboys.

Susie was smart, but some things were difficult for her. Maybe I needed to take time off, and get some much needed rest. We could share some time together.

Every night I stopped at Fanettes and drank cognac with Le Lynn. Tonight was no different. It bothered me to see her drink, and she was pushing herself by spending so much time at the bar. Saigon tea commissions were a good income for Le Lynn. We had no sexual relationship, but was sure it could be arranged. I valued her friendship.

After several drinks I always went to the rest room, and jacked a round of ammunition into the chamber of the Beretta, before the trip down De Tram street. It had become a nightly ritual.

I bid Le Lynn farewell and started for the apartment. I walked swiftly down De Tram. There were no cowboys in sight. I was slightly inebriated, but I was uneasy. I sensed something wrong. It was too quiet.

The silence was interrupted by the loud roar of motorcycles approaching from Tran hung Dao Street. I turned; three cowboys were bearing down on me. My hand instinctively reached for the Beretta. The noise was frightening, and the headlights were blinding. I flipped the safety, and rapid-fired three rounds into the ground in front of the Hondas. The cowboys sat silently on their bikes. I stood my ground with the gun pointed directly at them. I dared not show my fear, or they would surely attack. They slowly backed out of the street. I felt confident that Susie and I could live in peace.

When I got to the apartment Susie put her arms around me. "Bob, cowboys no come again. I know you shoot gun, and they think maybe you kill them."

After taking my shower I sat at the table, and drank straight whiskey. Despite Susie's companionship, I was lonely and homesick. I missed Sax, and I longed for Georgina and the kids. Drinking myself into oblivion only caused depression, and when I drank I was rude to Susie and everyone else. But I drank anyway. I needed some answers. I couldn't understand why I needed to drink so much, or why I was depressed. I was concerned for my Vietnamese friends, and their future independence. Would the South win the conflict? What was happening to my life?

The next morning I was hung over. My head was killing me, and I craved a drink of booze. I grabbed for my bottle and held it to my mouth. I drank myself back to never-never land.

Susie was mad, not only because of my condition, but because I didn't go to work. She shook her head in disgust, and said, "You dinky dao, and you lose job."

Susie left the apartment, and I stumbled back into bed in a drunken stupor. It was afternoon before I awakened. I immediately went to the shower, and found the cold water to be sobering and refreshing.

Susie was still gone, so I poured another whiskey. With the glass in my hand I settled into the lounge chair on the balcony to brood. I didn't give a damn about war or life in general.

Across the alley from the apartment house was a Buddhist Temple. The monks stood on the flat rooftop, and peered over the side at the outside world. Their heads were shaven and they wore long saffron-colored robes, and from the balcony I could make out their faces and hear their voices.

These young Vietnamese were studying to become monks, some out of faith, but it mostly protected them from the South Vietnamese military draft. As monks, they were exempt. Why should they have to face death in a meaningless war? Of course, thousands of American youth faced the same fate and held the same conviction about the draft.

Susie was gone for the day, and probably for the night because of my behavior. I continued my binge. I was exhausted from weeks of 11 hour days, the stress of traveling route 1. And I was homesick. I needed some time to myself.

There were two six packs of American beer in the refrigerator, and I still had two fifths of whiskey. I made repeated trips into the apartment to refill my drink, but always returned to the balcony. I glared at the monks and showed them the 32-20 revolver that lay on my lap. In my drunken state of mind I wanted to intimidate them, to prove my superiority over the young novices. I wanted to show them who I was. I had another drink.

I had a high tolerance for alcohol, and sometimes wouldn't appear to be drunk. I didn't slur my words, and my equilibrium was good, but my behavior was intolerable. Of course, I'd had years of practice. I decided to pay my monk neighbors a visit.

I went into the apartment and put my revolver into my belt. I slipped on my favorite yellow sport shirt, letting it hang loosely over my pants to conceal the weapon. I made my way down the stairs, and strutted out into the street.

I paraded into the Buddhist Temple, and was amazed to find the room was bare except for a large gold statue of the Buddha.

There was a spiral staircase leading upwards, and without hesitation I ascended to the second floor. Much to my surprise several monks were sitting around visiting with uniformed ARVN soldiers. I hadn't realized these young people were so human. I bowed politely.

"I am an American, my name is Bob, and live next door. I wanted to meet with you."

It was like old home week. Everyone shook my hand. Nearly all these young monks spoke English, and for a minute I was speechless.

The surprise of seeing soldiers in uniform, and the monks' hospitable reception had a sobering effect. I told my audience where I lived in the States, and how long I had been in Vietnam. I explained that I worked for a civilian company at Long Binh in warehousing.

An ARVN soldier came forward, and introduced himself. He was short and muscular, built like a tank, and looked in superb physical condition. He was good looking, and his features resembled Caucasian more than Asian.

"I am Lieutenant Hehn. We wrestle with arms on table like in U.S." He pointed to a coffee table, and gestured with his arm, bending it from the elbow with his fist clinched.

"Lieutenant, do you want to arm wrestle?"

"For sure papa san. I show you something. O.K.?"

Hehn beat me, but not without a struggle. I asked him how he knew about arm wrestling. He told me he had trained in America for a year with the U.S. military, and had learned many American customs. He had seven years service in the military. At the present he was on leave and was visiting with his family in Saigon.

We sat on a couch, and some of the others gathered around to visit. Then everyone suddenly jumped to their feet and bowed in unison as an older, heavy-set Vietnamese entered the room. He head was shaven, and was clad in a white robe and leather thongs. Hehn leaned close and whispered into my ear. "Bob, this is Big Buddha; big, big, Buddha of all Saigon." Everyone respectfully stood back and remained absolutely motionless.

The Buddha looked me straight in the eye, and I politely bowed. At the same time my revolver fell out of my belt onto the coffee table, and shattered the thick glass that covered the top. I was so embarrassed. I was mortified, and I wanted to run to the rooftop and jump over the side.

I picked up the revolver, and stuck it back in my pants. The Buddha walked to a desk, and seated himself behind it. I'm sure he could tell I was absolutely mortified. I opened my billfold, took out the total of fifteen hundred piasters and laid it on the desk.

"I am terribly sorry. I will give whatever you ask for replacing the glass. Tomorrow I will come back and bring money."

The Buddha declined my offer. I bowed and backed out of the room, and ask Lt. Hehn to join me. We left together.

Susie was home with a girl friend, and didn't appear to be mad or upset. I knew I'd had made an ass of myself, and I apologized to her for getting drunk. Susie introduced her girl friend. "This is Leo. We have been friends long time."

I introduced Hehn to the girls. My story of how I met Hehn at the temple upset Susie. When I mentioned breaking the coffee table's glass top, she came unglued. She said we must move away.

Hehn pleaded my case. "Buddha understood the circumstances. He knew Bob was drunk, and forgave all." Susie only shook her head, and said nothing.

Susie served refreshments, and we visited. I could see that Leo and Hehn had developed interest for each other, and I thought they would make a handsome couple. The two left to get better acquainted, and Susie and I went to bed.

I signed in for work at Long Binh the following morning, and my eyes and bloated face proved a dead give away. Jack Hutson, transportation department supervisor, and Maxie Rubbin noticed my condition, but said nothing. I walked out to my area. The two mile hike helped clear my throbbing head.

As I made my rounds in the area, I noticed the equipment operators and laborers were idle. My absence had created problems. Only one crane and two forklifts were operating, and the laborers were waiting for orders.

The operators informed me that most equipment was deadlined, and was at the maintenance shop being repaired. No drinking water had been delivered to the area, and lister bags (waterproof canvas bags with spigots) hanging in various locations were empty. They should have been filled with water daily for laborer's use. I was angry at myself for letting my crew down.

I walked to the maintenance shop and asked why the equipment wasn't being maintained. A mechanic explained that half the American mechanics were in Saigon screwing off, and repair parts were in short supply. There weren't even spark plugs to keep the jeeps operating. The tire shop couldn't keep up with tire repairs, and new tires were scarce.

I walked up the road and stormed into Brown's office. He was sitting behind his desk with his feet propped on the top. He lowered a magazine. "Patterson, now what's on your mind?"

"What has happened around here? I just came from the shop, and everyone is gone. Most of the equipment is deadlined. There are no parts. How are the area supervisors suppose to do the job? How can my people work without water? The water truck hasn't been around for days."

Brown leaned back and folded his hands behind his head. "Patterson, keep your shirt on. It takes time to get things done."

"There's a war on," I yelled, "and the army engineers need bridging, and other major contractors need materials."

"Cool it. I run this place," Brown countered, "so get back to your area, and do your job." I walked out shaking my head. How was I supposed to do my job without equipment? How were my people supposed to work without water?

There were Americans that wanted this war to last forever. The longer the war lasted, the more money they could make on the black market. Brown could get emergency parts from the army, and he knew it.

American GIs were dying; these materials were critical to the success to the military effort. Convoys needed to be loaded promptly, so they could get back to their respective areas before dark. Convoys moving after dark were easy prey for the Vietcong. They were open to ambush, and American GIs were dying. I felt responsible.

After work I got drunk at Fanettes, and it was late when I staggered down De Tram to the apartment. The cowboys had kept their distance since our last encounter, and my gun display. All was quiet.

Susie wasn't mad, but was disappointed with my condition. I poured a drink and told her I had to change conditions at work. "Bob take shower. No drink. Must work tomorrow. Okay?"

The next morning Brown informed me that I would be receiving forty trucks an hour for off loading. Half the trucks would be loaded with psp matting, and the balance would be paving asphalt. "I need at least four cranes, and four to six forklifts. "I told him. Get me the equipment!" I went to other area supervisors for help, and borrowed two cranes and two forklifts. My crews stood by. They were loyal, they respected me, they were aware of the problem confronting me.

Philco-Ford flatbed trucks loaded with materials started arriving from Newport, the docks that were located at the mouth of the Saigon River. We went into action. Everybody knew their job. We worked ten hours without a break, and at times there were trucks backed down the road for three miles. We didn't give up, and the last truck was off-loaded at 1900 hours.

I didn't work the next day. I slept late, and in the afternoon Susie and I went to the Rex. I drank beer, and she browsed in the shop. I sat at the bar, and talked to a couple of colonels about the war. They were both drunk and talking shop.

Their mission in Vietnam was search and destroy the Vietcong. There was one hitch. They couldn't find the elusive enemy, let alone destroy him. They, like the rest of the American military, were frustrated and bewildered.

I bought Susie some earrings, and another sweater. We went home, and Hehn and Leo visited for the evening. He and I got pleasantly plastered, while the women were talking about their families and the war.

I asked Hehn how long he was committed to staying in the military. "Bob, a Vietnamese soldier is committed to the Army until he either is killed or so badly wounded that he can no longer fight."

Hehn had become a good friend, and he wanted peace. He wanted to marry Leo, have a family, go fishing, and play golf. He loved his country. He was just like American boys, fighting and trying to restore peace to his homeland. The word "communism" was rarely mentioned.

When I signed in for work the next day I said nothing to Brown, and immediately left the office. I walked slowly, and detoured into other areas to see what kinds of materials were warehoused.

The army had a huge complex that was loaded with goodies. Refrigerators and electric stoves, thousands of gallons of paint, and thousands of portable air conditioners were stored in conex boxes. They were stacked three high, and stretched for two square miles. Row after row of wooden crates identified only by Federal Stock Numbers were piled in seemingly endless rows. Millions of board feet of lumber were stacked side by side. Each bunk of lumber was tightly banded and rotting in the humid heat. It angered me to think that American forests were being stripped of trees so the lumber could rot in this stinking jungle.

Another storage pad housed water purification equipment and ice making machines with "Made in Germany" stenciled on each crate. Dozens of generators from three kilowatt to fifteen hundred kilowatt were stock-piled with "Made in Japan" stenciled on each crate. Thousands of drums of paving asphalt were marked "Republic of China." American taxpayers were supporting foreign companies. Why?

A mile to the east, at Long Binh, was a huge U.S. munitions dump. It was several miles square, and entirely enclosed with chain link fencing. Barbed wire was installed around the top, and a full company of U.S. infantry had been assigned to guard the area.

Vietcong dug "spider holes" under the fence into the dump to blow up pads of ammunition. Regardless of the number of troops guarding the ammo dump it was virtually impossible to keep out the VC. They could burrow like moles.

There were numerous other locations in Vietnam that housed large open storage complexes. To name a few: Cam Ranh Bay, Nha Tranh, Da Nang, Qui Nhon, Tuy Hoa, Hue, Ben Hoa and Tan Son Nhut Air Bases. The American taxpayers wouldn't believe the billions of dollars being spent. The pockets of rich American industrialists and crooked politicians were bulging with U.S. greenbacks. They had no consideration for the young American boys dying in this undeclared war.

The workload increased during the next couple of weeks. Equipment breakdowns were an every day occurrence. There was one nine-day period that lister bags remained empty of water for the laborers. Days dragged and working conditions worsened, and everyone was exhausted from the heat.

I was becoming a thorn in the side of PA&E bosses, and my friend Sax kept warning me just to keep quiet and do my job. "Bob, this is a 'mickey mouse' war, and you are fighting city hall. You can't win. Do your job and take care of your obligations back in the world." I knew my job was in jeopardy.

That night Susie was excited. The Tiger Lady was big news in Saigon. She had ridden her Honda up to an American captain, and shot him in the face. An American GI on guard duty nearby saw what happened, and opened up with an automatic rife. He was at close range; the bullets literally cut the woman in half. One less Vietcong.

It rained hard for several days, and the warehousing work came to an absolute stand-still. I was restless, and I was drinking heavily. It was hard to put the bottle down once I started, and my hands shook.

It always took three days to get back to normal. I kept beer on hand at work, this way I could ease off the alcohol and not get the shakes. I'd definitely become an alcoholic, and I had no idea how to cope with my problem.

Drinking had become a way of life, and my escape from reality. I drank for the next three days and nights, while it kept raining. Sometimes I would stay in the apartment, and sometimes I would go to Fanettes or the Rex BOQ. Susie went to the Rex with me, mainly to keep me out of trouble. I argued with the American officers about the war. But sometimes I felt sympathetic.

I understood the American GIs were ordered to fight. They were mostly patriotic, and good soldiers. But some would get drunk and brag about search and destroy missions or about killing for the plain enjoyment.

I had company on the fourth morning of my binge. Jack Hutson and Maxie Rubbin walked into the apartment. Maxie took one look, and shook his head. He was thoroughly disgusted. I was exhausted, and my hands were shaking. I was unshaven and dirty, and I had been guzzling beer since before dawn. I was drunk.

Susie excused herself, and Jack and Maxie seated themselves at the table. "Bob Patterson, is that you?" Maxie laughed. "What's with you, Bob?"

"I guess I'm feeling sorry for myself. I'm no damn good. I'm weak and a nobody."

"Patterson! Damn it. Get your head out of your ass," Jack said. We need you on the job. Brown's going to get you by the balls."

"It's only 0830 hours. We'll drive you to Long Binh," Maxie said. "We'll go straight to your area, and you stay out of sight. You've gotta sober up."

Susie came into the room. "Bob, please, I love you. I afraid for you. You lose job. You must give money to baby sans in America."

I showered and shaved, and the three of us left the apartment. Hutson nosed the company pickup toward Long Binh. We passed the main office at Long Binh and I ducked down. Jack headed straight for my area.

I ran to my office; I knew Brown was sure to be on the prowl. I unlocked my office, and went inside. I took a rock and broke loose the screen next to the hasp, just enough for my hand to slip through from the inside. I took the padlock, and placed it into the hasp, and locked it. I straightened the screen enough so Brown wouldn't notice. I became the man who wasn't there.

There was a hammock slung in the office, and I got underneath; not even Brown could detect me. The booze had taken its toll. I passed out.

Later I heard Brown calling my name. I didn't move. He called again and again. He walked away, but continued calling. He asked Hoa, my interpreter, if he had seen me. Hoa didn't answer.

After I was sure Brown was gone I unlocked the door, and walked outside. I strolled down the rows of lumber, and out onto the main road that surrounded the area. I needed to be seen.

I casually meandered along inspecting materials. Brown pulled along side and told me to get into the pickup. "Where the hell have you been, Patterson? You haven't been here for three days, and this morning I couldn't find you. Now you come bouncing up like a rubber ball."

"Lou, I've been sick with dysentery, but I'm here this morning. Sometimes I forget to sign the register. Is there anything wrong?"

I saw Jack Hutson after work. He asked, "Bob, y'all still on the payroll?"

"Is something wrong, Jack?" It had been a long day.

"Bob, I'll take you home tonight. I just bought a brand new 1968 Toyota Corona, and we'll take a spin. You need some fresh air."

Jack lived in a villa at University Village about five hundred yards west of Route 1. It was two miles east of Thu Duc, a city of fifty thousand people. Thu Duc was half-way between Long Binh and Saigon.

Villas at University Village had been built specifically to house the professors and instructors that would teach at the University of Saigon. The University of Saigon had been built before the start of the war, but it never opened. It was conveniently located on a hill near Thu Duc.

We pulled off Route 1 at the Thu Duc junction, and drove a short distance to the villa that Jack rented from a doctor. He pulled into the driveway.

"Jack, how much does this villa cost?"

"Bob, it's a hundred dollars U.S. green per month. Not bad. What I like, in addition to the country living, is that I'm close to Long Binh and close to Saigon."

The war had prompted the landlord doctor to move his practice to Vung Tau, a resort town on the South China Sea. Leaving the villa vacant wasn't wise, mainly for security reasons, and renting to an

American was the best alternative.

The villa was ideal. It was located in the country, on a banana plantation, and palm trees and mahogany trees had been planted for future harvest. I could see other villas secluded in other banana groves.

We walked through a screened front porch into a large living room that faced west, toward Thu Duc. The villa had a dining room, and three large bedrooms. Each bedroom had its own bathroom and shower. Another bedroom was located on the extreme north of the villa, just off the rear of the kitchen. The maid's quarters off the kitchen were more than adequate, and would definitely please Baby San. Each room had a ceiling fan.

The villa contained three refrigerators, two full sized ones in the kitchen and a smaller one in Jack's bedroom. The small fridge was equipped with a keyed lock to protect his beer and cigarette supply.

I saw other items of interest. A U.S. Army shortwave radio was on a table in the living room; M-1 and M-2 automatic rifles were partly concealed between the dining room wall and Jack's liquor cabinet. A white jeep was parked out front. Jack said the U.S. Army had supplied the items by barter, that is, in exchange for favors.

The jeep belonged to Bob Priest. Bob was an unemployed master mechanic, who had been working for RMK. Borrowing a jeep from the Army was one thing; painting it white was ludicrous.

Security was minimal at the villa. A four foot high fence interwoven with a thick, thorny hedge surrounded the property. The security system consisted of one large white goose. Jack said the old gander caused a ruckus whenever strangers approached, particularly after dark. You could hear him honk for a country mile. Some security was necessary, because Thu Duc was is the middle of Vietcong country.

A one car garage was attached to the villa. The yard had a lawn and a few flowers and shrubs, but wasn't well groomed.

Jack shared the villa with Yvonne, his Vietnamese girl friend and Larry Potter, who was also employed by PA&E. Some of Yvonne's relatives served as maids and housekeepers, and one was the groundskeeper. My first impression was that Yvonne ruled the roost. She had created a haven for herself and her entire family.

We drove back to Saigon after completing the grand tour of Jack's villa. He asked if I would be interested in living at Thu Duc. I could have the main bedroom. The offer was tempting, but I would need Susie's opinion.

I wasn't enthusiastic about Yvonne and her family. The clan would probably eat us out of house and home, and steal us blind. Everything would have to be kept under lock and key.

Jack parked the Toyota out front, and we walked to the apartment. I introduced Susie, and poured him a drink. I told Susie about the villa, and that Jack asked us to share it with him. She was thrilled.

Susie had lived in Thu Duc and had performed her song and dance routine at a theater in the city before the war. It would be like going home. "Bob, we move tomorrow?" she asked.

Jack left for Thu Duc. Susie started packing and I went to bed. My hangover was gone and I felt satisfied about the move. A change of scenery would be good, and Little Black Eyes was elated.

Chapter Nine

September arrived, and Susie and I were enjoying our new surroundings at University Village. It was convenient for me, and it was neat riding back and forth to work in Jack's Toyota. Some nights I'd take the bus from Long Binh to the Thu Duc junction. It was less than a ten minute walk from the villa.

I did miss going to Fanettes for cognac and visiting with Le Lynn. I wouldn't see Sax and Lon, go to the "I" House, or visit with Benny at the Royal Hotel. But I didn't have to roll out of bed in the middle of the night, and risk the bus ride to and from Saigon on Route 1, and I had extra hours of leisure each day. Hitchhiking was easy, as rides were readily available, and Jack went to Saigon regularly.

Doctor Nguyen Le Huu, our landlord, came one evening to collect the rent. He was a well educated and soft spoken medical professional, and had been informed that Susie and I were living at the villa. He was happy. We were responsible people, and would take care of his property. He yearned to return to his medical career at Thu Duc someday, when the fighting ended.

Dr. Huu had checked Susie's background, and she had an excellent reputation in the Thu Duc area. Jack had a reputation for heavy drinking, rowdiness, and shooting firearms inside and outside the villa. Had I known this, I would have hesitated about moving. Jack was all right though, and we understood each other. God knows I drank too.

Larry Potter and I were getting acquainted, and occasionally he would come out to my storage area and visit. I didn't know his duties at PA&E, and he always avoided the issue, but it was no concern of mine. We started having lunch at the U.S. Army's 9th Transportation Company mess hall together, and some times Jack joined us. The 9th Trans. had excellent food, and the mess sergeant was a great guy.

During lunch one day Larry asked me to get money orders for him at an Army Post Office (APO), and I obliged. He pulled up to an APO, and I went inside with a fist full of MPC notes.

I handed the clerk one thousand dollars. He studied the photo on my ID card, and without hesitation handed me ten one hundred dollar money orders. Larry had instructed me not to write anything on them. I was curious about the transaction, but I was learning to look the other way.

At Thu Duc the next evening Jack and I were sitting in the living room drinking beer, and Potter walked in with two men. They walked directly to his room. I noticed Larry was sweating heavily, and he looked troubled.

The two men left, and Larry came into the living room with a beer in his hand. He took a deep breath, wiped his brow, and flopped onto the sofa.

"Who were those two guys?" Jack asked. "I thought they might be the Russian KGB. The dark glasses and jackets with epaulets on each shoulder, and the wide belts and buckles made them look like James Bond."

"Those guys were CID, Criminal Investigation Division, the U.S. Army version of the FBI," Potter answered. "They've accused me of changing money on the black market, and wanted to search my room for evidence."

Jack spilled his beer as he leaped from the chair. His mouth dropped open and his eyes narrowed. "Why did you bring them here? You stupid ass! There isn't any doubt they saw our weapons. No way they could overlook this damn shortwave radio with U.S. Army written all over it. They couldn't miss Priest's white Army jeep out front." He hesitated. "Leavenworth isn't that far away. You're going to get us all into the gray manor."

Potter tried to cover his ass. "Jack, I had Patterson get the money orders. He hasn't gotten any for himself. The CID can't trace anything. I'm clean."

"What the hell are you doing, Larry? Are you making me a patsy?" I shouted. "What's with the money orders? I demand an explanation. Are you conning me?"

Jack grabbed hold of Potter's shirt. "Damn it, you bastard. Level with Bob. He's a friend. Don't get him all fucked up. Understand?"

Potter started sweating again. "I'm sorry, Patterson. Money orders bring big bucks on the black market. Damned near as much as U.S. greenbacks."

"Bob, have you changed money since you've been in country?" Jack asked.

"Yeah. I wrote a personal check to a French national at Gia Dinh. The exchange rate was much higher than at PA&E's pay office at the golf course. I made a good profit."

"You're getting the idea," Jack beamed. "I've sent many money orders home, all from the black market. Get them from different army post offices so the APO clerks don't remember your face; and they don't ask questions. These young Army kids don't give a shit anyway. We're only authorized to buy two hundred dollars worth a month, but sometimes I change a couple thousand. That makes me two to three grand profit a month in addition to my monthly wage with PA&E. You know—there's a war on."

Potter's hands were still shaking as he cracked open another beer. "Bob, you've got to try the market. You'll make more than working for any company in Vietnam."

"You got to be careful though," Jack said, cautiously. "The CIA and CID will kick your ass out of the country if you're caught. One other thing, about every six months the U.S. Government replaces current notes, and prints different colored MPCs. They give Americans twenty-four hours notice to cash in their notes for the new ones. The secret is to change money fast, and mail your money orders back to the States."

"Jack, have you ever been stuck with the old MPCs before you could exchange?" I asked.

"Bob, I've been stuck with a couple thousand in MPCs. But there's a risk in anything. If you're interested in changing money I'll show you the ropes."

"It sounds like a challenge. Everyone tells me this is a mickey mouse war. Money is the main objective."

"We'll leave work early tomorrow, and cruise Saigon for black marketeers," my Texan friend drawled. "Potter, damn you. You can sign Bob and me out tomorrow at Long Binh, so we'll get a full day's pay. Do you understand? Remember the CID is on your ass!" Jack smiled. "Larry, it won't only be the CID, I'll contact the CIA."

I'd never seen anyone sweat like Potter, and he was having trouble lighting a cigarette. It gave me a good feeling.

The following day Jack and I got into his car at Long Binh, and headed for the 9th Trans. mess hall. We ate a quick sandwich, and headed straight for Saigon.

When we reached the city Jack stopped the car at a newsstand. He bought a Saigon Post newspaper and placed two one hundred dollar money orders inside. He parked the car on Tu Do Street, and we went straight to the Continental Hotel.

We took stools at the bar, positioning ourselves to have a full view of the entire room. Each ordered a vodka collins, and Jack put the newspaper on the bar. A bartender named Charlie moved in close to Jack. He nodded, but said nothing.

"Charlie, I have two hundred dollar money orders. How much for MPC today? I don't need piasters, only MPC."

"I get you one hundred sixty-five," Charlie answered.

"Are you Cheap Charlie today or good ol' Charlie?" Jack smiled. "I can get a hundred seventy-eight at Johnnie's book store cross the street. You no lie. How much you give me?" There was a silence before the bartender answered.

"Jack, maybe I get one hundred eighty. I try for you. O.K.?"

Hutson agreed. "If you get one eighty, O.K. You no Cheap Charlie. You number one Charlie." The old bartender smiled.

The cagey old fox disappeared, and Jack and I casually sipped our drinks. I felt like Humphrey Bogart in *Casablanca*, but don't get me wrong, Jack was no Bogart!

There was no doubt that many shady deals had been transacted at the Continental. I suddenly realized I was becoming part of this corrupt, mickey mouse war.

Civilians had it easy. We hadn't been drafted right out of high school to take orders from some glorified general soaking up the sunshine by his swimming pool. We didn't have to carry M-16 rifles into the jungle and get our asses shot off. God, how I empathized with the American GIs. What were they fighting for?

Charlie reappeared in about ten minutes, placed the newspaper back on the bar, and walked away. Jack slowly looked around, picked up the paper, and put it under his arm. "Bob, I'm going to count the money. Keep your eyes open, and come back to the restroom if anything looks suspicious." I felt like the cat who'd swallowed the canary.

He returned without the newspaper, and we left. Jack cautioned me. "Always count the money. If you're short, get it straightened out pronto. If Charlie knows he can fuck you, he'll do it every chance he gets.

"That was easy, but be careful," Jack said. "Saigon is crawling with CID and CIA. I will buy three more money orders at an APO, so I will be ready to change again. I made one hundred-sixty dollars today. When I accumulate a thousand dollars I buy money orders, and send them home for deposit in my bank account. Simple and very profitable! It's our free enterprise system in Saigon."

We motored down Route 1 toward Thu Duc, and I questioned the money changing artist. "Jack, won't the army postal clerks get suspicious after awhile, and notify the authorities? Your face will become quite familiar."

"Bob, I don't worry about that, because there are numerous APOs, and I rotate each time. Sometimes I get GIs to buy money orders for me, and I pay them for their services." He hesitated. "Most of these kids that work at APOs don't much give a damn. They're draftees, and just want to go back to the World.

"If you really want to make the big money, have someone send you U.S. green in one hundred dollar bills from the States. Instruct them to write a short letter on typing paper. Wrap the greenbacks in the typing paper, onionskin paper, and in carbon paper. APOs can't x-ray the contents. It's illegal to have U.S. greenbacks in your possession. I can get two hundred fifty MPCs for one hundred U.S. green."

Susie and Yvonne met us at the door of the villa. Both tried to speak at once, and Yvonne finally won out. "Jack, Larry Potter come in after work. He get clothes, and say he move to Saigon. He try to make love to me."

"It's better this way," Jack said. "With Larry gone maybe we can stay out of Leavenworth. Dale Henderson wants to move here, and that is good."

Sax walked to my area the next morning to visit. He and Lon were doing fine. He said Lon and her brother managed an Esso service station not far from where they living in Saigon. The money was good, it kept her busy, and she felt important.

Sax cautioned me to be careful playing the black market. Joe Milletti had gotten caught changing money at Marcel's in Gia Dinh. Marcel was slapped in a local Vietnamese jail, and Milletti was escorted to the airport by the CID. He had to leave the country. Dale Henderson had talked to Joe before the authorities hauled him away in a military car, and Milletti was laughing about the incident.

Joe bragged that he had been in country for six months, and sent sixty thousand dollars back to his home in Spain.

"Marcel is a nice guy, but his chances of survival in a Vietnam prison is about a hundred to one," Sax said. "Be cautious, Bob, Milletti was lucky."

Since the rains of early September had stopped, we were able to increase our work load. Materials were coming in from Saigon Port and Newport daily and in large quantities. Joe Horton, the supervisor at Area 207 was transferred to Long Binh to help handle the huge load we were carrying. He was assigned to help me.

Several new men had been hired to work as supervisors at Area 208. Some were green, but some were seasoned veterans.

Two of the new hires were Koreans, and had been in country only a few days. Lee Bac Coon and Ye Yong Yong were natives of Seoul, and had never traveled outside Korea. Each seemed willing to work.

Lee Bac Coon was slender, about five-nine and extremely erect, like a well trained and disciplined military cadet. We talked, and it was soon apparent that he dreamed of living in America with his family.

Ye Yong Yong was a heavyweight, maybe five-eight and two hundred pounds. This guy was happy-go-lucky with a perpetual smile. He proved to be an excellent worker, and willing to tackle any task asked of him. I hoped that we could become friends, not only for his pleasant attitude, but because this guy was tough. Ye was a black belt in karate. He'd be handy to have around in times of need.

The two new American employees were George Lachapelle and Chuck Alexander. Each had been employed by RMK-BRJ, and had changed companies for the same reason as Sax. More money.

Both George and Chuck liked their booze and women. Lachapelle was from Seattle, and had been a successful insurance agent. His drinking problems had caused his business to fail. He was divorced, plagued with financial problems, and desperately needed a geographic location far away. He managed to get hired by Morrison-Knudsen out of Seattle.

George had fallen in love with an attractive Vietnamese girl, which probably compounded his troubles. He was torn between his affection for his ex-wife, and his passion for his beautiful and enchanting Southeast Asian woman. I understood George's feelings.

Chuck Alexander was originally from Boise, so our friendship was instant and everlasting. He was a Morrison-Knudsen hire out of Boise, and had also changed jobs for financial reasons. Chuck was about my size, and felt the same about the war as most of the American civilians here. The American rich were fattening their pockets at the taxpayer's expense.

"Alex, maybe down the road we can throw a wrench into the cogs," I said.

Alex shrugged. "We won't last with PA&E."

We signed out on the register, picked up our mail, and climbed on the bus. Hutson sometimes left work early, so I really couldn't count on him for a ride to Thu Duc.

The bus moved towards Route 1, and into no man's land. I opened letters from both daughters, Susanna and Paulina. Paulina, my thirteen year old, was always bubbling about school activities, neighborhood news, and how she and her brothers and sister were faring in general. She kept letters coming regularly, and this was good for my morale. She was a thoughtful and loving child.

Susanna was fifteen and growing up. She informed me that her mother had a boy friend. I was not surprised, but it hurt. It was inevitable that Georgina would find a companion, as I had done. Reconciliation with her looked fruitless at this point, and distance added to our diminishing relationship.

When I entered the villa Jack and some friends were drinking beer, and solving the world's problems. Wendell Hestead, PA&E's tire shop foreman, was sitting on the couch with Tom, his girl friend.

Wendell and Tom lived in a villa in University Village. He managed his tire shop operation at Long Binh in an expert fashion. He was also a native Idahoan, from Burley.

Lynn Berksnyder, an RMK geologist, and Tina, his Cambodian companion, were wrapped around each other on our large leather lounge. Lynn worked at the RMK rock quarry near Long Binh. He and Tina lived in a small cottage a mile down the road on the outskirts of Thu Duc.

Jack and Yvonne were arguing about who had snatched his new sheets and pillowcases, and left two pair of well worn rags in their place. Jack had trouble with theft, and no wonder with Yvonne in charge. I was fortunate to have Susie taking care of my possessions.

Dale Henderson sat off by himself, sipping his beer in contentment. Dale was quiet, stayed to himself, and was anticipating the completion of his PA&E contract. He missed his family in Denver, and wanted to go back to the World.

Susie was killing time in our room looking at pictures, and waiting for my arrival. I kissed her on the head as I advanced toward the refrigerator. I would drink a beer and shower before joining the others.

I popped a cold one, and devoured it in record time. I showered, changed into clean shorts, and Susie and I melded ourselves into the crowd.

We Americans living in the Thu Duc area had to think about our safety. Vietcong were everywhere, and we had no idea who might be our sly, and elusive enemy.

For all we knew, Vietcong might be members of our household; God knows they had infiltrated the labor groups at Long Binh. Susie had been born and raised in Hanoi, and Baby San, our maid, was a native of My Lai. Who could be trusted? Our firearms could only protect us from thieves, or from a small VC attack. If the enemy attacked in large numbers, Saigon would be our safest refuge. Susie and I could retreat to Saigon.

Berksnyder and Hutson were discussing the war situation. I had my own thoughts, and asked to be heard.

"Bob, you're new among us, but go ahead," Jack said. Berksnyder managed a smile.

Eyes turned my way. "Thanks, Jack. The VC haven't bothered us on the job at Long Binh, nor at our villa. The VC know that I'm American. They know my name, know where I work, know my social security number, and could kill me at will. But they have no fight with the American civilians."

Jack laughed at my statement. "Bob, does this mean the big Buddha is going to give your eulogy and bury you after the Vietcong blow you to hell?"

"Jack, why should the VC kill me when I'm protecting their interests? American civilians throughout Vietnam are stock piling materials, constructing office buildings, living quarters, bridges, new roads, multiple airstrips, a new Saigon water supply and sewer system, setting up communication systems, and taking care of the villas here at University Village. This is all being accomplished at the American taxpayer's expense. Ho Chi Minh is in Hanoi planning his strategy, knowing that although thousands of his countrymen will die in the war, he will drive the Americans and their allies to the sea, and he will unite North and South Vietnam. And the brand new American built infrastructure will be to his benefit.

"We're going to lose this damn war! American politicians are calling the shots, not the U.S. Military. Pentagon and State Department people are corrupt, and big business and the politicians are pulling the Pentagon's strings. The U.S. Military doesn't give the orders, and every General over here has his own swimming pool in a luxurious setting and doesn't give a damn. How can we win?"

I cracked a beer and continued. "Rich Americans back home are lining their pockets; they want this war to go on forever. They're not concerned about the little guy fighting in Vietnam, nor American taxpayers in general."

"Patterson, have you just about run down?" Berksnyder said.

I raised my voice, and shook my fist. "Lynn, it's not how you make your money in this world, it's that you've got it that counts."

The Vietnamese had lost their independence to the French in 1885, and except for Japanese occupation during World War II, the French ruled the Southeast Asian country for eighty plus years.

After Japan's World War II defeat, the Vietnamese people led by Ho Chi Minh, declared their independence. Ho Chi Minh, which means "He Who Enlightens", had his people's complete confidence.

Ho was first a Vietnamese Nationalist, and second a Communist, and he needed help from the United States to survive after he had declared his country's independence in 1945. President Truman had been in office for only four months, and hadn't had ample time to establish a policy in Southeast Asia. Therefore, he didn't acknowledge Ho's plea for assistance.

Since the U.S. didn't respond, the British freed the French who had been imprisoned by the Japanese during the war. The British armed the French, who then forced Ho and his Vietminh followers to retreat into the mountains. The French Government didn't accept Ho's declaration of independence, and once again gained control of the country. The U.S. Government disapproved, but to no avail.

In 1947 French generals expected to crush Ho Chi Minh's Vietminh guerrillas, later known as the Vietcong, within a few weeks. The U.S. supplied the French with 2.5 billion dollars in aid during eight years of fighting, only to see it end in a French defeat at Dien Bien Phu, a valley fortress that had been deemed "invulnerable." In 1954 at a Geneva agreement, Vietnam was divided at the 17th parallel, separating North and South Vietnam.

After the humiliating French defeat, and the loss of thousands of French troops at Dien Bien Phu, American leaders couldn't leave well enough alone. America had learned absolutely nothing!

Our Presidents, Dwight Eisenhower, John F. Kennedy, and L.B. Johnson, all contended that if we didn't stop Ho Chi Minh, communism would spread like a plague throughout Cambodia, Laos, Thailand, the Philippines, and all the way to Australia.

First, we sent Marine advisers to Vietnam in the early 1960's to assist the South Vietnamese. Then we sent in Marine troops, followed by Army, Air Force and civilian support companies. By 1967 we had five hundred fifty thousand troops, and eighteen thousand civilians in the country. At this point in the fighting, the Vietcong build-up was getting larger, more American GIs were dying, the rich American industrialists were stuffing their pockets with fortunes in greenbacks, and the American taxpayer was getting poorer. Did the U.S. fight on or retreat?

"Look who the American draftboards are selecting to fight in this conflict. They're taking young blacks out of the urban ghettos. They are drafting hispanics, and low-income whites. They are taking kids with low scholastic averages out of colleges. Is the American Government dealing in ethnic cleansing, both at home and in Southeast Asia?"

I was exhausted after my tirade. "Susie, let's go to bed. Tomorrow is here soon enough." She smiled and we bowed out, leaving our friends in a more somber mood than a couple hours earlier.

Every morning in pitch blackness Jack, Dale, and I headed up Route 1 towards Long Binh. Jack would tune in the car's radio, and every morning it was the thing. Some nut on Armed Forces radio would start with "Gooooooooooooood Morning Vietnam!" He would make a few wisecracks, and then come on with "back in the World" music. This guy made you feel like living, what a sense of humor.

After breakfast at the 9th Trans we would drive on to Long Binh, sign the register, and tramp off to our respective pads.

At the day's end I would to walk to the office. One day I took a shortcut through a U.S. Army depot. This was a lucrative area for black marketeers. Crates and conex boxes (metal containers) were filled with goodies containing military clothing, jungle boots, bayonets, electric stoves, refrigerators, hand tools, small generators, flashlights, drums of paint, and much more. The military didn't use Vietnamese security guards to protect against pilferage, they insisted on using their own people. Of course, it didn't make a helluva lot of difference. It was like having the fox guard the hen house.

There wasn't a GI to be seen, but I stumbled onto a PA&E employee loading crates onto a flatbed truck with a forklift. A Vietnamese driver was in the truck cab. The forklift operator didn't see me, so I watched in amazement for several minutes. The man finished loading the truck, approached the driver, and handed him a fist full of greenbacks. Papa San, you go Saigon! De de mau. De mau lin." Who would you guess? Mangie!

I approached my long haired friend, and he nearly jumped out of his skin. "Hi Bob, what are you doing in the army section?"

"Well, Mangie, I'm taking a shortcut to the office. It's damn near quitting time. What the hell are you up to?"

"I just came over to help the army. They're a bit shorthanded."

"Bullshit! The way you steal material, you could get in the Guinness Book of World Records as the only kleptomaniac in the world with a forklift!"

"Are you going to report me to the authorities, Bob, or what?"

"In the first place I only work here, and I'm not CIA or CID. Just be careful. We both know the consequences."

We got into Mangie's jeep and went to the office. I got out and turned to him. "Don't worry, but take care."

On the bus that evening I put Mangie out of my mind and fell asleep immediately. The long days in the heat were taking their toll. After we turned onto Route 1 and headed toward Thu Duc, a sniper's bullet slammed into the windshield opposite papa san; The old guy didn't even flinch. I awoke abruptly, and probably ruptured myself when I jumped straight into the air. Papa San floor-boarded the bus, and kept his foot down all the way to Thu Duc.

The VC were firing mortars and small arms fire onto the highway. There were several civilian vehicles and an American army six by six truck burning off in the barrow pit. We were like sitting ducks, but I still believed the enemy didn't want to kill us. They'd kill American soldiers, but I didn't think they'd kill American civilians taking care of their interests. Still, I was damned happy to get off the bus and head for the villa. Papa San roared off down the highway toward Saigon.

After dinner that night I kept thinking of Mangie and the black market. I was curious how much money a 1500 KW generator would bring on the black market. There were eight new 1500s in my area, and none had been uncrated.

I had issued one to Trans Asia Company several days earlier. The generator weighed twenty two thousand pounds, and it was loaded onto a forty foot lowboy truck using a Super-40 Hyster. Lee Bac Koon, my Korean friend had been the Hyster operator.

Degelco Trucking Company could easily be hired to transport the generator to any destination in South Vietnam. The security guards could be bribed for a nominal fee to get it through the gate at Long Binh. It would be a piece of cake.

I wrote all the specifications on paper, and asked Susie to check it out in Saigon the next day. What would a 1500 KW bring on the black market?

I didn't sleep well that night. My mind was preoccupied with delusions of grandeur, but my conscience was working overtime. I envisioned stacks of neatly wrapped U.S. greenbacks. But I was afraid of the CIA, and envisioned the federal prison at Leavenworth.

The next morning I signed my name on the register, and went directly into Brown's office. My conversation sounded like a broken record, the same one I'd been playing for months. "Brown, you're the boss, and you call the shots, but when will there be water for my laborers? When do I get equipment? When are you going to get off your dead ass, and get this place organized? One of these days you're going to have a riot on your hands." I stomped out, and I knew I had embarrassed him in front of everyone.

When I arrived at my area the other American supervisors had already heard about me spouting off to Brown. Each encouraged me to hang in there; they were behind me. Lachapelle and Alexander suggested I go to labor relations at Tan Son Nhut. They promised every American at Long Binh would stand behind me. It was tempting.

Things were buzzing. The undeclared war was escalating; more and more troops were being assembled at Long Binh, and huge quantities of materials were arriving daily at the storage area. It was a steady stream of one and a half ton Philco-Ford flatbeds pouring in from Saigon Port and Newport docks. Stacks of material stretched for miles. Hundred of millions of U.S. taxpayer's dollars were being squandered for what? And thousands of American boys were dying.

We started receiving floatation devices, which were used as helicopter landing pads in the rice paddies. They inflated automatically, so choppers could come in fast, land, pick up or off-load men and materials. We already had several thousand of these devices stockpiled. Why were we receiving more for storage? Maybe a procurement expert in the Pentagon made a mistake, or perhaps he had an interest in the company manufacturing floatation devices.

The U.S. had gotten into one helluva situation. They could save face if they'd pull out of Vietnam now. This conflict could go on for years. But how could America pull out when big business pulled politician's strings?

We received barbed wire and nails for five straight days. U.S. Steel was written all over the cartons of nails, and on the barbed wire. In my area alone there was enough barbed wire stockpiled to encircle the earth more than once.

It was Saturday night, and my crew had completed our most productive week. It was time to celebrate. Jack, Dale, and I drank whiskey long into the night, and we bragged to each other. We talked about home and about the war, and about our loved ones. We were not embarrassed when we cried about young American soldiers dying.

The following morning was Sunday, and my hangover was the deciding factor not to go to work. Susie and Yvonne always laughed when we had a party, because they knew the consequences. They loved to see Jack and me in agony with hangovers.

After tomato juice, bacon and eggs Susie asked to speak in private. "Bob, honey, I go Saigon like you say, and black market cowboy give me paper."

I couldn't believe what I read in the note. The black market cowboys would give two hundred seventy-five thousand dollars in U.S. green for each 1500 KW generator that I delivered.

Susie's eyes met mine. It was hard to comprehend two hundred seventy-five thousand American dollars. This would keep Susie and me forever, and help her children and mine for years to come.

"Susie, I think I can get the generators past the security guards at Long Binh to their destination. But we are talking boo coo money. Maybe the cowboy will take the generator and keep the money. If they give us the money, how do we get it out of Vietnam?"

Susie and I had the same thought. The risks were enormous. We weren't thieves, and our chances of leaving the country were nearly impossible. Bob and Susie would probably get killed.

My companion came close and I put my arms tightly around her waist. "Susie, do you love me?"

"Bob, I love you too much. If you good for me, and I good for you, that all that matter."

"Are you afraid to die, Susie?"

She looked away. "If I no see and they kill me, I do not know. If I see, then I am afraid for my baby san. I not afraid for Susie."

"We're doing all right. I send money home to my children. You have your baby san, and Tuyet is in school. We don't steal the generator. We don't need trouble."

Susie eyes sparkled. "I am happy, and we no need trouble."

I didn't work the next four days. I drank beer, and Susie and I spent time at the Rex, and we had dinner at the "I" House. Susie stayed in Saigon to visit, and I returned to Thu Duc. Brown would be furious.

The fourth morning I joined Jack and Dale, and we went to Long Binh, and back to reality. Dale signed my name on the register, and he told Brown I had gone to the motor pool.

The ex-pug growled. "Patterson is going to pay his dues."

The big man wasn't long arriving, but I was ready for the onslaught. "Good morning, Mr. Brown."

Brown walked up, and put his face down into mine. "Patterson, I'm not going to waste time. I told Mr. Kraig I needed men to work nights, and you're elected. You start tomorrow night at 1900 hours."

"I'm looking forward to working nights. The nightshift hasn't kept up its end of the work load." I turned and walked away.

While They Died

Chapter Ten

It was late afternoon when I prepared for work. Susie helped buckle the shoulder holster strap under my left arm. I pushed the small Beretta semi-automatic in place and slipped on my shirt, hiding the small weapon.

Susie talked as we walked hand in hand to the road leading to Route 1. She was very protective. "Bob, remember, VC everywhere. It be boo coo dark. Stay close to mama san workers, and don't leave Long Binh until daytime." She reached up and pecked me on the cheek. Squeezing my hand tightly she reassuringly added, "No sweat Bob, you be O.K. Big Buddha take care." I watched the small figure return to the villa.

It was damn good to know Big Buddha was my protector, and he was looking after me.

PA&E's bus arrived shortly after I reached the highway, and Papa San, the old driver, looked surprised to see me. I smiled and nodded. He had become a reliable friend.

I knew several Americans on the bus coming from Saigon. They asserted that the night shift was a piece of cake, and I sure didn't want them to know I was uncomfortable about working nights.

When we arrived at Long Binh the day shift took our places on the bus for their trip to Saigon. Brown was getting into his pickup to leave; he turned my way and grinned. "Patterson, have a pleasant evening in the moonlight with the Vietcong." I gave him a cheery thumbs up.

I walked through no man's land to my tiny office and unlocked the door. I wanted to make sure everything was intact. I had asked Sax to be on extra alert, since he was on the day shift. Joe Horton and Ye Yong Yong were also close by during the day, as was Lachapelle. No reason to worry, but there were several guns and cameras stored in the footlocker, as well as precious pictures and letters from my family.

Some of the mama san laborers that had been loyal and reliable to me on day shift were now on the nightshift. They were milling around, as were the equipment operators, waiting for orders.

It was soon dark, and the only lights were those on our equipment and one 3KW generator that revealed a small flood lamp.

Philco-Ford flatbeds loaded with drums of paving asphalt started arriving for off-loading. Thank God I was familiar with the operation, because the decreased visibility could be hazardous for the laborers. But lights would invite the Vietcong.

Two cranes were placed facing each other about forty yards apart. Both had barrel hooks attached to the boom cable to accommodate off-loading of five drums at once. Chuck Alexander supervised one crane, and I took charge of the other. It was Alex's first night too, and I wasn't surprised Brown had also elected him for nightshift. He was crotchety as hell, and had missed several days due to an extended party in Saigon. We had a lot in common, fortunately or unfortunately, and I was glad to have him aboard.

Trucks were backing into position for off-loading, just like clock work. The operation seemed to move satisfactorily, even with poor lighting, but I continually cautioned the laborers to stay away from drums swinging from trucks to the storage pad.

Once in a while a truck failed to back in properly, so I would prod the driver along. Some drivers lacked driving experience, and others hampered the operation on purpose. They were Vietcong, and were probably born and raised in Hanoi. Why they wanted to upset the apple cart I'll never know; hell, they'll eventually own everything anyway, after the Americans and their allies are driven out of the country.

It was inevitable that sometime during a shift something was bound to go wrong. One old papa san driver wouldn't back his truck in for off-loading. He rammed a truck to his rear, and then stalled crossways in the path of another truck trying to maneuver into position for off-loading. Several drivers left their trucks, and started waving and jabbering like crazy.

I yelled to Alex to be on guard. I thought the confusion was deliberate. Alex yelled back. "Get that old SOB back in line. He's the trouble maker."

Damn, I was mad. I walked over to papa san. "You rotten old bastard, back that truck into place! De de mau!"

I never swore at these people, but I was out of control. Papa San glared defiantly. He boldly walked to the cab of the truck, picked up a tire iron, and started my way. Alex yelled, "Bob, look out! That son-of-a-bitch is coming after you."

Work stopped abruptly. Cranes ceased operating, and everyone seemed to be waiting for a climax like an old western shootout. Old papa san kept coming toward me, and I knew he was serious. I slowly reached up, and started unbuttoning my shirt to get the Beretta. I was mentally prepared to shoot, but God knows I didn't want trouble. They might all react, and with no MPs near by, it could prove fatal for Alex and me. We wouldn't stand a chance against these people even if armed with automatic rifles.

One old mama san moved in close to my side, as I started to expose my firearm. She looked at papa san and the tire iron, and then back at me. Suddenly she said something in Vietnamese. Papa san turned, and walked back to the truck. He laid his weapon on the floorboard, climbed into the cab, and backed the truck into position for off-loading.

Alex waved and gave a thumbs up. My knees were weak, and sweat clouded my eyes. Everything started operating again. Had I just plain out-bluffed the old man, or was old mama san aware that I was armed? Maybe she wanted me around for awhile. She smiled proudly, and returned to her job.

Finally, trucks ceased arriving from Newport, lights were turned off, and it was quiet as a morgue and pitch black. The mama san laborers slowly walked to my office. The diminutive women curled up together, and soon were fast asleep.

It would be easy for someone to walk up in the darkness and slit my throat, but I solved that problem. I crawled right into the middle of the mama sans. Nobody was going to harm these little people. They were my protectors. Alex joined me soon enough, and we slept soundly. Daylight awakened me, and for a moment I thought I was in another world.

A week passed with no more mishaps. It was impossible to be as efficient as the daytime crew. It was slow and cautious work without adequate lighting. I was satisfied though, and Brown didn't give me trouble. Trouble, however, was never far away.

We always took our lunch break at midnight. The Americans would jump into a weapons carrier for the ride to the 9th Trans mess hall. Lights would be turned out, and the laborers and third nationals would sleep until our return.

One night shortly after my confrontation with the old papa san, we were returning up Route 1 from our lunch break, when we noticed a red glow in the sky in the direction of Long Binh. "My God, Alex, our storage area is ablaze." The driver went hell bent, and headed straight for the fire.

The inferno was devouring everything in its path, and spreading rapidly. I hollered to my compatriots. "Forget the water hoses! Get the damned Army in here with bulldozers so we can bank up around this section. We've got to cut off the fire."

It looked hopeless. The fire had spread to the thousands of drums of paving asphalt. The ground sloped towards the jungle, and the flaming asphalt was running down into the creosote-preserved poles and piles stacked at the bottom of the slope. Metal barrels filled with oil were exploding and shooting straight into the air. Conex boxes filled with oil-base paint and paint thinner caught fire. The situation looked absolutely futile, and it resembled a spectacular Fourth of July fireworks display.

Banking dirt around the burning holocaust with army bulldozers prevented total destruction. We maneuvered army fire trucks close enough to contain the blaze, and at least we kept it from spreading into the lumber section and our main offices. Twenty-five per cent of the material in 208 was completely destroyed; The estimated cost of the material would run into the tens of millions.

My small office was totally destroyed. I lost treasured pictures of my family and some personal letters, and other supervisors lost camras and firearms.

The next morning the area was crawling with news media, top military brass, and key PA&E personnel. I questioned several third nationals, who said they heard small arms fire and had seen tracers hit asphalt drums. My thoughts centered around the American civilians, and on what I had seen and heard here. By destroying materials at Long Binh, it would be impossible for anyone to get an accurate inventory. The next morning the day shift started clearing the burned out area. More material would be stock-piled to be looted by the Americans and the Vietcong.

There were advantages working nights. I had more time with Susie, and spent time visiting with the Vietnamese people. We discussed the tragic war, and how the French had mistreated them during their occupation of Southeast Asia. I gained their confidence, and I was accepted.

One Saturday, just two weeks after the fire, started out as one helluva busy night. Several contractors needed materials, and three military units gave me requisitions for important items that needed expediting. The night was warmer than usual, and there was a full moon.

The military was in a hurry, so I concentrated on satisfying them before dealing with civilian contractors. I didn't envy the truck convoys inching their way through the jungle after dark. Two GIs were assigned to each six by six truck in a convoy, a driver and another GI riding shotgun.

These were eighteen year old kids waiting for their trucks to be loaded. Each wore a flak jacket, and each carried an M-16 rifle. Night time was bad news for convoys traveling through the jungle. The

Vietcong took a heavy toll, and many young American GIs died.

We civilians would usually hear about convoy casualties after the Vietcong ambushed and destroyed the trucks and slaughtered the GIs. Enemy mortar and machine gun fire made a bloody mess of convoys.

On this Saturday night one U.S. Army supply expediter, Sergeant Dixon, came pushing his way through to my office. It was already crowded, and I didn't need a hassle from anyone. To complicate matters the good sergeant was on the sauce, drunk and belligerent. He demanded that I fill his requisition pronto.

"I have orders from General Bradford at MAC-V Headquarters for two 3KW generators," he growled. "Mister, I mean now!"

"General Bradford will have to wait his turn," I said, politely.

"You damn civilians think you own this place. Get off your ass."

I ignored the supply sergeant and continued issuing materials. GIs standing around saw what was happening, and one husky buck sergeant confronted Dixon. "These civilians have a lot of guts working their butts off under adverse conditions, and they aren't even armed. Get lost!"

Dixon returned two hours later. He was calmer and sober. He and I went looking for his generators. They were packed in small crates, well hidden in the darkness. We finally located the items and loaded them onto a small four by four trailer that was hitched behind his jeep. The vehicle crept back to my office in the incredibly bright moonlight.

It was daylight by the time the transaction was completed. Dixon apologized for being so discourteous earlier in the evening, and admitted he had been drinking Black Velvet.

"Hell, Sergeant, that's my favorite beverage. It isn't the best, but it's smooooooooth". A hearty laugh dissipated any remaining animosity.

We talked, and I told him about living at University Village with Susie. I was hesitant to tell about my relatively good life in Vietnam, since I knew Dixon was living in an entirely different world.

He told me about working for General Bradford at MAC-V Headquarters, and what a bastard he was. The general didn't give a damn about the war. "The top brass at Mac-V all have clean sheets, swimming pools, good food, and boo coo con gai, that is, many

Vietnamese women of their choice."

It was September 24th, and a beautiful Sunday morning. Sergeant Dixon and I decided to venture to Thu Duc. We would pick up Susie, return to Long Binh, and spend the day with him. We could have lunch, return to the villa, and I could still get a few winks before work that evening.

The sergeant went to his jeep and retrieved a fifth of Black Velvet. "Mr. Patterson, let's have a little fortification before we leave for the villa." He smacked his lips.

He cracked the seal, twisted off the top, and handed me the bottle. Without hesitation I took a huge, gurgling blast. Damn it was hot stuff. I grabbed for the water jug. My eyes watered, as the alcohol burned its way to my stomach.

My friend tipped the bottle bottoms up, and held it in that position for a considerable time. My God, what a belt.

"Damn, Sarge, let me try that again, if there's any left." I grabbed the neck of the bottle tightly, and savored another gulp.

The sarge took another hearty swig, and smacked his lips. "Bob, we best head for Thu Duc before we're both in never never land."

He stopped the jeep at the office, and I hurried inside to sign the register. We both felt like taking on the whole damn North Vietnamese Army.

Dixon poured the coal to the small, narrow wheeled jeep, and I hung on for dear life. We whizzed past an MP checkpoint yelling and waving, I wanting all to know of our happiness on such a gorgeous morning. The narrow dirt road was bumpy, and Sarge was having difficulty controlling the speeding jeep.

"Dixon! My God! Slow her down! We're gonna crash!" I grabbed the bottom of the seat with both hands.

He lost control, and the jeep careened to the right. The left front wheel hit a deep chuck hole, and the vehicle flipped.

My body was hurled backward through the steel frame, and I helplessly became airborne. I hit the ground with a sickening thud, and the pain was sudden and excruciating. I was wedged tightly in a deep ravine that had been carved by the monsoons. I tried desperately to free myself, but I blacked out. God only knows what happened to

Dixon.

Two MPs stationed at the checkpoint that we had passed moments ago came running over. "You O.K. buddy? I'll give you a hand." He and his companion couldn't budge me. "This guy's stuck. You take one side and I'll take the other and lift. Hell, he's not conscious".

My eyes briefly opened. "One—Two—Three——pull"! I let out a yell you could hear forever. The two lifted in unison and freed me from my immediate predicament. They left me lying at the side of the road as the agonizing pain forced me into darkness again.

One MP stayed with me, and the other ran back to the checkpoint to radio for an ambulance. I rallied—I faded away. "Sir, hang in there. We'll have you out of here soon. Try to keep calm." Blood was running down my face, and the MP dabbed at it with a piece of gauze from his first-aid kit.

The ambulance skidded to a halt. Two medics kneeled down, and gently lifted me to my feet. I collapsed in a heap. I was drifting in and out of consciousness. The medics lifted me again, dragged me to the ambulance, and leaned me against the hood, but I fell to the ground in torturous pain. "Please, don't touch me," I begged, pitifully, "My God, please!" They finally got a stretcher, and gently lifted me aboard.

We bounced along toward a military dispensary. The road was potholed, and it felt like there were no springs under the ambulance. The pain caused me to black out again and again. I thought the truck would never stop.

The attending doctor at the dispensary ordered the medics to carry me inside the building for observation.

"Take this guy to the 93rd Evacuation Hospital," the doctor said softly, after completing his examination. "He definitely needs x-rays, probably a spinal tap, and God knows what else. Don't waste time. He's in serious trouble."

We went hell bent to the 93rd Evac. Every time I regained consciousness, the pain sent me back into nothingness. I dreamed I was on a bucking bronc, my feet were stuck in the stirrups, and I couldn't get off. We stopped, and the medics gently slid the stretcher from the ambulance.

I asked for morphine, and a young doctor obliged. In a deep

southern accent he asked my name.

"Bob Patterson. Are you a doctor?"

"Yes, I am Captain, I mean, Doctor Morgan." He smiled down at me. "I've been sent here from the World just across the ocean. Where do you hurt?"

"Doc, I hurt all over, but the real bad pain in is my chest and the middle of my back."

"We're going to get some blood samples, take a spinal tap and some x-rays. It'll hurt some, so don't be ashamed to yell. We're real used to that here at the 93rd."

I looked at the bright lights of the emergency room. I still couldn't fully fathom just what was going on. I saw the MPs. "What happened to Sergeant Dixon? Where is my friend?" I never heard a reply. Blackness again.

The next time I opened my eyes Dr. Morgan was standing over me. I was in a room crowded with young men laying side by side. There must have been at least sixty GIs.

"Who is your next of kin, Mr. Patterson?" Dr. Morgan asked.

"Doc, PA&E has all that information; I'm not going to die. I'm staying right here." I tried to smile. "Where you from, Doc? I know it isn't New York." I was trying not to think about the pain.

"I'm from Southern Virginia, and I mean deep South."

I struggled with the pain. "Doc, I've got relatives in Virginia and North Carolina. My dad was born in Durham. I'm from Idaho, y'all."

The morphine diminished the pain, and I was quiet. Doc told me I had to sit up. He wanted to listen to my lungs. He placed his hand in the small of my back. "One-two-three—up we go!"

I let loose a blood curdling yowl. Doc moved the stethoscope around my chest, then on my back, listening intently.

"Mr. Patterson, you have pneumonia. We'll put you on a breathing machine, and try to keep fluid from building up in your lungs. You have two fractured ribs on the front left side next to your sternum. You have four fractured ribs on the back left, next to your spine. We'll check you over again, try to determine what other internal injuries you might have incurred. All things considered, Mr. Patterson, you're one helluva lucky man. With tender loving care and the grace of God you'll pull through."

"I'll make it, Doc. Did you hear how Sergeant Dixon fared? Is he hurt?"

"Never heard of the man. He didn't come to the 93rd."

Sleep didn't come easily the first night. I asked for pain pills several times. Breathing was difficult, and the wheezing in my lungs sounded like the death rattle. I worried about Susie, and I knew she was probably wondering what happened to me. Jack will find me. Were my kids all right back in the world?

Doctor Morgan came by early in the morning. "Bob, it's time to sit up. I want to check your chest, then we'll see if you can drink some juice. In a couple hours a nurse will bring the breathing machine. It'll be uncomfortable, but it's absolutely necessary."

He put his hand under my back. "One-two—three—Up we go." There was no way that I could contain myself, and out came the horrible scream again. God, it was embarrassing. There were a lot of GIs in the quonset hut, and some were in terrible shape. Some were missing limbs, some were blind, some had shrapnel and bullet wounds, and had their guts blown out, dysentery, and God know what else. And here I was making strange and pathetic noises.

The nurse arrived a couple of hours later with the breathing machine, and I knew the worst was about to come. She didn't waste any time. It was once again one-two—three. It was painful, but this time I had managed not to yell. She stuck a hose into my mouth, and the machine automatically forced me to breathe in and out. Every breath forced my rib cage to expand and contract. It was excruciating, and the GI next to my bed turned away. After it was over I apologized, but he said nothing. They all knew the meaning of pain.

The latrine was about fifty yards from my bed, so whenever nature called I had to slide out of bed, walk the full length of the quonset hut, cross the street, and enter an eight holer. Nurses were busy, so I couldn't ask them to assist. It took me a full two hours from the time I started, until I was safely back in the bed. Thank God I didn't have dysentery.

The following morning I asked a nurse to slip pillows under my back. I requested pen and paper to write home and inform my family that I would be off work for awhile.

I slept for a time, then a voice awakened me, and I was looking face to face with two large military police. A sergeant asked my name, and how I was feeling.

"I'm Bob Patterson, and I've really felt better."

The sergeant took a paper from his shirt pocket and read aloud. "Bob Patterson, a civilian, employed by Pacific Architects & Engineers, is charged by the United States Government for violation of the following U.S. Army regulations: Misappropriation of a government vehicle, driving while intoxicated, with no valid driver's license, and destroying government property. One jeep, one four by four trailer, and two 3 KW generators completely destroyed." "Sarge, I can't believe this could be happening to me. I wasn't driving! I'm an American out here in the jungle, trying to do a simple job, and I get hit with this crap."

The sergeant shrugged. "Sir, I'm only following orders. I don't like this either."

"Sarge, one question. Where the hell's Sergeant Dixon?"

"The MPs at the checkpoint that tended to you said you were alone in the vehicle." I shook my head in disbelief. "Will you please try and find the man who was driving the jeep?"

Both MPs looked at me. "Sir, we'd like to believe you. We'll check it out."

"I don't want Dixon to get in trouble, nor do I want trouble. One thing for sure, I'm not going any place." I turned away.

The two MPs left, and I lay there wondering if I had been alone in the jeep. My memory of that morning was sketchy. I remembered the sergeant, and I recalled filling a requisition for materials. I couldn't have had much to drink by my standards. There hadn't been time. I had to think, and sort things out.

The nurse brought the breathing machine, and then I had lunch. My lungs felt better, and I had an appetite. I'd make it, but if the Government pressed charges I might be better off dead.

After dozing for several hours I had another visitor. I opened my eyes, and thought I must be hallucinating. It was an ugly face grinning from ear to ear with its bald head, hairline mustache and little beady eyes. It was Hutson! The Texan drawled, "Bob, I hear the U.S. Government has you by the balls. Is that right?"

"Jack, I don't know for sure. They've pressed charges, but a couple of MPs are investigating the circumstances. I'm trying to sort things out. I took a pretty hard jolt, and my mind isn't too clear. What does misappropriation of a vehicle mean?"

"Bob, that means that the jeep was taken without proper authority. The Army is saying it was stolen." I shook my head in disbelief.

"Is there anything I can do for you?" Jack asked.

"Yeah. Get Susie, and bring her here to the 93rd. I could use some help getting out of bed. These nurses will do anything for me, but I can't ask. There are too many GIs who need help."

"I'll have her here early in the morning. She's worried about you. Hang in there."

I awoke the next morning to a soft voice. "Bob, this is Susie. Jack bring me to Long Binh."

"Thanks for coming Susie. I have missed you." Tears filled my eyes, and I took her hand.

"Bob, I miss you, too. Jack say you need Susie."

"Susie, if you come every morning, it will be good for me."

"I come to you. Jack say he bring me to Long Binh every day to you. Soon you come to Thu Duc."

Susie stayed the morning. Now I had something to look forward to each day. The American nurses liked Susie, and they visited with her when time permitted. The GIs envied my good fortune.

The days settled into a routine. First, the long walk to the latrine, breakfast, breathing machine, and a doctor's visit with his stethoscope. Doctor Morgan was a good man, and I kidded him about his "y'all." He was amazed at my speedy recovery, and estimated I could possibly check out in two to three weeks.

Susie arrived early, and she helped me walk outdoors. I was feeling stronger. I napped in the afternoon, while she visited with GI patients.

When Susie left on the fourth day, the two investigating MPs came by to talk. The big sergeant greeted me. "Good afternoon, Sir. You're looking much better than when we were here before."

I nodded anxiously. "Fellahs, did you talk to Dixon about the accident?"

The sergeant didn't answer my question, but he did have good news. "Mr. Patterson, the U.S. Army had decided not to press charges against you. There is some doubt as to the violations, and there is little evidence supporting charges against you. We're sorry to have caused you any inconvenience. Good luck, sir."

Jack came by in the early evening, and I told him the Army dropped charges against me. I asked him to drive me to Thu Duc.

Hutson questioned my request. "Bob, do you honestly think you can endure the pain?"

"Doc Morgan said I shouldn't go, he says I need the breathing machine, but it's my decision. He gave me a month's supply of pain killers, and I'll take morphine before we start out in the morning."

Hutson gave me a confirming nod, and shook his head in disbelief, as he walked out of the ward.

Jack and Dale popped through the 93rd Evac's door shortly after I had finished breakfast. Dale threw a clean shirt and pants at me. "Let's go papa san! Hutson and I are very valuable employees of PA&E, and have to rush back to work. Brown knows you are checking out, and even said hello."

My two friends helped me dress, and I thanked the hospital staff for putting up with me. Doctor Morgan shook my hand, and said his services were available at any time.

Jack and Dale steadied me as we walked toward the shiny new 1968 Chevy pickup. They seated me in the middle, and Jack gingerly strapped the safety belt in place. We started down Route 1 to Thu Duc.

It seemed an eternity driving down the busy, treacherous highway. Jack hugged the right side of the road, allowing traffic to pass, and finally the truck turned off Route 1 toward Thu Duc. Susie and Yvonne were waiting eagerly in the driveway, and when they saw us, pushed open the gate. They each welcomed me with a smile. It was good to be home.

While They Died

My bed was prepared with fresh clean sheets, and several pillows were stacked against the headboard. Susie undressed me, helped me slip on a pair of shorts, and then gently settled me back on the pillows, just like a pro.

My little keeper kissed me on the forehead, and whispered into my ear. "Bob, I fix Chinese soup. Soup make you strong, so you go work. Must make money for your baby san."

"Susie, you dinky dao. You crazy. You say must make money-money-money. Choi oi. Very funny." We laughed.

"Bob must do what Susie say. I make you strong. Maybe you can boo coo bum-a-lum in bed someday. Make much love. Choi oi!"

I finished my soup, and Susie removed the pillows from under my back. It was effortless to slip off into never never land. I slept until just before dark, and suddenly the villa filled with people.

There was Wendell Hestead, my friend from Burley, and his girl Tom, Berksnyder and Tina, Lt. Hehn and Leo, and of course, Jack and Yvonne. It was a pleasant surprise.

Everyone burst into the bedroom, and gave me a grand welcome home. Beer cans popped open, bottles of vodka and bourbon appeared—and away we go! Fortunately or unfortunately, I couldn't drink because of the medication.

My good friend Hehn and I had much to talk about, and Susie and Leo went into the kitchen to share their moments. Hehn had been engaged in fierce fighting just south of Da Nang. The Vietcong were well fortified, and they dealt the ARVN and American troops heavy casualties. The enemy was elusive. They would hit and run, and they kept pouring more and more North Vietnamese regulars into the South. It didn't look good. Hehn said he was on leave for two weeks, and he would share time with Leo and his family. He looked worried, and he was exhausted.

My friends disappeared into the living room, and someone put a tape on the Sony tape recorder. Things were swinging, and the party progressed. It was after midnight when it tapered off, and everyone left, except for Hehn and Leo. They would take a taxi back to Saigon in the morning.

Six days after the accident and I continued to improve. The rasping sound had all but disappeared in my chest. I was physically stronger, and my appetite was good.

Susie prepared a gratifying breakfast, and then it was off to the shower. She lathered my body thoroughly, and was characteristically gentle. The large bath towel delicately dried my bruised and sensitive flesh. She finished the task and left, as I could complete the morning ritual without assistance.

This was the first time I had really inspected my body for damage caused by the accident. The full length mirror revealed a long cut on my forehead, just above my left eye, and the entire left side of my body was skinned and bruised. The damage began at the neck, down the arm and side, and continued to my ankle. My left buttock and leg were badly swollen, and my family jewels and penis were as black as the ace of spades. I was shocked, and I let out a holler. "Oh my God, I've lost my manhood!" I couldn't recall having an erection since entering the hospital, and sweat began running down my face and my stomach knotted.

Susie helped me back onto the bed, and because of our relationship I revealed my physical problem. "No can make love. I finish sex. No can get up anymore. No can do. I'm ruined."

She laughed so hard tears ran down her cheeks. She couldn't stop the hysteria and had to leave the room. Hell, this was no laughing matter.

Susie returned and very casually slipped off her clothes, never once taking her eyes off me. She laid close to my body, and fondled me, and I was aroused. She very gently seduced me, and she was undeniable proof that I still had my manhood.

Several days passed and Brown stopped by the villa to check on my recovery. He was shorthanded at Long Binh, and needed my expertise. I was flattered. But he could see I was incapacitated, and my recovery would take time.

I flinched when Susie helped sit me upright in bed. "I'm sorry Lou. My ribs are sore as hell."

He sympathized. "Bob, take some time, and I'll keep in touch. Incidently, I want you to start working days when you return. This way I can keep an eye on you." Susie smiled at Brown as he left. I didn't know how to take his remark.

Boredom set in. I walked in the yard and out to the highway. I watched television, and drank beer. Bo Priest, the unemployed RMK-BRJ master mechanic, dropped by occasionally to have a beer on his way to Saigon.

Bo was from Missouri. He was about five-ten, and carried a hundred fifty pounds. He was in his mid forties with graying hair, and sported a large, full sized mustache. His eyes were light blue, and always appeared about half closed. He was quiet, had good humor, and lived one day at a time. He walked with a stiff left leg, which he noticeably favored. This guy had guts, was frightfully cool, and was the kind you didn't want to cross. There was no doubt he could shoot you right between the eyes, and never lose a moment's sleep.

By late October, my ribs were mending satisfactorily, and I could soon return to work. I had written to Geogina, and enclosed a check for five hundred dollars. I asked her to send back five one hundred dollar bills through the mail. I instructed her to wrap the bills in carbon paper so that the APOs couldn't x-ray it. Dale returned from work one evening and handed me the letter with the five crisp one hundreds carefully concealed. I didn't tell anyone about the money, not even Susie.

Priest came by one morning, and I asked if I might ride to Saigon with him. My finances were low, and I needed both MPCs and piasters.

We climbed aboard the white jeep, and headed for the city. "Bo, why did you steal this jeep from the United States Army and paint it white. It's ludicrous!"

"Well, Bob, I look at it like this. It's obvious the Army thinks there isn't anybody so idiotic to steal a vehicle, and then paint the damn thing white.

"Another reason for not giving a damn in Vietnam is because of 'the friendly handshake'. The American Government has a U.S. Aid program, a give-away program to help the Vietnamese civilians. USAID in American Government language stands for "United States Agency for International Distribution."

"Anytime you see a decal sticker on a vehicle or equipment with the hands clasped together, you can rest assured it is USAID. Saigon is literally crawling with jeeps, and other equipment bearing the 'handshake' decal. The agency also distributes food, clothing, medical supplies, and other goodies throughout the world. USAID does good, but it gets carried away. The U.S. taxpayer needs relief, too."

Bo agonized when he talked, mainly because it hurt to discuss how much of the taxpayer's hard earned money the American Government was giving away. My friend shrugged, "Hell, Patterson, I don't mind stealing shit over here. The way I see it, part of it belongs to me anyway."

The jeep pulled into a parking place off Tu Do Street, and Bo and I walked to the Continental Hotel. I had three one hundred U.S. greenbacks concealed inside a Saigon Post newspaper, just like my friend Hutson had done. We sat down at the bar, and ordered whiskey-coke. I had learned my lesson well.

Charlie, the bartender, recognized me immediately. He sauntered over, and nodded. "Sir, you change money today?"

"Papa san, I have three hundred American green. I want two hundred in MPCs, and one hundred in piasters."

This guy was cool. He raised his eyebrows and shrugged. "I get for you two hundred fifty for MPC, and two hundred ninety in piaster.

This top dollar. Everybody want U.S. green."

I looked at Priest, and then back at Charlie. "What you think, Bo?"

"Sounds like a damned good exchange to me. I'd go for it."

"O.K. Charlie. You number one today. Thanks. Ca mon."

"Patterson, you're a first class pro," Bo said.

We ordered another drink, and Charlie slipped the paper under his arm, and vanished. I was flabbergasted. Three hundred dollars profit on the MPCs, and one hundred ninety thousand profit on the piasters. Not bad for ten minutes work.

Charlie returned with the money stashed in the newspaper. I sauntered towards the rest room, and counted out the loot in the privacy of a stall. I returned to the bar, and nodded my approval to Charlie.

Bo and I drove to the International House for lunch. He had never been in the place, and marveled at the different nationalities of people and at the rows of noisy slot machines. We ordered cold American beer and good old fashioned American hamburgers with onions. Bo sat quietly taking it all in and I'm sure he was wondering how I became a member.

It was an eventful and prosperous day in the city, but it was always good to get back to tranquility in the country. I gave Priest fifty MPCs, and thanked him. He left for Thu Duc where he and Mop, his girl friend, lived.

I went into the bedroom and cracked a beer, when Susie quietly appeared. "Bob, you have nice day in Saigon? You find pretty con gai, and you boo coo bum-e-lum?"

"Choi oi, very funny mama san. I no butterfly."

I handed her the stack of money. "You keep one hundred fifty MPCs for Susie. Give to me fifty MPC, and keep the rest for later." The money was safer with Susie than it would be at Fort Knox.

One old mama san maid was really acting strange lately, and I asked Susie if the old woman was crazy. "Sometimes old mama san chew betel nut, and go dinky dao, same as Bob when he drink whiskey." I got the point.

After some research I found out that betel nut was produced from the betel palm tree. The Asians mixed lime juice with the betel nut, and used it as a stimulant. If used in large amounts the mixture could cause intoxication, and discolor the teeth. Believe me, black teeth were very common in Southeast Asia. The dentist gave you a choice of denture color- black or white.

It was early November, and Lou Brown had come again to check on my progress. I was sitting in bed sipping beer. He smiled and nodded a greeting.

"Bob, it looks like you are ready to come back to work. Heard you've been to Saigon a few times."

"Yeah, I needed rent money and a few things from the commissary. I'm much stronger, but I'd like a few more day for my ribs to heal."

Lou turned to leave. "I want you back on nights for awhile. There is a ship due from the States loaded with paving asphalt, psp matting, and lumber. It's going to take lots of bodies to get it warehoused. See you in a week?"

"How about November 10th? That'll give me ten more days."

"You be at Long Binh in ten days or forget it." He turned and left without another word.

My concern was my ribs. I was looking forward to work, because I was bored stiff. Walking was easy for me, but riding in a jeep bothered me. Any sudden jolt was still very painful. Maybe I could get more pain pills from Dr. Morgan.

The old white goose, our trusted sentry, had been honking a lot the past few nights, and Jack, Dale and I talked about it at dinner time. Dale's bedroom was in the back of the villa, and the goose kept him awake. It could be Vietcong, or just local prowlers looking for something to steal. These people stole for survival and they were professional.

One night just before I started back to work, there was a hell of a pounding on my bedroom door. It was Yvonne. "Bob, Susie, get up! Get up!" Then I heard her yelling at Dale. "You get up. Dale, you get out of bed!"

Jack was already in the living room when Dale and Yvonne entered. Susie and I followed. Baby san, our maid, came running into the room, and she was scared half to death.

"Somebody steal anyting," Yvonne said. "Maybe VC come to house and take."

"Yvonne is right," Jack said, "somebody has ripped us off. Our television is gone; both Sony tape recorders are missing. My work boots are gone."

Susie and I nosed around and other valuables were also missing. All our liquor was gone from the cabinet, except for a half bottle of vodka. Knives were gone from the kitchen. I hadn't heard anything, and I'm a light sleeper. Susie hadn't heard anything, and that was really unusual.

"Why the hell didn't they take the M-1 and the M-2 rifles?" I asked.

Dale shook his head. "The goose didn't honk. I'd have heard that for sure. I'm not accusing anybody, but this has got to be an inside job. That gander would have warned us of a stranger in the yard."

Dale left the room. Jack and I tried to piece things together, but neither was Sherlock Holmes. Yvonne was the first one up to alert everyone. I knew she would steal from her own grandmother, and I'd caught her lying numerous times. I turned toward Yvonne and glared. "Did your people take? I think you know. Out with it, Yvonne!"

She looked shocked to think anyone would accuse her. "Bull shit me Goddamno, I no teel anyting!" I couldn't help but burst out laughing.

Then a gunshot rang out. I grabbed the 32-20 Colt, and Jack ran for the M-2, then Dale strolled in from the back yard carrying the M-1 rifle. "I shot the son-of-a-bitch." Everyone stood in silence, not knowing what he meant. Who did he shoot?

I walked to the kitchen window, and peered out. By a dim porch light I saw the goose. It was laying with its chest pointed towards the ground, and its ass was sticking straight up in the air. I knew what Dale meant. The household would have goose for dinner tomorrow.

Several days later Susie found a hole cut in the fence behind the villa. The thieves had carried their loot out through the hole and disappeared into the jungle. The only reason the goose remained silent was because the gander knew someone in the party of thieves. This had to have been a household member, but who? It would remain a mystery.

The time had come to return to work, and I considered myself fortunate to be alive. I would miss my Beretta. Either the MPs or the 93rd Evac crew had confiscated it. I never asked about it. It was illegal for a civilian to have a firearm in the first place.

Susie and I walked together toward the main road to Long Binh. I had been saving a surprise for her, and it was difficult not to contain my excitement. We had a few minutes before the bus arrived, so we stopped in the coolness under a large mahogany tree.

I turned her body toward mine and put my arms around her, drawing her close. Tears of gratitude filled my eyes. "I love you Susie, and thank you so much for taking care of me during my recovery. I would never have made it without your tender and loving care. There will never be anyone like you."

Susie turned her face upward. "Bob, I love you." I opened her hand, and placed two crisp U.S. one hundred dollar bills into the palm. She smiled and put the money into her brassiere. "Tomorrow I go Saigon and change "green" for boo coo money, and I keep for my baby san."

Everyone welcomed me back to the job at Long Binh, and I was anxious to start work. I hadn't worked for thirty eight days, but the area looked in good condition. It was clean, and materials were in place. However, I was informed equipment breakdowns were still frequent, and the laborers weren't getting their water bags filled. I checked the lister bags, and the water inside was stale. It should have been replaced daily. Brown's neglect was intolerable, and I knew we would soon have another confrontation.

Alex had been transferred to the day shift, and several new hires were on nights. It didn't seem to matter who was working anymore. My main concern was deadlined equipment, long overdue for maintenance, no water for my laborers, and materials not expedited promptly and efficiently. I started keeping a record of Brown's performance for future reference. He was in for a rude awakening.

Activity was at a standstill this night, so the laborers huddled in close to each other and went to sleep. They reminded me of small children in a nursery at nap time, all snuggled together in complete innocence. Staying close to the mama sans gave me a sense of security. At least I wouldn't be singled out to stop a sniper's bullet.

Susie had made me bring a jacket this evening, and I put it around my shoulders. A pneumonia relapse was something I didn't need. The only light was coming from a crane restacking materials. I sat under my "lean-to" for a longtime, once again suffering from a severe case of nostalgia. I had a bad case of homesickness. The darkness of the jungle had closed around me, and an occasional bird call was my only link with my present surroundings.

A week passed, before I was in trouble again. I had drunk too much rot gut the night before, and Susie was mad. I had gotten bombed, and didn't remember all that was said. I do remember Susie saying, "Bob, you dinky dao! You drink boo coo, and you no say nice things to people. I go away, and maybe I no come back." Losing Susie was unthinkable. Maybe she was trying to pound some sense into my thick skull.

A ship had arrived at Newport loaded with materials to be warehoused at Long Binh. This task was accomplished in short order in spite of equipment failures. My crew and I had a good working relationship, and were able to solve numerous problems. I think Brown was amazed how we completed the project with few problems.

The last Philco-Ford flatbed was off-loaded, and I slowly walked back to the office. I signed off, and went to the bus stop. Papa San was always on time.

The driver didn't have to be told to stop at the Thu Duc junction. He opened the door, and I jumped to the ground. My body was healing from the jeep accident. My ribs were still sore, but my lungs were normal.

The sun was shining as I sauntered toward the villa, and opened the screen door to the front porch. A stunning Vietnamese beauty looked up in surprise. Her hair and make-up were flawless, and her short, snow-white skirt exposed perfect legs. My tiredness left me.

"Morning, mama san. Who might you be?" She ignored me. I asked again.

Looking away, she answered. "My name is Minnie, and I wait long time."

"Do you wait for someone?"

Tears filled her eyes. "American army captain say he meet me. I wait long time. He no come. Soon I take taxi to Saigon."

"Honey, my name is Bob, and I live here. I work nights at Long Binh. I just finished work, and come home. I go back tonight. You understand?"

"You say name Bob? I know you, Susie's boy friend. Yvonne tell me, and she say you and Susie have boo coo fight, and Susie no come back Thu Duc. Maybe I stay with you. O.K.?"

"Minnie, come into villa with me, and I drink beer, and we have chop chop together."

Her tears dried quickly, and her eyes brightened. I took her hand, and she followed me into the living room.

Yvonne scampered by pretending not to notice us, but I'm sure the cogs in her corrupt little brain were working overtime. She and Susie had a personality conflict. Susie knew Yvonne, and her conniving, deceptive methods. Yvonne also knew Susie would kill me if I had another woman, and Yvonne wasn't beyond blackmail. Furthermore, Yvonne would love to get even with me for accusing her of stealing. Getting intimate with Minnie could be costly.

Baby San was reluctant to serve breakfast. She didn't smile and was nervous. I cracked a cold beer, the little maid shook her head, and scurried off to her quarters.

Several beers made it easier to forget Susie, at least for the present time. My friend was becoming warmer, and I sensed her intensity. I suggested we retire to the bedroom.

"Minnie, it is more private."

"Bob, honey, I understand."

Now my mind was working overtime. Oh! I'm doomed to die and go to hell. I loved Susie, but she has left me, and what an opportunity. She did walk out, and maybe she'll never come back. What the hell difference does it make? This is war.

Minnie and I were in bed together in record time. What a pleasant way to spend the day. We stayed in the bedroom until late afternoon.

Reluctantly I told Minnie I had to shower and get ready for work. She went into the living room wearing black panties and a matching black brassiere. Nothing else covered her body; she knew it paid to advertise.

I had to get Minnie off the premises. Of course, I'm sure Yvonne was already beating out the news on her drums. I showered quickly, dressed for work, and opened a much needed beer. I walked into the living room, and Jack and Dale were standing there laughing like a couple hyenas. The cat was definitely out of the bag.

Jack laughed like crazy. "Wow! Dale and I sure are happy we left work early today. We just met Minnie, and she's pretty nice on the eyeballs!"

I sank into a chair. Minnie immediately came over and sat down on the arm, moving in close to me. I hadn't noticed that Jack had his Polaroid camera in hand. Before I could move, the flash bulb went blink, and then blink again. I jumped up. "Jack, I'm already doomed. Please don't show the pictures to anyone."

Hutson and Dale were delirious with laughter. "Minnie, please go put clothes on. Jack and Dale, they dinky dao."

The commotion finally calmed, and Minnie went into the bedroom. Baby San called that chop chop was on the table.

Minnie came out of the bedroom fully dressed, and seated herself next to me, across the table from Jack and Dale. Dale was behaving himself, but Jack was a horny old bastard. He was eating dinner, but his eyes were fixed on Minnie. His stare was embarrassing to her and me.

Jack's behavior left a lot to be desired. "Bob, she sure does have nice boobies on her. Most of these little ladies over here are either flat-chested, or they're wearing Hong Kong bras. You know, the ones made of that soft spongy stuff." He laughed. "Minnie, you wear Hong Kong?"

"Hutson, she understands English, so be careful. She's our guest."

"Come on, Patterson. Are they the real thing?"

"Minnie, Jack has to know if you have Hong Kong or real thing. Go ahead, and show him. It make no difference."

Minnie was no neophyte, and it was obvious she wanted to live with an American. Slowly and deliberately, looking Jack straight in the eyes, she unbuttoned her blouse. Taking both hands she pulled the blouse apart, revealing two unblemished and perfect breasts.

I was thoroughly disgusted with Hutson. "Dammit, close your

mouth. Now you know." Dale's face flushed, and he excused himself. Jack grinned and kept gawking as Minnie buttoned her blouse.

After finishing dinner I motioned for Minnie to follow me into the bedroom. "Thank you Minnie for staying with me today. It made me very happy, but you must leave and not come back. I like you, but there is Susie."

"I don't think Susie come back. She boo coo mad, and she go away. I come tomorrow, and I stay with you, and I make you happy. I am good woman. I come tomorrow."

"Minnie, please don't make this more difficult. If Susie comes back she will kill you and me. I know Susie. Please, I must go work now. Xin loi, I'm sorry about that."

Spending the day with Minnie could have been the biggest mistake of my entire life, but if there's any consolation, it was a pleasurable adventure. "Hi ho. Hi ho. Off to work I go!"

It was business as usual at Long Binh. The day crew had off-loaded a ship load of cement. Thousands of pallets of cement were carelessly stacked everywhere. The night shift would have to rearrange the mess.

Brown came by for a look. Philco-Ford trucks were backed up for two miles, and there were broken bags of cement, and pallets of cement scattered all over the area. I was disgusted.

"Lou, what happened? Didn't anyone work today, or are they just trying to beat me to death with disarray? I can't believe this. It will take days to straighten it out."

"Mr. Patterson, I am sorry. There was a shortage of forklifts today. We had fourteen deadlined: ten with mechanical problems and four with flat tires, and there is a shortage of tires. What can I say?"

"It's not easy to warehouse at night. Our progress is hampered by poor lighting, and I don't have enough equipment operators. Lou, I'll do my best under the circumstances."

"Bob, take tomorrow off with pay, and start back on days. The third nationals and locals really work for you, and I need this section in shape. Kraig is coming from Saigon next week for inspection. Can you do it?"

"O.K. Lou, but you have to promise to give me decent equipment and fresh water for my laborers." We shook hands for the first time.

But I would continue to keep records.

We worked hard all night, and managed to off-load the backlogged trucks of cement. The area was still a shambles, but if Brown kept his word, it would be in order for Kraig's inspection.

I boarded the bus, and slept. Papa San awakened me at the Thu Duc junction. It would be good to work days again.

When I walked into the villa Minnie was sitting in the living room with a small suitcase on her lap. My God! How could I have been so stupid? My luck was going from bad to worse. My life was like a yo-yo.

"Morning to you, Papa San. I come to stay with Bob. I make you very happy."

"Good morning to you Minnie; you look nice today. I go get beer, and we talk."

I walked into the bedroom alone, plopped down on the bed, and shook my head. Then all hell broke loose. Susie dashed past the bedroom door, shaking her fist, and yelling in Vietnamese. She grabbed Minnie by the blouse with one hand, and slapped her hard in the face with the other. The poor frightened girl picked up her suitcase, and retreated.

I reached into the refrigerator for a cold beer. Susie charged through the bedroom doorway like a grizzly bear, and I turned just in time to look into two black, glaring eyes with murder in them. I threw the beer straight in the air, and tried to protect my ribs. Fists clenched, Susie was swinging both arms wildly, aiming for the most vulnerable parts of my body. I couldn't believe the strength of this little tiger.

She ran to the bed, and pulled the 32-20 revolver from under a pillow, and began waving it erratically. She was hysterical.

"Susie, if that thing goes off, Bob be no more. Let's talk!"

The gun pointed directly at my vitals. "You butterfly. You make love to her. I know because I stay in maid's quarters with Baby San. I no go Saigon, and I no want to leave Bob. You bad man." I took the gun from her, and threw it on the bed.

She went to her handbag. "I have pictures of you and con gai." She thrust the polaroids into my face. Oh, my God. She had the pictures of Minnie and me that Jack had taken the day before.

"Honey, please give the pictures to me. I throw away. We forget everything. Xin loi. I am sorry."

"Maybe I keep, and I show everybody. They think you no good man. Maybe VC shoot you."

"Please forgive me, Susie. I love you. Maybe I open beer, then we talk."

She snapped. "No can have beer. You bum-e-lum with con gai. You butterfly." She began to cry.

"Bob, come to me. Put your arms around, and I give to you one picture."

"Now what do I do."

"You tear up picture, and throw away." I followed orders, and waited for further instructions.

"Take other picture, and tear up." She laid her head on my shoulder. "You promise no butterfly ever?"

"I promise Susie; I no butterfly. Now can I have beer?" She reached up and pecked me on the cheek.

I was glad Brown had given me the day off before I started the day shift. I needed to share the day with Susie. We arose early and prepared to journey to Saigon. It was a lovely morning, and we sat quietly in the taxi holding hands.

Susie had given the taxi driver Lon's address. It seemed like ages since we had seen her. We paid the driver, and wandered through a maze-like section of Saigon's residential district. The one and two room dwellings, hidden from the main street, were mostly old structures, but they were home to thousands of people thankful for a place to live.

Susie knocked, and the door cracked open. Lon threw her arms around Susie. "Sax, come see who here. Bob and Susie"

"Come in papa san and mama san," Sax beamed. "Good to see you. Did Brown send you here to spy? I screwed off today."

"No, but I'm going back on days starting tomorrow morning. Brown needs a good man, and he actually gave me today off with pay."

"Bob, I've told you before. You do your job. You run a good crew, and nobody knows materials any better. But Brown and his henchmen will win. They don't want anyone to do a good job. Remember,

America's fat cats are making boo coo bucks. They want this war to last forever."

"Sax, I've been keeping a journal of the disarray at Long Binh, and I believe I'm doing what's right. Lives are in jeopardy."

"Do what you have to do. Every American at Area 208 is behind you one hundred per cent. Maybe you can get better conditions for the third and local nationals."

Susie and Lon went off by themselves chattering like crazy, and Sax and I started talking war. Both agreed that events weren't happening the way they were being reported by our military leaders and the politicians. We definitely weren't winning the war. Perhaps we weren't losing, but the Vietcong and the North Vietnamese regulars were beefing up their forces. It was scary to think about five hundred-fifty thousand American troops in Vietnam with Washington fat cats and politicians calling the shots.

"How do you get along with Jack Hutson at Thu Duc?" Sax asked. "I warned you that moving there was bad news. You should have stayed with Susie at the apartment on De Tram Street. Thu Duc is VC country, and if they attack, you'll never get out alive."

"We agree; Saigon is much safer than University Village, but we are close to work and we're happy."

I shook my head. "Jack told me he has VD. If Yvonne finds out, Jack best head for Mongolia. He takes penicillin capsules like normal folks take vitamins. I take my vitamins in the morning, and Jack pops a penicillin capsule, and laughs about it. He's had VD twice in the past two months. It's probably the same dose."

The chatter stopped, and I invited my friends to the International House for lunch. Lon and Susie split a hamburger, while Sax and I drank beer.

After lunch I took Sax to the manager's office where he made application for an "I" House membership. The manager assured him a card within thirty days. We all walked out into the street, and went our separate ways.

Susie and I took a taxi back to Thu Duc, and reminisced about our first meeting at the Casino Bar. We missed our apartment on De Tram Street, and I missed Fanettes Bar.

The PA&E shuttle bus stopped at Thu Duc junction right on time. It was approaching daylight, and I climbed aboard for the always hair-raising trip to Long Binh. My compatriots cheered, and several shook my hand and welcomed me back to the day shift.

Alexander beckoned for me to sit beside him, and informed me of conditions at my area. "Bob, you will inevitably have problems with Brown. Once everything is in order again, he will limit your water supply, and equipment will be hard to come by. This guy's something else. He's after your ass."

"Alex, I'm not going to be concerned about Brown. I'm keeping a daily summary of all activities, and I'll probably go to labor relations at Tan Son Nhut in the end. Right now I'm disturbed about not having a firearm on my person. My Beretta was confiscated after my accident."

"Bob, I have a 6.32 cal. Pic. It's German made. It hasn't been fired much, and there's a full box of ammo. It's yours for the asking."

Alex happened by my area later in the day with the gun. We wandered off into the lumber section to look at the weapon. The Pic was small, but it was surprisingly heavy, and well manufactured. I inserted the clip, removed the safety, and fired six rapid rounds into the lumber pile. It performed well. Alexander and I made a deal.

I was ready for a white glove inspection. Brown was satisfied with the appearance of the area, and Tom Kraig was due to arrive. Equipment maintenance was still a problem, but things had improved. Brown kept his promise, and lister bags were filled each day with water for the laborers.

Alex and Sax had warned me about Brown. I was convinced the following Monday morning that things weren't going to change. He had transferred all three of my labor crews to another section. The old crews voluntarily returned to my area, so now I had six crews.

Hoa, my interpreter said the crews refused to leave. They had been here for a long time, and liked working for me.

Brown pulled up in his pickup. "Patterson, how are you getting along with your new crew?" A hundred fifty laborers surrounded the truck. My leader didn't wait for an answer.

Thursday Lou came to the area, and still insisted on the labor switch. He was determined to make things as bad as possible for me.

I was disgusted. "Lou, do what you think is best. This is Thanksgiving, and Alex, Lachapelle, Ruppe and I are taking the day off."

Ruppe commandeered a PA&E pickup and we all headed for the 9th Trans. The mess sergeant had invited us to turkey dinner with all the trimmings. Everyone enjoyed the meal, but we were all thinking about our families back in the World.

After dinner Alex and I walked to Route 1, and hitched a ride to Thu Duc junction. He'd never been to the villa. He was impressed, but the lack of security at the Village caused him to shudder.

We retired to the living room, and I introduced Alex to Susie. Baby San served cold beer.

"Patterson, you have done quite well for yourself since arriving in Vietnam, without a job. Maybe you should accept the system at Long Binh and concede to Brown. Fighting him will probably cost us both our jobs."

"Alex, I've considered the consequences, but if we can prove to labor relations the inefficiency and corruption at Area 208, maybe we can win. Besides, you're not obligated to be part of this."

"Bob, you may be right, but fighting city hall is almost always a losing battle."

I stubbornly insisted on laying out a plan, despite my friend's warning of the repercussions.

"Alex, meet me tomorrow at noon at the Rex BOQ. We'll draft a letter to labor relations. I've kept accurate records of mismanagement. Are you with me?"

"I'll be there and we'll do this letter thing together, O.K.?" We shook hands.

We popped a beer and drank a toast to our future success. Susie looked at me in dismay. "Bob, where you work when you finish PA&E?"

Sleep didn't come easy for me that night. I was thinking about drafting the letter to labor relations, and about my kids back in the World. Susie cuddled up close. I was concerned for her, and for our future. If I took a job with another company, I could be sent to the Delta or up north to Cam Ranh or some remote area. What would happen to Susie? She couldn't go with me, because I'd be living in barracks.

Alex was drinking a beer when I approached his table at the Rex. "Good afternoon, Bob. Draw up a chair, and I'll spring for a beer."

"Thanks. We'll have a blast after presenting this to labor relations."

My letter was directed: To Whom It May Concern, Labor Relations, Pacific Architects & Engineers, Tan Son Nhut, Saigon, Vietnam. I listed my grievances, and the hardships to the third and local nationals, mainly the lack of daily water. I emphasized one nine-day period in particular that laborers received no water. Convoys could not be loaded efficiently and quickly, because of the lack of available equipment. Loss of life was inevitable under the circumstances, because trucks were being ambushed by the Vietcong at nighttime. Truck convoys could easily be loaded in early morning using well maintained equipment, and travel to their destination in daylight.

"Alex, I'm not trying to cause trouble for Brown. I'm trying to improve working conditions for the laborers."

"When shall we invade labor relations?" Alex was feeling no pain.

"I won't stay in Saigon tonight, but I'll meet you at 0730 tomorrow at the USO on Tu Do. We'll have breakfast, and then go straight to Tan Son Nhut." I didn't touch the booze; I needed a clear head.

My trip back to University Village was stressful, and my thoughts focused on the letter. I had committed myself, and I knew there was no turning back.

The USO was a good place to meet. The food was always good, and it was secure. An old East Indian sat in the entryway and checked IDs. He sported a heavy beard, had a warm smile, and could have easily passed for Santa Claus.

Chuck Alexander was sitting at a table reading the Saigon Post newspaper. "Alex, you heeded my advice, and stayed sober yesterday afternoon?"

Alex and I didn't talk on the way to Tan Son Nhut. My friend and I located the civilian labor relation offices and entered through a large plate glass door. We asked the Vietnamese receptionist to see the official in charge.

Fifteen minutes passed before we were greeted. "I'm Hubert Skaggen with labor relations. May I ask your business?" He put out a soft, clammy hand, and smiled weakly.

"I'm Bob Patterson, and this is Chuck Alexander. We're with PA&E at Long Binh. We have something to discuss in private."

Skaggen had a plush office that could have been located on Wall Street, rather than, Vietnam. The sign on the desk read: Hubert Skaggen, Executive Vice President, Labor Relations, Tan Son Nhut.

"Mr. Skaggen, Alex and I have written a letter to labor relations. It concerns conditions at Long Binh, and we need your help."

Skaggen nodded, and I handed him the two handwritten sheets of paper. He leaned back in his leather chair, and began reading. I intently watched for his reaction. The more he read the straighter he sat in the overstuffed chair. He was getting the message loud and clear.

"Gentlemen, these are strong words. I'll give this serious thought. Come back in a week or two." He was clearly trying to brush us off.

Alex and I remained silent. Five minutes passed and small beads of sweat formed on Skaggen's forehead. The parasite cleared his throat. "Gentlemen, I realize the seriousness of your statement, and I feel that immediate action should be taken. Tomorrow morning I will send two of my best men to Long Binh. They will be instructed to discuss this serious accusation with Mr. Brown. I want to get to the bottom of this."

"Mr. Skaggen, we don't want you to send two men to Long Binh. We want you to personally go to Long Binh. Don't talk to Brown, talk to GIs, the third nationals and the laborers. Talk to American supervisors like Alex and myself. Brown is the problem, not the solution."

"Gentlemen, you can rest assured that there will be action, and soon. Please allow me to analyze your letter, and I will make a decision. Is this fair enough?"

"Skaggen, we'll return to our duties at Long Binh and wait for your answer." We could see the handwriting on the wall. This was City Hall.

The next morning Alex and I signed the register, and walked to our areas. Alex was in charge of the lumber section, a half mile from my district. Communication between the areas was difficult, so our only alternative was to wait.

One week passed, and no word from labor relations, but Brown had made himself scarce. It was December 8th, and Christmas was on my mind.

Other supervisors no longer fraternized with Alexander and me, and I was beginning to feel we had the plague. Our fellow supervisors knew something that my friend and I didn't know.

The following morning when Alex and I signed the register, Brown motioned us into his office. He seemed pleased about something.

"Sit down fellahs, I have news for you. I received word this morning that you're both being transferred to the general office. Kim, our trustworthy courier, is waiting outside to personally escort you. Mr. Brunnel in personnel will be expecting you, and he will inform you concerning the disposition of the transfer." We left the office.

"Alex, this is the beginning of the end. One thing for sure, Brown wants to give us a speedy send-off."

Alexander had never ridden with Kim, and didn't understand just what I meant about a speedy send-off. We climbed into the back of the jeep, and the crazy Korean pushed the gas peddle to the floorboard. Alex got the message.

We entered the main office, and were greeted by the pretty little Korean receptionist. I didn't think she would remember me, but she did. "Good morning, Mr. Patterson, you come to see Mr. Brunnel?"

"Yes, I come to see Mr. Brunnel, and so has Mr. Alexander."

"Been long time, Mr. Patterson, since you be here. You look good. Is nice to see you."

"Thank you. Can we see Mr. Brunnel now?"

We followed her to the personnel manager's office. She knocked on his door, bowed politely, and left.

Brunnel cleared his throat. "Come in Mr. Patterson, Mr. Alexander." He shook hands, and asked both to sit down. "Fellahs, I have no personal animosity, but I do have a job. Chuck Alexander and Bob Patterson, you are both being terminated for cause."

"Mr. Brunnel, being terminated for cause is pretty serious," Alex said. "This means it will be difficult for Bob and me to get work with another company. Am I right?"

"First, I'll tell you the grounds for this drastic action. Alexander, your records indicate insubordination. Mr. Brown and you have a personality conflict. I am sorry, and there's nothing I can do."

"Mr. Patterson, your work records indicate insubordination and extreme absenteeism. I see here that you missed a total of thirty eight days in succession."

"Sir, the thirty eight days absent was due to a jeep accident in September."

"Like I said, I'm only doing my job. Come back in three days and I'll have your severance pay. Incidently, when you return remind me about being terminated for cause. I'll see what I can do."

"Mr. Brunnel, did labor relations talk to other American supervisors about conditions at Area 208?" I asked.

He only shook his head. "There was some discussion with other supervisors. Not one American spoke in your behalf. Sorry." City Hall had won the battle.

Alex and I downed several beers at the Rex BOQ, and discussed our present situation. "Alexander, I am sorry for dragging you into the Long Binh mess. I wish there was something I could do."

"Bob, I went into the fracas with my eyes open, so don't blame yourself. Perhaps conditions will improve; we did our level best. I have contacts in Vietnam, so the employment situation isn't critical. How about you?"

"I have no job prospects. I'm going to take a few days, and think the matter over. My concern is my family back home. They need the income every month. I can manage for two months before the big crunch. Right now I best get to Thu Duc, and tell Susie." We shook hands.

It was dusk when I walked from Thu Duc junction to the villa. Susie asked what happened at Tan Son Nhut. She sensed something was wrong, so I told her.

There was a moment of silence. "I know you lose job today. I am sorry. Bob, you smart man. You no have trouble to get job."

"Thanks, Susie. Maybe I make mistake. Tomorrow we will go to Long Binh, and get my personal effects. We will go to Saigon. Maybe I will buy something pretty for Susie at Rex. O.K.?" I received an enormous hug.

It was early when Susie and I walked to Route 1. It was no effort to hitch a ride with Susie along. In moments we were picked up by a Philco-Ford flatbed loaded with materials for Area 208.

My little companion greeted the Vietnamese driver, and they chattered all the way to Long Binh. I admired the scenery, and marveled at the beauty of Southeast Asia.

My little German Pic automatic was in my pocket, just in case. I had hesitated bringing the firearm, and would avoid a confrontation. I didn't think Brown would do anything foolish. I had to keep cool.

The Vietnamese driver stopped at the shack where my personal effects were stored. Lachapelle and Taylor were supervisors in my area now that I had been terminated.

Lachapelle unlocked the shack, and I removed my belongings. "Bob, I am sorry we didn't back you up," George said. "Labor relations interrogated several Americans, and nobody had enough guts to stand up and fight. We heard you and Alex had been terminated, and everyone backed down. Why should they lose their jobs as well? I am sorry."

"Thanks." I gathered my personals and left. I didn't look back.

I entered the main office, while Susie waited at the main gate. I stood in the center of the room. Kim Choung Un glanced up, and casually returned to working on inventories, and my friend Jack Hutson peered over and waved. I slowly walked into Brown's office.

"Mr Patterson, I've been expecting you. Labor relations informed me of your sudden departure from PA&E's payroll. What's on your mind, friend?"

"Lou, you won. I know that somebody's got to be paying you to screw up daily operations, and I know there are Americans that want this war to go on forever."

Brown grinned smugly. "Patterson, you're a nobody. You little guys just don't get the message. There's a lot of power backing this war. Don't push your luck."

I was confronting a man who out-weighed me by sixty pounds, and an ex-pug. With both hands on his desk top, I leaned over into his face. "Stand up and fight like a fuckin' man!"

Alex yelled from the doorway, "Brown, stand up you bastard, and fight like a man!"

Brown turned ghostly white. "Patterson, I know what you carry in your pocket. I'm not about to get up." He was absolutely petrified.

I turned to Alex. "Let's get out of this cesspool before I vomit."

Susie was waiting. "Honey, let's go home, it's all over."

"Bob, you scared me! You were mad enough to beat Brown into oblivion, or maybe shoot him," Alex said. "I'll see you in Saigon."

Susie and I climbed aboard an empty flatbed and headed back for Thu Duc. The driver took us to the front gate, and wished us good luck. I went directly to my beer stash, and popped a cold one.

"Susie, tomorrow we go to PA&E's office and get my severance check, and then we go to Rex. I buy you something for American Christmas. You understand Christmas?"

"For sure, Bob. You remember I have American boy friend before. He is papa san to Hai, my baby san. Everybody give something for Christmas."

My God! Only twelve days until Christmas. This was a helluva time to be unemployed.

Susie and I left early for PA&E's office. After a forty five minute drive the taxi stopped at the entrance. Susie came inside with me, and took a seat in the air- conditioned room.

"Morning to you, Mr. Patterson. You bring body guard, so you no have trouble with Mr. Brunnel?" The little secretary inspected Susie from top to bottom.

"I like Mr. Brunnel. He is a good man."

The manager greeted me cordially, and shook my hand. "Mr. Patterson, I am sorry about what's happened. I'm really in no position to comment, but will say I admire your guts and your concern for others."

Brunnel handed me the severance check and my passport, which had been kept in the company vault for safe keeping. "The check should help until you can reorganize. You must surrender your PA&E identification cards. I want the PX and commissary card, and the personal ID with your picture."

Alex had cautioned me about giving up my ID cards. My activities would be extremely limited without the IDs. Two major reasons were obtaining money orders at APOs, and liquor and cigarette rations.

"Mr. Brunnel, in mid September I was in a near fatal jeep accident. I lost everything, even my billfold. I don't have my ID." Lying didn't come easy.

"Patterson, you should have contacted me. I would have replaced them. I won't press the issue."

"You've been a straight shooter with me from the start, and I appreciate it. There is one favor."

"Mr. Patterson, what might that be?"

"Sir, would you give me a release on my contract? I've got five kids, and I'm dead in the water without it. No major American contractor will hire me."

"Dammit, Patterson! You really make it tough on a man. Oh, what the hell." He filled out the release form, and I was overjoyed.

I thanked Brunnel for his consideration and hurried to the front office. Susie and I walked arm in arm out into the warm sunlight.

It was still early in the day when we took a table on the crowded patio at the clubhouse. I ordered a coke for Susie, and a vodka collins for me. What a beautiful morning, and what a great way to start the day.

We were watching the golfers tee off from the first hole when George Lachapelle approached our table. He grinned sheepishly. "Bob, what in the world are you doing here? How are you, Sweet Susie?"

"George, I could ask you the same thing. I just finished dealing with Brunnel in personnel. I got my passport and severance check, and a contract release. Now I can look for a job."

"That's great news, Bob, and that gives me an idea. I'm playing golf with Barney Coin, a superintendent for RMK-BRJ. He is my former boss."

"What's that got to do with me?" I asked.

"I'll feel him out for a job. I'll come by Thu Duc tomorrow night after work." George and his friend walked to the number one tee.

Susie and I took a taxi to the Rex BOQ, and I drank beer and visited while she shopped. It was amazing how everything was coming together. I bought her a gold ankle chain to express my love and appreciation for her companionship.

I told Susie we would return to Saigon soon, and visit with Sax and Lon. I was anxious to hear from Lachapelle, but things moved slowly in Vietnam, and Christmas was coming.

While They Died

It was December 14, 1967. How quickly the time had passed since April 24th, and the beginning of my venture in Vietnam. I was wiser in some respects, and felt confident about finding a job in the near future. One thing to remember in Vietnam, nobody was in a hurry to do anything.

Bo Priest came through the front gate in his white jeep. Favoring his stiff leg, he slowly eased out of the vehicle, and entered the living room through the front door. His timing was perfect, because I needed a ride to an Army Post Office.

"Bob, I hear you've joined the ranks of the unemployed. I ran into Hutson at Long Binh, and he said that you and Alexander made a believer out of Big Lou Brown."

Bo liked this kind of bunk, particularly when someone my size would even think of standing up to a tyrant. God knows I was only trying to prove a point to Brown, but at any rate, I had bonded a positive relationship with Priest. This was good. He had guts and transportation, and we would support each other in a time of necessity.

True friendship could be the difference between life and death with so many uncertainties in a country at war. Bo Priest was a friend, and I had allayed any skepticism or mistrust for the man. I valued his boldness and frankness.

There were several military installations in the immediate vicinity that were convenient for supplying treated drinking water. Local tap water was unfit for human consumption, so Jack and I hand-carried a supply in five gallon plastic containers. Each military compound had an APO, so money orders were readily available.

I mailed two letters at the APO, and picked up two hundred dollars in money orders for future reference. Changing money on the black market would help supplement my income until I became employed, and since Bo's finances hadn't been good since his unemployment, I gave him some incentive for furnishing the transportation. Ten percent of the profits seemed to be agreeable.

George Lachapelle and his driver stopped by the villa after work in a PA&E pickup, and he came bouncing through the front door and yelling, "Beer, Beer, papa san. De mau len!" He was filthy from head to toe, and enjoying every minute of it. This was a far cry from his white-collar background in a lucrative insurance business. He liked the adventure in Vietnam, and the money provided he and his family with necessary cash.

I handed him a cold one, and he immediately devoured it. "Damn, don't stop now, Bob. I have a terrible thirst." It reminded me of my days at Long Binh, and I really missed the action.

"George, I've been curious of what transpired between you and the RMK-BRJ superintendent. How do things stack up?"

"Well, Bob, you know how slow things happen over here. Barney Coin is leaving for the States in a couple days for the holidays, and he'll be back on January 10th. You go to RMK's main office at Number 2 Duy Tan in Saigon on January 11th, and Barney will talk with you. No promises, but it looks good."

"One more thing, and remember this. When you get to RMK's office talk to Coin, completely ignore Bob Hyenberg, the personnel manager. The guy is weird, and thinks he's God's gift to the universe. He'll screw up things proper for you."

"Thanks. I can visualize a drastic cut in salary, but a bird in the hand is better than a flock in the bush. I'll only be working six ten hour shifts a week. I heard Alaska Barge isn't hiring. First things first, but maybe in the future. Alaska Barge is a good outfit, and they give a man a respectable paycheck. I'll settle for Raymond-Morrison-Knudsen, Brown-Root and J.A. Jones. What a conglomerate!"

"Bob, take care, and good luck. I won't be far away. I'm off to Saigon." With a beer in hand he waved goodbye. It was good of Lachapelle to give me the lead. I'd have to pace myself until after the holidays.

Jack and Dale were making plans for the holidays, and both were going to their respective homes in the States. Since I had idle time, they asked me to get confirming plane reservations and tickets for them at CAT, our local Saigon travel agent. They each gave me personal checks for twelve hundred dollars for round trip tickets. Each wanted to depart Saigon on December 22nd, and return on January 4th. The transaction took a good two hours at CAT Travel Agency.

I was anxious to venture to the Rex BOQ for cold beer and American food when I finished. It was still early afternoon when I stepped off the elevator at the fifth floor. When I entered the near empty ballroom, my eyes focused on the only person planted at the bar.

"Chao co, papa san." I plunked down on a stool next to Sax Ruppe, and ordered an American beer. "Sax, this is getting to be a habit with you missing work. How's it going out there in the boondocks?"

"The Army Engineers have paved the road from Route 1 to Area 208, so that accidents like yours won't occur. PA&E is sprinkling the roads around the storage pads every day to keep the dust down, laborers are getting their daily water ration, and downtime of equipment is minimal. Everybody is talking about the change, and saying Bob Patterson is the man of the hour. Hell Bob, you're a hero!"

"Sax, this is good news, particularly for the locals and third nationals. It'll also help the army convoys. Maybe GIs will live longer. They won't have to transport materials through the jungle at night."

Ruppe was inebriated, and I was confident I would join him soon enough. "Shit, Patterson, like I said, you're a damn hero, and I'm proud to be your friend."

"I'm not going to dwell on PA&E getting their heads out of their asses. I might be a hero, but you still have a job."

Ruppe slugged down the beer. "Yeah, that's a bad deal, Bob. We should have backed you up."

"Hell Sax, you guys did stand behind me, about five miles. You can thank them." He was silent for a few minutes.

"Bartender, I want to buy my buddy and me a beer!" He put his hand on my shoulder. "Look, Bob, we're still friends. Forget it, and let's have a party."

Ruppe and I shook hands, and moved to a corner for some privacy. The place was starting to get noisy, so we ate lunch, and after several beers it was time to leave.

Sax suggested I stay with him and Lon for the night. Curfew wasn't far away, and it was scary riding in a taxi to Thu Duc after dark. I accepted his invitation, but he had to promise to have Lon verify with Susie where I spent the night. I didn't need boo coo trouble with little black-eyed Susie. Lon got home from work the same time that Sax and I arrived in a taxi. We were happy-go-lucky.

"Hello Bob," Lon said, "good to see you, and how is Susie?"

She looked at Sax in disgust. "No work today, huh? Pretty soon you no have work, and be same same Bob. We have no money, and we get hungry, and have no house to live."

My friend laughed, and assured Lon he wasn't going to lose his job. "Honey, tomorrow I go to work at Long Binh for sure." He laughed heartily, and slapped her on the butt.

She gave him a huge hug and smiled. "Sax, you dinky dao. Choi oi!"

Sax poured two whiskey-cokes, and then got serious. "Bob, I want to tell you something important. Listen closely. You know that Lon and her brother manage an Esso service station on Hai ba Trung Street not far from where we live? After Lon comes home at night from work, she tells me, "every day I see boo coo VC come Saigon. They bring guns and everything for to fight war."

"I've pieced together what she's trying to tell me. The Vietcong are coming into Saigon in funeral processions, and hiding their weapons in caskets. They're bringing in AK-47s, ammo, mortars, machine guns, and God only knows what else. They're burying these weapons in the cemeteries. VC are getting jobs with American companies, and are even working as taxi drivers. God only knows how many are working as bartenders. They learn about troop movements from American civilians and GIs that frequent the bars."

Sax poured another drink. "Funeral processions in Vietnam are commonplace, and they are huge. They believe the larger the procession, the wealthier the family, and they hire professional mourners. These mourners are actually paid to wail and grieve. The more the merrier. But the disturbing difference is that now some of these mourners are Vietcong trained in Hanoi. They aren't local nationals."

My friend was getting drunker, louder, and more excited. "You see, there are thousands of Vietcong coming into Saigon, and the build-up is getting huge. With thousands of VC infiltrating the city, it looks like an offensive is about to erupt. Bob, what'd you think?"

"Hell, Sax, it doesn't surprise me. These devils are smart, they're tricky, and they all look alike. Why don't you go tell General Westmoreland about this, and he'll probably give you a medal? Maybe two medals."

"Bob, I don't think any Vietnamese will tell everything he knows, not even Lon or Susie. They want to protect us, but in turn, they have an obligation to the Republic of Vietnam. These people are patriotic and no different than Americans under the same circumstances. Agreed?"

"Sax, Westmoreland would have you committed to the funny farm if he were approached about our discovery. You couldn't get within five miles of him in the first place. The big show is building momentum, and all hell is going to break loose. It's going to be mighty interesting."

Lon and Sax were tired, and he would be up early for his trip to Long Binh. I bid them a pleasant good night, and crawled up the steep stairway to a small room in the attic.

The room was adequate, but it wasn't pleasant. I'd slept there before. Rats got into the attic through a hole in the gable end of the house. They would awaken me as they very slowly stalked across the sheet that covered my body. These weren't small animals. Their average size a foot long with an eighteen inch tail dragging along behind. It kept me alert. When I felt them crossing the bed, I'd backhand them with my fist, and listen to them squeal when they hit the wall. I was glad I had taken my plague shot. Pleasant dreams!

Susie was waiting for me when I got to the villa at Thu Duc the next morning. "Good morning, mama san. I stay Saigon last night."

She ignored me for several moments. "Susie know you no butterfly with con gai in Saigon. I shoot you if you bum-e-lum. Choi oi! Lon send friend to Thu Duc last night, and tell me you stay with Lon and Sax in house with boo coo long tail rats." Sometimes Susie had one helluva sense of humor.

It was December 21st, and Armed Forces Radio was playing Christmas carols. Everyone seemed to temporarily forget about the war. Dale and Jack were home early for the day, and wouldn't return to work until after spending Christmas in the States.

Jack and I broke open a fifth of Black Velvet, and officially started celebrating the holiday. Jack had brought home a bag full of firecrackers, powerful little explosives, and we were having a ball setting them off out in the yard.

Dale was busy packing his clothes, but was preoccupied about a venereal disease that he may have contracted. It was called non-specific urolithiasis. U.S. Military doctors were baffled. GIs who had contracted it were denied leave to go home, and nobody wanted to discuss the subject.

Dale was worried about going home to his wife and three children because of the disease. There was little known about it, and there was no known cure. Penicillin wouldn't touch it. Sometimes the disease had the symptoms of gonorrhea, the discharge showing positive under a microscope, and other times the discharge would test negative.

Jack and I consumed nearly a fifth of booze, and I cautioned my friend. "Jack, better knock it off. You have to catch a plane early tomorrow morning. Yvonne is in your bedroom waiting to help you pack. Let's eat; no more rot gut."

Hutson didn't heed my words, and cracked open another fifth of bourbon. He was like many of us. Once he started drinking, he wasn't about to stop.

Yvonne yelled at him. "You drunk. No help you. I go away, and maybe I no come back." She was gone.

Jack was slurring his words, and was belligerent. Dale and I tried to get him to eat, but to no avail. We each took an arm, half dragged him into his bedroom, and told him to sleep it off.

"Bob, I've got enough on my mind without worrying about Hutson. I'm trying to figure what to say to my wife about why I can't have sex, because of this damn disease." Dale jerked his thumb towards Jack. "He's your nightmare."

Jack managed to take a shower, and changed clothes. He walked into the living room, swaying, still unstable, and far from sober. "B-B-Bob. I'm going to Saigon to see Minh at her bar, a-a-nd get me up early in the morning."

"Jack, listen to me. Minh's Bar is no place for you tonight. She won't tolerate your drunkenness. You are in terrible shape to drive your car, and being drunk makes you a sitting duck for the cowboys. Stay at the villa! You've got a plane to catch back to the World!"

"Go to hell, Patterson. I'm going to Saigon."

"If you're going to town take my automatic. You'll probably get your head blown off." I disgustedly shoved the gun into his pocket along with a hand full of firecrackers. "Good night Jack, lots of luck. Xin loi."

Jack disappeared out the door. The Toyota engine roared, the tires spit gravel as they spun out through the front gate.

"You do everything. If he no come back, we look for him tomorrow," Susie said, calmly. "Go to bed. Jack is dinky dao, and he won't hear what you say."

It was early morning, and a loud pounding at my bedroom door made me slide my hand under the pillow and retrieve the 32-20 revolver. I leaped out of bed, and flung the door open. I couldn't believe what I saw. Hutson was standing in the doorway.

He was one sorry sight. Jack was crying hysterically. He had a black eye, his nose and lips were badly swollen, and his face was cut in several places. His wrists were skinned and still bleeding. His white shirt was in shreds, both pant legs were nearly ripped off, he was barefoot.

It wasn't funny, but Susie was laughing. "Welcome home, Jack.

Did you have good time at Minh's Bar? Maybe army tank hit you. Choi oi!"

I went to the refrigerator and got two beers. "Jack, sit down and start from the beginning."

"Not everything is too clear, but some guy was messing with Minh, and I intervened. Minh asked me to leave, and I think I hit her. The MPs came crawling out of the woodwork, and I started on them. The next thing I remember, I was sitting in an army jeep handcuffed to the frame. The cuffs were hurting my wrists, and I couldn't see because of blood running down into my eyes. They gave me a citation, and turned me loose. I got a ride to Newport on a Honda, and a GI truck brought me to the junction. Here's the citation."

It read: Drunk and disorderly, striking a Vietnamese citizen, resisting arrest. Confiscated one 6.32 Pic Automatic firearm, one clip, nine rounds of ammunition, sixteen firecrackers.

"Jack, where is your diamond ring and your car?"

"Bob, I don't know much about anything. I'm going to bed. We'll talk in the morning. I won't be catching that plane for the States tomorrow; I have to go to PA&E's general office and face the charges."

The following morning Susie went out to the Thu Duc junction, hailed a taxi, and the three of us headed for Saigon. Jack wanted to go straight to PA&E's office at the golf course. Susie and I went to Minh's Bar. Maybe we could get information about Jack's idiotic escapade.

Minh greeted us cordially. "Chao co, Susie and Bob. I know why you here, and I am sorry about your friend. Jack boo coo drunk."

"Minh, I want to apologize for Jack. We tried to make him stay at Thu Duc, but he wanted to see you. Maybe he has love for you. I don't know."

"I have boy friend, and Jack and my American friend say bad things. Jack want to fight, and I tell him to leave. Jack hit me, and I call MPs."

"Minh, somebody steal Jack's diamond ring, and twelve hundred dollars, and he lose his car."

"Jack have ring when he leave bar," Minh said. "I don't know about money and car."

"Thank you, Minh. Susie and I will go now, and try to find car." It was embarrassing for me, particularly since I was an American and considered a guest in Vietnam.

Susie and I hailed a taxi, and cruised up and down the streets in the immediate vicinity. I thought Jack probably went straight to Minh's Bar, and I didn't think anyone had stolen the car. After two hours of an unsuccessful search, we had the driver take us to Thu Duc. We anxiously waited for Jack's return.

My friend was downhearted when he walked into the villa. PA&E had terminated him for cause.

"Jack, you stay here tomorrow, and Susie and I will go to Saigon. We'll find the car. You probably parked on a side street. I'll get you another plane reservation. Go home for the holidays, and when you come back you'll find a job."

Jack nodded his approval. "I wish I had listened last night. I can't figure what happened to my ring and cash. The diamond was worth twenty-five hundred bucks, and somebody ripped off twelve hundred in cash. Besides, I lost your gun."

"Minh said you were wearing your ring when the MPs dragged you out of the bar. Maybe your ring and cash were stolen right here at the villa. It has happened before when you were drunk. Think about it."

Hutson waited for Yvonne to return. Late in the afternoon he called her into the living room, and asked Susie and me to join them. He confronted his girl friend point blank. "Yvonne, I think last night you take my ring and money."

"Jack, I no teal anyting!" Yvonne yelled.

Susie and I looked at each other and smiled. Jack knew, but how could he prove anything? We opened a beer, and settled in for the night.

Jack took my advice and stayed at the villa, and Susie and I went to search for his car. I went to CAT and talked to Annie about another plane reservation for Jack. She told me to come back late in the day, and maybe she could do something.

We found the Toyota parked on Ngo Duc Ke Street, just across from the Saigon River. It was partially hidden under a tree, and the only apparent damage was four flat tires. .

Christmas was two days away, and Susie wanted to shop. I went to a military PX to buy Susie and Baby San each a gift.

I finished shopping, and returned to CAT to pick up Jack's reservation for Christmas Eve. I thanked Annie, and she wished me a happy holiday.

It was dark when I parked the car at the villa. Jack came to meet us, and I handed him a confirmation on his plane reservation.

When Jack was safely on the plane and headed for the States, Susie and I drove the car to Thu Duc. I tuned the radio to Armed Forces Radio and we listened to Christmas carols.

It was quiet at Thu Duc with Jack and Dale gone. Yvonne went to Saigon to stay with relatives, and Susie, Baby San and I would spend Christmas alone. Sax had to work, and Lon would be busy at the Esso service station. I liked the solitude, but we were in VC country. It was eerie.

Early Christmas morning I called to Susie and Baby San, and they came into the bedroom with enormous smiles. There was a gift for each, and they accepted graciously.

Baby San quickly opened her package, and inside was a gold Timex watch with an expansion bracelet. She had never had a watch, and she thanked me with tears in her eyes.

Susie opened her package, and she too received a watch. I bought the best Seiko available at the PX. She was thrilled, and she and Baby San thanked me.

Susie went to our closet, and returned with two packages. "This from Baby San and me. Open please, papa san."

I opened the packages. One gift was a genuine tiger claw inlaid with gold and attached to a gold chain. The other was a gold ring with a jade inlay. The Vietnamese believed that bright jade meant good luck.

Susie excitedly explained, "Bob, ring have bright jade on top, and heart on side. This mean good luck from the bottom of my heart. I leave tiger claw with Big Buddha of all Saigon. He bless, and he say no harm come to you. VC no can shoot you." I was deeply moved, and the three of us exchanged hugs. It was a tearful event, and I was grateful to have warm and caring friends in this far away land.

Later in the evening Lynn Berksnyder and Tina, and Wendell and Tom dropped by the villa for drinks. We played American Christmas songs on Dale's new Sony tape recorder. It had been a quiet and enjoyable day. We all wished each other good luck.

New Years came and went. Bo and I made three trips to Long Binh to get money orders, and changed money in Saigon. I sent money to the kids, and had enough in reserve to be comfortable for a while longer.

Susie and I were enjoying our solitude. She spent most of the day in Thu Duc visiting relatives and friends, and I lounged around the villa watching TV and sipping beer.

It was late afternoon, January 4th, when a taxi pulled up out front of the villa. Jack and Dale had returned from the States. We shook hands, and settled down in the living room for some serious beer drinking. I asked how the American people back in the World were accepting the war.

"Bob, the war isn't well accepted by the people," Jack said. "Young men are burning their draft cards, and defecting to Canada. College students are protesting, and citizens in general are asking President Johnson what the hell we're fighting for? Young people are demonstrating in the streets all over America and chanting to the President: 'Hey, Hey, LBJ, how many kids did you kill today! Hey, Hey, LBJ, how many kids did you kill today!'"

"I was talking to friends in Denver," Dale said, "and they are watching the GI body count on TV. More and more caskets are coming back to the States. Martin Luther King gave a speech, and he asked General Lewis Hershey, our great selective service director, why the poor, and the blacks, and other minorities were being drafted, and the rich and college kids were being exempt. Evidently our Government is weeding out what they consider the less desirable of the good old United States of America.

"Draftboards are something else," Dale said, his voice shaking. "The bastards are sending young men from towns and rural areas, and kids from the ghettos to be slaughtered. The school dropouts and the kids with low scholastic averages are being picked. It looks like an excuse for "ethnic cleansing."

Jack and Dale were surprised that Americans back home were so naive and gullible. America was becoming divided. Jack chug-a-lugged his beer and continued. "Congress is asking President Johnson how he can continue to send troops to fight without a declaration of war. Congress, in turn, is appropriating funds to escalate the conflict. In October, Johnson recommended to raise taxes, and this really upset the American people."

"I've never been in the military, and after being over here I'm not sure if I would fight," Dale said. "Is communism taking over the world? I again agree with the American civilians, who say this is a "get rich" war. If this was World War II, and we were fighting to save our freedom, I would volunteer. Bob, what would you do?"

"Pearl Harbor was attacked when I was fourteen years old. Kids became men overnight during World War II, and thousands of men and women were drafted. But we also saw a lot of draft dodgers that found ways to stay at home. I lost a brother in that war, and I learned to hate Germans and Japanese. I attended military school, and entered the service when I was eighteen. I trained hard, and hoped I would see combat, but the war ended. If I were of draft age now, I'd have reservations. I've always been patriotic, and I was raised to respect my flag and love my Country, but I don't think the communists here are a big threat. This is a "get rich" son-of-a-bitch. Jack, you're a retired combat soldier. What do you think about fighting?"

"I have no doubt that I would fight," Jack said. "This war is wrong, but being an American and being patriotic means everything to me. Yes, I would fight."

Jack went to his room, and returned with a small package. "Bob, I owe you and Susie for helping me before Christmas."

The package contained a .25 cal. Browning automatic, and two boxes of ammunition. It was nickel plated with pearl-handled grips, and it was expensive.

The next morning Dale went back to work at Long Binh, and Jack and I went to Saigon. Our first stop was RMK's office at Number 2, Duy Tan, Saigon. Jack had worked for RMK before. He knew the top brass, and they were aware of his ability and experience. He had worked on a crusher at RMK's rock quarry.

Jack went to the second floor to see Dick Bowden, who was Jack's previous superintendent, and I waited in the lobby at RMK's information desk.

The young lady at the desk asked if I had been helped. I informed her I'd like to see Mr. Hyenberg, the personnel manager. The receptionist walked to a glassed-in office towards the rear of the room and returned. "Please follow me."

The personnel manager looked young for his age, and still had peach fuzz. "I'm Bob Hyenberg. How can I help you?"

"I'm Bob Patterson, and I'm looking for a job. I've been employed by PA&E, but we severed our relationship. Here is my current resume, and a release on my contract."

Hyenberg carefully read my resume. "Mr. Patterson, you have a good background in building materials. Why did you leave? PA&E pays top wages."

"Mr. Hyenberg, I was absent from work for thirty-eight days due to an accident. PA&E no longer wanted my services."

"Patterson, according to your resume we have something in common. We both hail from Boise, Idaho, but you can rest assured this will have no bearing on whether I hire you. Here is an application form. Fill it out, return it promptly, and remember that I do all the hiring at RMK."

Jack returned from the second floor carrying an application form. "How did it go, Jack?"

"Bowden seemed pleased to see me, but is reluctant to hire. When I left RMK they were busy as hell, and needed my experience. He thinks I left the company high and dry, but he gave me an application form, and that is some encouragement."

Lynn Berksnyder and Tina were at the villa when Jack and I returned from Saigon. Jack and Lynn had worked together at the quarry for RMK, so it appeared that Lynn might have some influence with Bowden. His input could be a deciding factor to rehire Jack.

I left Berksnyder and Hutson to themselves when Susie called me into our bedroom. "Bob honey, Susie go to Saigon to stay with my baby sans for the TET. This is Chinese New Year. My people will come to my house, and we be thankful together."

The TET had been mentioned during Christmas, and Susie told me that it was similar to our Christmas and New Year. It would commence at midnight on January 29th.

At the end of the year, at midnight, the Vietnamese celebrated their "GAO Thus", the end of the old year and the beginning of the new one. It was quite different from celebrating New Years Eve in the U.S.A., where hordes of people jammed the streets to roar in the New Year with noisemakers and car horns, and celebrate in bars and taverns.

In Vietnam everybody remained at home and participated in silent ceremonies. The whole family assembled around a huge censer of fragrant incense smoke. With spring flowers around them and a cloud of smoke overhead, they meditated about their ancestors who fought to create and preserve their homeland. They thought about dear friends who were far away. They paid their debts, and they repented of any bad deeds. They started the year with a clean conscience.

Firecrackers would explode to welcome the returning "Spirit of the Home". On the "Head Day" of the year, as the Vietnamese usually call it, they paid visits, wishing each other a happy New Year. Many people went to pagodas to pray to Buddha that peace would reign among their families and over their country. They brought home branches of fresh plants as a "symbol of happiness".

On the second day the people commenced amusements and games, which lasted almost a week. They participated in wrestling matches, buffalo fights, kite flying, and a number of different native dances. But the main celebration was always the TET. Since time immemorial, it had been observed throughout the country by all the people— scholars and commoners, rich and poor alike. Games and amusements differed according to wealth and social status, but to all, the meaning of the TET remained the same, "To recall the past and prepare for the future".

Susie informed me that Baby San would be going home to her village of My Lai to spend TET with her friends and family. She would be gone until April. She wanted to help her elderly parents with chores before returning to Thu Duc.

An old mama san would stay at the Thu Duc villa, and would be in charge of the kitchen, laundry and cleaning, and would keep an eye out for intruders.

I certainly didn't relish the thought of going through interviews again. I should have listened to Sax, and rode with the tide at PA&E. I would still have a good paying job.

Jack and I bid Susie and Yvonne farewell, and headed for Saigon to seek out Bowden and Coin with hopes for employment. Fighting had intensified, and it was very apparent as we drove along Route 1 between the Thu Duc junction and Newport Docks on the Saigon River.

Several vehicles had been destroyed, and were still burning. There were numerous empty ammunition casings laying about on the highway. The Vietcong were much closer to Saigon. In the past I wasn't too concerned about my safety, but now everyone was growing uneasy.

U.S. Huey gun ships, jet fighters, and propeller driven Skyraiders were much more prevalent overhead. Rockets were being fired into nearby villages, and bursts of machine gun fire were frequent. Artillery shells were bursting, and we didn't know if they were ours or theirs. Vietcong sniper fire increased, and bullets were finding their targets. My Buddha-blessed tiger claw was hanging around my neck. No harm could come to Bob!

Two RMK-BRJ cat-skinners had recently been killed at the rock quarry not far from Thu Duc. Vietcong had infiltrated through spider holes, and cut them down with automatic weapons.

We arrived at RMK's office, and Jack went upstairs to Bowden's office. I inquired for Coin's office at the information desk, and an American receptionist directed me to the second floor.

As I turned to walk up the stairs Bob Hyenberg blocked my way. I tried to walk around, but he refused to allow me to pass.

"Excuse me, sir," I said.

"Patterson, I specifically told you that I am the personnel manager, and I do the hiring. Maybe I didn't make myself clear."

"Mr. Hyenberg, I'm certainly not looking for trouble. I was personally instructed to contact Mr. Coin about a job when he returned from the States after the holidays. Please don't try to stop me."

I placed my briefcase on a nearby chair and spread my feet apart, preparing for combat. My teeth were clenched tightly together, and my face reddened. The receptionist stood close by, wide-eyed and silent.

Hyenberg stepped aside, and I proceeded up the stairs to the second floor. I hoped that I wouldn't need anything from this guy down the road. It would be futile.

Barney Coin's desk was crowded with papers, and he appeared deeply engrossed with daily business. He asked what I wanted.

"Mr. Coin, my name is Bob Patterson, and George Lachapelle told me to personally contact you about getting a job with Raymond-Morrison-Knudsen, Brown-Root, and J.A. Jones."

"Lachapelle told you to see me?"

"Yes, Sir. I just bypassed Mr. Hyenberg in personnel, and he is fit to be tied. I didn't mean to cause him trouble."

"Don't worry about Hyenberg, he's harmless. How is Lachapelle, and is he staying sober?"

"Yes, George is sober, and he's a good man. We worked together at Long Binh when I was employed by PA&E. I'm no longer with them.

"You have a family, Patterson?"

"Yes sir. I'm divorced, and I have five kids back in the States."

"Need a job pretty bad, huh?"

"Sir, would you please consider looking at my credentials? Here is an application that I had previously picked up from Bob Hyenberg. Also, attached is a release on my PA&E contract."

"I'll look at your credentials, but no promises. Why did you leave your previous employer?"

"Mr. Coin, I was terminated for cause. PA&E used extreme absenteeism for the cause, as I was off work for thirty-eight days. I was in a jeep accident. I have no excuses, Sir. My performance at Long Binh was above average, and I'm sure Brunnel at PA&E personnel will verify it."

Coin looked at his calendar. "Patterson, be in my office Friday, January 26th. If your papers are satisfactory you can start processing for hire. One thing is in your favor, RMK doesn't recognize PA&E as a major contractor. Have a nice day, Patterson."

"Thank you, Sir. I appreciate your consideration. I'll be here."

The Toyota quietly hummed towards Thu Duc, and Jack and I were both preoccupied. I'm sure we had similar thoughts. Will we be working in the near future?

Susie and Yvonne were anxiously waiting for our return. "Bob, you and Jack go work soon?" Susie asked.

"It looks good, Susie. All we can do is wait."

Employment was close at hand, so I gave Susie fifty thousand piasters. "Give this to Baby San for the TET. She will need when she go home to My Lai. Give her my love and good luck."

"I give to her money, Bob. She need to help mama san and papa san. You make her very happy."

Jack and I kept busy while we waited to hear about our jobs. We hit several APOs for money orders to change on the market. CID was constantly on our minds.

Hutson and I left for Saigon early on the morning of January 26th. I entered Coin's office at exactly 0900 hours, and he handed me the necessary papers to start processing for hire. We crossed the hall into another office, and I was introduced to Jake Harris, RMK's personnel coordinator.

"Jake, this is Bob Patterson who was recently terminated for cause by PA&E. He could be a valuable employee, and has extensive building material experience. Keep and eye on him, and make sure he doesn't miss work. He missed considerable time on his previous job, and that is something that will not be tolerated."

"Patterson," Jake said, "if your papers are satisfactory when you return to my office, I will decide where to locate you. We may keep you in the Saigon area or send you up country to Da Nang or Nha Trang."

I thanked Harris, and returned to the lobby. Jack was making time with one of the secretaries and didn't seem too pleased when I interrupted. "Jack, I need to take a physical immediately. How did you make out with Bowden?"

"I take a physical, and report to the rock quarry on Monday morning. I'll have my old job as supervisor on the rock crusher. I'm taking a drastic salary cut, but I'm back on the payroll."

At the medical clinic, we were ordered to strip, and the check-ups began. The process didn't take long, and I was told to return Tuesday, January 30th. The doctor would read my x-ray when he returned from Da Nang.

Jack and I returned to the villa. Susie was preparing to go to Saigon to spend the celebration with her family and friends. She would be painfully missed, even for a few days.

My little companion kissed me. "Bob, I miss you. Take care, and good luck from the bottom of my heart." I watched her board a lambretta to Saigon.

Baby San, our maid, left for My Lai, and wouldn't return until April.

Chapter Thirteen

An uneasiness was developing among the Vietnamese household workers. Each was preparing to go to their respective homes for the TET, except for the old mama san that Susie had asked to stay at the villa. I watched Yvonne's mama san and papa san bustling around the kitchen and in the maid's quarters.

Jack and I asked Yvonne why everyone was in such a hurry to leave Thu Duc. "Everybody go home for the TET, but they boo coo afraid. They think maybe Vietcong come soon and make trouble."

"Honey," Jack said, "South Vietnamese President Thieu and U.S. Ambassador Bunker have made a thirty-six hour truce with North Vietnam. Everybody can be happy, and celebrate the TET without trouble. The Vietcong will not fight during Happy New Year. The truce will start from the evening of 29th through the morning of January 31st. In turn, the Vietcong leaders have announced a truce to last from January 27th until the morning of February 3rd. Nobody make trouble during the TET."

Yvonne suddenly became enraged. "VC fight very soon. They kill many South Vietnamese people and American GIs. Vietcong love their country, and will fight. They not afraid of Americans, and they will die for Vietnam." Yvonne's fists were clenched, and she was yelling. Jack and I were dumbfounded and remained silent.

"I not dinky dao. I know many things about where and why Vietcong fight. You hear on radio about boo coo fight at Khe Sanh. Americans have many soldiers there, and Vietcong kill them. They fight at Hue, and everywhere in Vietnam. Vietcong come to Saigon and make boo coo trouble. I no say more."

I had just become a firm believer that Yvonne was one hundred percent Vietcong, but I wasn't alarmed about Yvonne's affiliations. Jack was providing for her and her baby san. She wasn't going to bite the hand that fed her family. Her stealing from Jack was easy pickins', and probably self-satisfying. Yvonne was ornery.

Dale returned from work at Long Binh, and said the ARVN and American troops were on full red alert, but only for precautionary reasons. They didn't think the Vietcong would violate the truce. Not many local nationals showed up for work, but that was understandable with the TET celebration only three days away.

Dale, Jack, Yvonne and I piled into the Toyota on Sunday January 28th, and headed for the Hy Tho race track. Yvonne's parents and relatives were gathering for the New Year, and Jack had promised to take her home. The house was located on Lu Gia Street, just off Nguyen van Thoat. This was on the north side of the Hy Tho race track in Cholon, the Chinese sector. None of us were familiar with the area, so Yvonne was giving Jack directions.

We were on Nguyen van Thoat when the traffic became so congested that it virtually stopped. Yvonne said she would walk to the house, and that we should turn around, and return to Thu Duc at once. She wasted no time getting out of the car, and waving goodbye.

It was scary to be entangled in this mess. All three of us were aware of the danger of crowded places. The Vietcong loved to cause havoc by tossing a bomb into crowds.

"We've got to get back to Tran quoc Toan Street," Jack said, anxiously. "I can find my way to Gia Dinh and to Route 1. This is a bitch! I've never seen such confusion. My God, cars everywhere, and thousands of people just milling around like lost sheep just before an approaching storm."

I tapped Jack on the shoulder from the back seat. "Hell, Jack, the only alterative is to turn around. The traffic is creeping slowly. I'll get out and stop it, and then turn this sucker around."

"Patterson, you're out of your cotton pickin' mind!"

I jumped out the right side, and walked around to the other side. Cars were bumper to bumper, and the honking was deafening. I prayed I wouldn't get crushed as I stepped between two cars. I faced the front bumper of a car driven by a well dressed Vietnamese, raised my hands, and waved and whistled. The car stopped dead, and within moments a space developed wide enough for Jack to come into action.

"Jack, start turning into this opening." I held my ground, and Jack slowly maneuvered the car into the gap. I ran into the opposite lane and stopped the closest car, and motioned for Jack to back up. I yelled for him to move forward, and he slipped into the unending line of honking cars.

We reached Tran quoc Toan Street and Jack merged the car into the slowly advancing traffic, and somehow managed to turn into the lane. Thank God, we were headed for Gia Dinh. It was long after dark when the Toyota pulled into the driveway at our villa.

The three of us sat motionless in the living room for several minutes, shaking our heads in disbelief of the experience. Old mama san peered out from the kitchen, and smiled broadly. All was quiet at the villa, and interrupted only by an occasional jungle bird talking to its mate.

The following morning was Monday, January 29th, and Dale walked to Route 1 to catch his bus to Long Binh. Jack headed for RMK's rock quarry in the Toyota for his first day's work. I would hitchhike to Saigon, and check out RMK's office. I thought perhaps my x-rays might have been examined.

I walked into RMK's medical clinic on Duy Tan, and the medic shook his head. "Bob, I think it will be several days before your x-rays will be read. Doctor Johnson is at our Cam Ranh Bay installation up north. Wish I could give you a more positive answer. Sorry."

"Mac, will you inform Harris in personnel of the holdup? I don't want him to think I'm goofing off. I'll see you on Friday." I returned to Thu Duc.

Jack and Dale arrived at the villa after work, and both were excited. They had heard rumors that Vietcong troops had attacked Bien Hoa

Air Base not far from Thu Duc. Dale said there was gunfire at Long Binh, and American and ARVN troop movements were seen along Route 1. Maybe Yvonne was right about a Vietcong attack, or perhaps it was only a few communist insurgents harassing the local natives before the TET.

We drank beer, and I prepared spam sandwiches for dinner. After our meager meal we adjourned to the living room and tuned in the television for news. There was troop movement on the road to Thu Duc, but nothing out of the ordinary.

We retired to our respective bedrooms. I listened to the radio, and thought about my kids back in the World. I missed Susie, and hoped she was enjoying TET. The celebration would officially begin promptly at midnight on this 29th of January, only two hours away.

Several hours had passed, when old mama san came into my bedroom, and whispered in my ear. "Papa san, papa san. Va day. Va day."

I slipped on a pair of shorts and followed her into the dining room. She pointed towards the window, and I quietly walked over and looked out into the darkness. By the light of the moon, I could see maybe fifty Vietcong milling around out in the yard. Each VC was armed with a Russian made AK-47 automatic rifle. My heart started pounding like crazy, and I slowly eased away from the window. I put my fingers to my lips. I could see her eyes by the reflection of the moonlight. They were large as saucers.

I picked up an M-1 rifle, and stuck the 32-20 revolver in my belt. There was a full case of 30 cal. ammo sitting on the floor of the living room. I walked into Jack's bedroom, and whispered to him. "Be quiet. There are boo coo Vietcong out in the yard. The crap's hit the fan. I'll get Dale."

We assembled in the living room with one M-1 and two M-2 rifles. We each had several clips of ammo handy just in case the VC decided to enter the villa. Under the circumstances we were all reasonably calm.

"We stay quiet, and don't move," Jack said. "Don't do anything unless they come inside, then we'll defend ourselves." Dale and I grunted our approval.

I silently walked to the liquor cabinet and removed a fifth of vodka. I reclined into my chair, cracked the seal, and pressed the bottle to my lips. I took one helluva slug. Jack and Dale took note of my actions, and immediately followed suit.

We didn't made a sound for three hours, except for an occasional gurgle from the vodka bottle. We were tired, and our enemy had departed. "Why didn't the Vietcong kill us?" Maybe it was confusion, or perhaps they had better things to do.

Dawn arrived, and so did the war. The truce had been broken, and Vietcong had attacked on the eve of the TET.

There were a dozen U.S. Huey helicopters in the sky, and several allied tanks were moving down the road towards Thu Duc City. The Hueys were firing machine guns and rockets into the jungle, and we could hear small arms fire. Mortar fire had erupted to the west and to the north, and artillery shells were swishing over our heads.

Dale walked to Route 1, and caught a ride to Long Binh, but Jack decided not to go to work at RMK's quarry. It was too risky, and he didn't share Dale's insanity.

I thought of a speech that President Johnson had made on December 22nd. *"The enemy has not yet been defeated, but he has met his master in the field."* Our fearless leader had best rephrase that statement.

Upon the recommendation of General Westmoreland, the hawks in the U.S. Congress wanted to send additional troops to the slaughter. If only the politicians would let the military fight the war. Why send more troops when such action could provoke the Russians and Chinese? We needed to be careful. All hell was going to erupt. I felt sorry for the American GIs, their allies, and the South Vietnamese who were fighting and dying.

Our water supply and electricity had been cut off. Jack and I parboiled what meat was in the refrigerator's freezing compartments to prevent it from spoiling. The fighting had escalated, and the food supply would be important. The radio had been turned on for reports from AFVN (Armed Forces Vietnam Radio).

The radio announced that the Vietcong had occupied the Saigon Radio Station. Three North Vietnamese battalions had attacked three gates at Tan Son Nhut Air Base, but security guards and the 8th Airborne Battalion repelled the enemy. By daybreak members of the U.S. 25th Infantry Division had moved into the airport, and heavy losses had been inflicted on the enemy, forcing them to retreat. VC were trying to overrun General Westmoreland's headquarters. The truce had been broken, and enemy troops had attacked the U.S. Embassy. The attack on the Embassy had been repelled, several American MPs had been killed, but Ambassador Bunker was safe.

The radio continued the report. The Vietcong and North Vietnamese regular troops had attacked nearly every province in South Vietnam, and had hit nearly every populated city. The old capitol of Hue was under intense fire from the enemy. The Saigon Radio Station had been attacked and destroyed, and all enemy troops that had occupied the facility had been killed.

As many as fifteen Vietcong battalions had infiltrated Saigon, Cholon and part of Gia Dinh Province. They also occupied the Hy Tho race track, where we had taken Yvonne just hours before.

Thousands of VC had infiltrated Saigon, and in some precincts of the city many Vietnamese civilians had been murdered. The enemy had been going from house to house, and when they found anything that resembled "American fraternization" the occupants were killed.

I thought of Susie, and knew that trying to locate her would be futile and dangerous. She was streetwise, and being raised in Hanoi may give her an advantage with the enemy. But she had many articles in her house confirming her association with Americans.

Our villa inside University Village was located just a few hundred yards from an important water storage facility. This was a crucial water supply source for downtown Saigon, and the Vietcong wanted desperately to destroy it. U.S. helicopters were constantly orbiting the area, and American and ARVN troops were sent in to protect the valuable supply. Four chinook helicopters carrying troops from the 101st Airborne landed across the road, and trucks were standing by to disperse them throughout Thu Duc City. Jack and I watched the activity from our front porch of the villa, but a high fence surrounded the reservoir, so we couldn't see exactly what was occurring inside.

We inventoried our liquor and beer supply, and it appeared adequate for several days. The food situation wasn't good, but it was sufficient under the circumstances. If everything else failed, we could drink ourselves into never never land.

Dale hadn't returned from Long Binh, and it was now Friday, February 2nd. We didn't consider that he might be in danger. Long Binh was a huge U.S. Military complex, and it wasn't likely the enemy could infiltrate the perimeter. In addition to United States 2nd Field Force headquarters, the 199th Infantry Brigade was at Long Binh while three infantry divisions, the 1st, 9th, and 25th were based in the surrounding area.

I tuned in Armed Forces Radio: "*Today at 1200 hours over ten thousand of the enemy have been killed in the recent series of attacks on the Republic. President Johnson said he could see no reason to stop bombing North Vietnam. Defense secretary Robert McNamara addressed congress, and Green Bay Packer's coach Vince Lombardi has died. North Vietnamese and Vietcong forces have sustained heavy loses trying to overtake Allied Forces in South Vietnam. The body count of enemy forces killed as of midnight, February 1st stood at ten thousand five hundred fifty three. Allied sources reported nine hundred seventeen killed, that included six hundred thirty two ARVNs, two hundred eighty one Americans, and four free-world forces. Two thousand eight hundred seventeen allied soldiers had been wounded. The kill ratio was eleven point five enemy killed for each allied soldier. This is only a prelude of what is to come. President Johnson said if allied bombing did not stop the enemy in the northern provinces that there was no reason why more troops wouldn't be sent to Vietnam.*"

Soon the Vietcong would pull back to re-group, and I could go to RMK's office to finish processing for hire. I was anxious to know where RMK would be sending me. Fighting was heavy west of Marble Mountain south of Da Nang, but the reports indicated fighting was light at Nha Trang. It had been one of the first areas attacked by the Vietcong, but according to AFVN Radio it was now secure. At any rate I needed to get to Saigon soon.

It was the evening of February 2nd. I sprayed for mosquitos, turned the ceiling fan on high, and plopped down on the bed completely exhausted. We could hear mortar fire from the southwest, and flares continued to rain down into the yard just outside the villa. Artillery shells consistently swished overhead, and an occasional small fire round would ricochet off the villa. A good night's rest was overdue, and sleep was inevitable.

Curfew was still in effect according to the last radio report, and all allied forces in South Vietnam were on full red alert. I didn't think I'd get to Saigon tomorrow.

Our cooking stove was out of propane gas, our drinking water supply was critical, but electricity and tap water was periodically available. On Saturday, February 3rd, Jack and I cranked up the Toyota, and drove to the Route 1 junction. U.S. military police that were directing traffic informed us a Long Binh trip would be relatively safe, so we turned north onto the treacherous highway.

We stopped at the 9th Trans Company, filled several containers with treated water, and the mess sergeant gave us cans of spam and a case of army C rations, eggs and bread. Then we went to a post exchange for goodies. We purchased our beer ration of three cases each, six bottles of hard liquor and our cigarette ration. We located two propane bottles for the stove, and followed a GI six by six truck full of ARVN soldiers to the Thu Duc junction. In short order we were safely back in our villa.

The radio reported that more Vietcong troops had moved into Thu Duc City in the night, but there wasn't activity until dawn. Propeller driven Sky Raiders stepped-up bombing and strafing in the area, and U.S. jet fighters were firing rockets. I counted twenty tanks and fifteen trucks loaded with allied troops moving in the direction of the fighting. Sitting on the front porch sipping a cold beer with no obstruction in my view made me feel like I was "King of the Hill." It reminded me of an old World War II movie.

Hundreds of Vietnamese refugees, mainly women and children, were moving down the road towards Route 1 carrying their personal belongings. The noise was deafening, and I felt sorry and helpless. Thousands of desperate people in need of help, and I could do nothing. It was apparent they were confused and frightened beyond belief.

The radio news reported that there were forty seven thousand people homeless in the Thu Duc and Saigon areas. I needed to find

Susie. I wasn't sure if the highway to Saigon was passable. but I knew I had to try. Susie and her family wouldn't ask for help, but I was worried, and wouldn't rest until I knew they were safe.

Small arms fire once again could be heard ricocheting off the stucco of the villa, and mortar fire was coming in from the jungle. The mortar attacks were erratic, and God only knew where they might explode. It hadn't occurred to me that I could be injured or killed trying to get to Saigon—but Susie's safety haunted me.

Dale returned from Long Binh Tuesday, February 6th, exhausted, and filthy dirty. But he was his usual cool self. He slid into the lounge chair and sighed. "I'll take a beer, fellahs, and I'm overdue for a shower.

"Hell really broke loose at Long Binh, and that's why I didn't come back to the villa." He devoured one beer and we promptly handed him another. "PA&E is still receiving materials from Newport and Saigon Port, but it's been costly. We lost sixty Philco-Ford ton-and-a-half flatbeds, the materials, and the drivers. They absolutely vanished into thin air."

Dale drained yet another beer, and I obliged once again. We wanted to hear more about his experience.

"Tom Kraig called out to area 208 on the radio this afternoon, and told all personnel to report to the main office in Saigon at their earliest convenience. The unofficial report says that eighty-four American civilians have been killed on the job throughout Vietnam. PA&E wants a physical body count, so I've got to get to Saigon tomorrow."

"I want to go to RMK's office," Jack said, "and Bob's concerned about Susie. We'll all go."

The morning of February 7th, I showered, dressed, ate a few morsels of food, and we were off to the big city.

The fighting had scaled down on Route 1. There were VC bodies laying along the roadside, and demolished vehicles were smoldering, but there was no incoming fire. The only visible activity were jet fighters flying sorties and helicopters scouting the immediate area.

All hell was breaking loose in Gia Dinh, on the outskirts of Saigon. There were no civilians on the streets, but ARVN and American soldiers were going from building to building mopping up Vietcong stragglers. Automatic rifle fire was deafening. Several allied tanks were firing rounds into buildings. Grenades were exploding.

Jack yelled loud and clear, "De de mau! Let's get the hell out of here." The wheels squealed, and the car sped through the streets. We weaved in and out of demolished vehicles, rubble, and spent ammo cartridges. Once we crossed onto Buu huu Nghia Street things quieted down. Nothing was said until Jack stopped the Toyota at the curb on Duy Tan street near RMK's offices.

I informed my friends that I would find my way back to Thu Duc. Jack would take Dale to PA&E's office at the golf course.

RMK's Doctor Johnson had returned from his trip up north, and had examined my papers thoroughly. "Patterson, it looks like everything is in order. You've passed your physical examination, but your x-rays indicate you have had quite an accident."

"Doc, I was in a helluva jeep accident in September at Long Binh, but I feel fine. There is some soreness but I'm all right."

The doctor shrugged and cautioned me. "You best be careful, Patterson. Another jolt could give you some serious problems. Good Luck."

My next stop was Jake Harris in the main office. I handed him my medical papers, that he stamped "Approved for Hire". "O.K. Patterson. Sign this eighteen month contract for one thousand a month. Come back tomorrow and complete your processing, and I'll decide where you'll be located."

Now I had to concentrate on finding Susie. I went directly to the Royal Hotel, where I found Benny standing at the registration desk. He warmly embraced me.

"Bob, what you do in Saigon. Why you not in Thu Duc. VC scare you away?" He laughed heartily.

"Benny, I need your help again. Susie came to Saigon before the TET to stay with family, and I am afraid she have boo coo trouble. Her address is 322/482B Phan dinh Phung. Do you know about the fighting, and can I get there?"

"You are my friend, and I no think you should go, but you will not listen. I have taxi driver friend who will take you to Phan dinh Phung. I come back soon." I told him I would wait in the bar.

Benny instructed the taxi driver where to take me. Under no

circumstances should the driver leave without me.

"Many VC in Saigon. No trust anybody, and Bob, you be boo coo careful. You no want Chinese haircut." He ran his finger across his throat.

I hadn't realized that Phan dinh Phung was so near to downtown Saigon. We crossed Hung thap Tu and Tran qui Cap streets. The Tourist Hotel was close by, and it was comforting to know where I was going.

My driver friend turned right off Le van Duyet onto Phan dinh Phung. He drove to number 322 and abruptly stopped. He nodded, and pointed down a narrow driveway. The small houses were all fused together, and each was numbered. I found 482B. "Oi! Oi!" I yelled.

I fumbled with my crude Vietnamese as a middle aged woman emerged from the doorway. "Toi khong biet. I don't know. I look for Susie. You biet?" She didn't understand.

I quickly rushed back, and approached the driver of the taxi. "Va day, va day, papa san." I was surprised when he opened the taxi door and followed.

The woman was still standing in the driveway. "You know Susie? My name Bob. I look for Susie. Biet?" She and papa san exchanged words. He bowed to the woman and motioned for me to follow.

Papa san continued driving farther from downtown Saigon, and stopped on Ky Dong Street just off Truong minh Giang Street, and the main road to Tan Son Nhut Airport. The area had been devastated by one helluva fire fight, and most buildings had been completely destroyed. Small fires were still burning and heavy smoke hung motionless in the air. Several cars had been riddled by machine gun bullets, and the street was deserted except for several small children playing in the rubble.

The driver shrugged his shoulders, and looked at me sadly. "No more, papa san. Xin Loi. Take me to Hai ba Trung Street." I stopped in the vicinity of Sax and Lon's house.

It was midafternoon and time was running out. I only had about two hours to get news of Susie and get back to Thu Duc before curfew. I tramped through the back alleys until I located Lon's house, and banged on the door. "Papa san, mama san. It's Bob!"

Lon slowly opened the door and peered out. A broad grin appeared. "Sax! Bob here to say hello!"

"Patterson, how in the hell did you get here? There's VC all over the place!"

Sax was planted at the table with his hand wrapped around a whiskey-coke, and a forty-five semiautomatic placed at his finger tips. He was watching television.

I told my friends I had come to Saigon early in the morning on business. Dale had to make an appearance at PA&E's main office, Jack had to see his boss, and I finished processing for hire at RMK's main office.

I told Lon that I had been to Susie's house, but she was not home. I was told to go Ky Dong Street where I might find her, but no Susie. "Do you know where to find?"

"Bob, Ky Dong is where her sister live. I think maybe Susie at her mama san house. Maybe I go see?"

"Lon, be careful."

"I don't have trouble. Susie's mama san live close. I come back soon. Bob, no worry. I find Susie for you."

"Lon knows what she's doing." Sax took a drink of booze. "I don't worry about her." Lon beamed, and waved goodbye. My friend was pleasantly plastered.

Ruppe poured me a generous whiskey-coke, and we discussed the beginning of the TET offensive. He commented how accurate Lon's observation had been concerning the Vietcong entering Saigon in funeral processions.

Over two hours passed as we waited for Lon's return. Sax poured several drinks, and we were uneasy. "Sax, I hope I wasn't wrong asking Lon for help. I could never forgive myself."

It was after curfew when Lon burst into the house with Susie close behind. Tears were running down her cheeks. "Bob, Honey, I miss you, and I happy VC no kill you."

I gently pushed her back. She was thin, and looked exhausted. "Susie, I worry about you, and know I must find you."

I thanked Lon with a tremendous hug. It was like old times when we lived together on De Tram Street. There was a closeness, and trust that would endure even this crisis. We huddled together.

Susie told how the Vietcong had been in her house on Phan dinh Phung for five hours, but hadn't harmed her or her baby san. She became frightened, and went to her sister's house on Ky Dong. The VC came again and American helicopter gunships fired into the area. She and her children had run toward her mama san's house on Hai ba Trung Street. Hai, her son, had been shot in the arm, and was being treated at the hospital. Tuyet, her daughter, was ill, but was recovering at her mama san's house.

Susie kissed me, and said that she must leave. She promised that very soon she would come to Thu Duc. I gave her money, and she disappeared into a labyrinth of ancient houses.

It was well past curfew, and too risky to venture to Thu Duc, so Lon asked me to stay the night. The following morning I thanked Sax and Lon for their hospitality. It was Thursday, February 8th, and I was anxious to finish processing at RMK's office.

I walked to Hai ba Trung and caught a taxi to Duy Tan. I picked up my U.S. Department of Defense and RMK ID cards, and went to Harris's office for instructions.

He told me that my papers hadn't been processed, and I would have to return the next day. I couldn't believe it, but nobody was in a hurry to do anything. I thanked Harris and departed.

I hailed a taxi, and went to Thu Duc. The driver was reluctant to cross the Saigon River bridge at Newport into VC country, but a thousand piasters persuaded him to chance the treacherous journey.

Susie had arrived home, and was busily putting the place in order. She greeted me with a gigantic hug. "Bob, I miss you too much, and I happy to be home."

The fighting intensified, machine guns and small arms were firing, and Huey gunships suddenly appeared in the immediate area. Skyraiders began strafing and firing rockets into Thu Duc. Allied jets and choppers were attacking Tu Tien, a small village just east of our villa, and artillery shells were exploding.

Heavy black smoke billowed up from Tu Tien, and the village was quickly leveled. I wondered how many local Vietnamese people had been killed, including women and children.

Fighting was closer, and shell fragments ricocheted off the exterior plaster of the villa. The noise was deafening. I was wearing the tiger claw around my neck; luckily I had been blessed by the Buddha.

Finally Armed Forces Radio reported there were Vietcong to the north and east, but that Thu Duc City seemed relatively quiet. American and ARVN troops had secured the area. Helicopter gun ships were still firing on Tu Tien and the entire village was ablaze.

In late evening the fighting ceased as abruptly as it had started. Occasional small arms and mortar fire could be heard, and flares were lighting the sky. It was too quiet. Jack kept the M-2 rifle at close hand, and I had the M-1 within reach. We didn't want to encounter the VC, but if they entered the villa we would welcome them with automatic rifle fire.

Next morning I made my way to Route 1 to hitch a ride to Saigon. Within minutes I was in a classy little car, and the driver even obliged to stop at Duy Tan Street. Bob Hyenberg watched as I started up the stairs to Jake Harris's office. I couldn't understand this guy, and I certainly didn't need trouble.

Jake thumbed through my papers, and I signed in various places. I didn't read the documents, I just wanted to go to work.

"Patterson, Nha Trang is getting hit pretty hard by Vietnamese regulars and the Vietcong, so I've decided to keep you in the area for the present. I want you to check in with Ray Norton at RMK's warehousing complex at the Island. Do you know how to get there?"

"Yes, I live in Thu Duc, and it's only a couple of miles from my villa. I've passed there many times while traveling Route 1."

The man glanced at his calendar. "Be at the Island on February 11th." I nodded, and we settled the deal with a handshake.

I returned to the villa, and Susie was all smiles. "Bob, I know you have job, and you send money to your baby san. Where you go work?"

"Susie, I have good news. You know RMK Island? I will work there in warehousing." She rewarded me with a kiss.

I broke the news to Jack and Dale when they came home from work, and that I would start on February 11th at the Island.

"Hell, that's Sunday. Why then?" Jack asked.

"Maybe Harris made a mistake. I don't know, but I'll be there

Sunday morning and find out."

Jack and Dale popped a beer, and I walked to the liquor cabinet and grabbed a fifth of Black Velvet. I raised my drink and gestured a toast. "Chin Chin, and good luck."

"Patterson, are you going to start on the rot gut, and you haven't worked one day yet?" Jack asked.

"A few drinks won't hurt. I know what I'm doing." Susie quietly left the room. I downed the booze, and poured another drink. Now I had an excuse to celebrate my success of finding a job. This wasn't new for me. I could always find a reason to drink, whether times were good, or whether times were bad. In reality I was escaping my weaknesses in life. Alcohol numbed my senses, and I could enter my fantasy world. When I sobered up, I started all over again.

I didn't realize that my alcoholism was progressing, and when I drank I would become powerless over alcohol, and my life was unmanageable.

Why did I continue to drink when I knew how difficult it was to stop? I couldn't put the bottle down and leave it alone. It was baffling. I needed some answers. Jack's behavior and mine paralleled each others when we drank. Why?

Jack and Dale deserted me, and I was left staring at a blank wall. After finishing half a fifth I stumbled off to bed. Sweet Susie was asleep.

Sunday morning I arose early, showered, dressed and slipped the little Browning automatic into the shoulder holster. Susie was humming "Summertime", our favorite song, and was fixing breakfast when I walked into the kitchen. I ate, kissed her goodbye, and hiked to Route 1.

I arrived at the Island office, and an older American greeted me. I told him Jake Harris had instructed me to contact Ray Norton at the Island, and that I was a new hire. He shook his head. "Come back Monday. Somebody has made a mistake."

Monday morning I went to the Island early. Ray Norton was sitting behind a desk in the office, and was preoccupied with shipping and receiving documents. He looked at my papers, and said that I would start in the electrical warehouse.

"Patterson, we can use your experience, but the VC are harassing my men with small arms fire from across the river. It's safe enough here at the office, but it's spooky out there in the warehouses. The tin siding on those buildings doesn't stop bullets. Come back in a few days, and maybe the snipers will be gone."

Drinking was my favorite pastime, and for the next week I stayed to myself. Susie went to visit her mama san and children, and Jack and Dale were working long hours.

Susie returned to the villa on February 18th. I was to report to the Island the following day, and she didn't want me to miss my appointment with Norton.

Monday morning I was hungover. The booze had taken its toll. I needed a beer, but Susie shook her head. "Bob, please go work. You drink, you no work. Go now." I didn't debate the issue; I trudged off down the road towards Route 1.

The three men sitting in RMK's office at the Island looked at me. It was obvious what I had been doing for a pastime. "I'm a new hire, and I've been sent by Jake Harris in Saigon. Is Ray Norton around?"

"I'm Ernie Timmons. Norton isn't here. He completed his contract, and is back in the States. Who are you?"

"I'm Bob Patterson, and I have papers."

Timmons looked at my hire slip. "Where the hell you been, Patterson? Harris said you either backed out of the contract or you were dead. You look about half dead." He and his two compatriots laughed at my pitiful appearance.

"I was here last week. Norton told me to come back later because of the VC snipers across the river. I've been marking time at Thu Duc, where I live. What's going on?"

"You better get your ass back to the main office and see Jake Harris," Timmons said. "He'll be interested to hear what you have to say."

I got a ride with an employee going to RMK's office, and within the hour was standing before Harris. His interrogation wasn't sympathetic, and I was definitely on the losing end.

"Patterson, Barney Coin cautioned me to keep an eye on you, and sure as hell you didn't show up for work. What's with you?" This guy was really pissed off, and Norton, my only alibi, was stateside.

"Jake, I went to the Island on February 11th. That was Sunday. I went back the next day, and Norton told me to come back in a week. Hell, I've been under fire as much as any of those bastards at the Island. Why didn't Norton put me to work? Why did he tell me to come back in a week?"

"Patterson, I don't know, and Ray is in the States. Coin is really pissed, and I'm under the gun." Harris hesitated. "Bob, I don't know why I should, but I believe you. Get your butt out to RMK's complex at Long Binh tomorrow morning, and in the meantime I'll contact Chuck Bruno. He is our warehouse superintendent at Long Binh, and he needs help. Patterson, don't crap in your nest; you've pushed your luck, and it's running out! Get the hell out of here."

While They Died

The taxi droned along the road towards Thu Duc, and I gazed out the window, preoccupied and deeply engrossed in thought about my immediate future. Will I have to move into a barracks at RMK's complex at Long Binh? Leaving Thu Duc was a chilling thought. My freedom is in jeopardy. It was unthinkable not to have Susie at my side. Oh, we would see each other, and she would still be my companion, but I wouldn't have the intimate daily companionship. I desperately needed her perpetual closeness for encouragement and affection.

Susie greeted me as I walked into the living room, and I nodded, but couldn't meet her eyes. I went straight to the bedroom, opened the refrigerator door and grasped a most welcomed beer. The lid popped and I drank desperately. I tossed the empty can into the waste basket, and popped another. Susie came into the bedroom and watched as I drained the second beer.

"Bob, you have boo coo trouble? You lose job?"

"No Susie, no lose job, but I go Long Binh tomorrow, and see bossman. Maybe I have to move to RMK house, and you will go back to Saigon. We will know tomorrow."

My anxiety plagued me all night, and I was depressed the following morning. Susie kissed me goodbye. "Bob, boo coo good luck to you, and no worry." I bolted from the villa and walked towards Route 1. I hitched a ride on a Philco-Ford flatbed headed straight for Long Binh, and jumped off at the road leading to RMK's complex.

The complex reminded me of my army days. Two story barrack-type buildings stood in rows, complete with outside latrines, and even a mess hall. The area was neat and clean, and had been well kept. Further to the north of the housing area were several warehouses and a motor pool.

My God! Maybe I'll be wearing a uniform, saluting my superiors, and marching to and from work in military formation! I'd developed a damn poor attitude even before I'd started the new job.

Another military-type structure housed Chuck Bruno and his staff. I entered the recently constructed wood-framed building, and identified his office by the "private" sign stenciled on the door. I knocked and waited for a response. I knocked again, and a soft voice from within the room politely beckoned, "Please come in."

Pushing the door half way open I announced my presence. "Bob Patterson here. Jake Harris said he would contact you about a job placement." By the sound of the voice I had visualized some meek, frail little guy wearing horn-rimmed glasses. This immense hulk stood, smiled, and shook my hand.

"Sit," he said. "So, you're Patterson?"

I handed Bruno my papers, and planted my butt on the only chair in the room. I watched as he read my application. His hand kept twisting the ends of a heavy, handlebar mustache, that curved up at each end. His brown hair was clipped in an exceedingly short crewcut, and his penetrating eyes were embedded in deep sockets. He was at least six-four, and he weighed about two-ten. His broad shoulders were straight, and his chin was pulled in and down in a military posture. He stared at me out of the top half of his eyes. I wouldn't dare judge his character with a first impression; however, I will admit he resembled a soldier trained in the ranks of the French Foreign Legion.

He spoke softly, but with authority. "Bob Patterson, you have just volunteered to be RMK's Long Binh expediter. Do you know the definition and duties of an expediter?"

"No, Sir!"

Bruno picked a Webster's dictionary off his desk, thumbed through it briefly, and started reading: "Expediter: one that expedites; spec: one employed to ensure adequate supplies of raw materials and equipment or to coordinate the flow of materials, tools, parts, and processed goods within a plant." Still sitting straight in his chair and twisting the mustache he laid the dictionary on the desk, and then looked at me with a faint, self-satisfied smile on his thin lips.

The silence bothered the hell out of me. "Look, Chuck, if I'm at liberty to call you by your first name, I'll be your expediter, O.K.? Just explain my duties, and I'll go to work. I live at Thu Duc, and I don't think I want to move to Long Binh and live in barracks."

"Patterson," he said, calmly, "call me whatever suits you. Here's what I have in mind. Jack Pounders, our current expediter, is completing his contract, and wishes to seek employment elsewhere. You will travel with Jack for a week, and become acquainted with your responsibilities. Be here tomorrow morning before 0800 hours, and we will see what transpires. Pounders is a good man and will be damn hard to replace." He looked down at papers on the desk, and motioned with his hand for me to leave.

Within the hour I was back at the villa telling Susie about Bruno and my job. "Everything be O.K., Bob." She came close, and pecked me on the cheek.

Bruno didn't intimidate me. I think he wanted my reaction about being an expediter, but he would give me a chance to prove my worthiness. I knew I was worthy to be employed by Raymond-Morrison-Knudsen, Brown-Root and J.A. Jones Construction Companies, American taxpayer's "pride and joy" in Southeast Asia.

Wednesday morning, February 21st, I strutted into Bruno's Long Binh office. My hangover had dramatically subsided, and I might live if not overly excited.

Bruno eyeballed me like I was a shavetail second lieutenant, and then gestured towards another man standing off to the side of the room. "Patterson, this is Jack Pounders, your most able instructor for the next week."

Pounders and I exchanged greetings, and each took a chair in front of Bruno's desk. This guy was even larger than Bruno. He was six-six and probably two-forty. I didn't feel intimidated, but I did feel damn small sitting between these two monstrosities.

Pounders reminded me of the Jolly Green Giant, and had the sense of humor to match. I liked him, and felt comfortable in his presence. My morale climbed to a new high, and I was confident of a good relationship.

Jack looked at his watch. "Bob, we best hit the road for Saigon. We have a long day." We walked out together to his RMK pickup truck.

There was a man sitting behind the wheel, so Jack and I walked around to the passenger side. "Bob, you'll fit better in the middle. O.K.?" Our bodies molded together like three sardines. "Con, meet Bob Patterson. He's my replacement."

"Bob Patterson, we be friends. O.K.?" The oriental grinned from ear to ear.

"Damn right we'll be friends, especially with you in the driver's seat. You can rest assured we'll be number one friends."

Con was about five-four and one hundred-ten pounds with exceptionally large round eyes for an Asian. He volunteered information about himself. "I am Chinese, not Vietnamese. I live in Cholon, and I have wife and two baby san, and I am number one RMK truck driver. This O.K., Mr. Bob bossman?"

"Bob, I'll assure you that Con is an excellent driver, and his name implies exactly what it means," Jack said. "This guy is one helluva con artist, which will be most helpful in fulfilling his duties. Expediting material to the job-site is very important, and if the material is not available, find same and deliver it at all costs! Remember that!"

Bruno had given Pounders several material requisition forms that had to be approved by the RMK engineering section on Duy Tan Street in Saigon. After this transaction we would proceed to the Island to pick up materials. The orders contained everything from automotive spare parts and freon refrigerants to transformers and compressors. We would make occasional stops at RMK's rock quarry to deliver parts. The quarry was where my friend Jack Hutson worked on the rock crusher.

Con cruised the new Chevy pickup down Route 1 towards engineering, our first stop. He was a good driver, and when we reached the low lands and the rice paddies, he accelerated, and drove like hell. Speed was important because of Vietcong snipers along the way.

Two full round trips each day would rack up approximately a hundred plus miles. I calculated the odds of survival while driving the most treacherous highway in the world six to eight hours a day, six days a week. That evening Con stopped at the Thu Duc junction and I got out. I thanked my friends and walked to the villa.

Susie ran to the gate and greeted me with open arms. She had seen me coming, so a whiskey-coke with ice was sitting on the coffee table in the living room. "Bob, Honey, you work hard today, and I have boo coo fresh crab fixed for you. Drink whiskey and take shower. We eat. O.K.?" She was happy. It reminded me of our good times on De Tram Street in Saigon.

I reminisced how Baby San, our maid, would parade into our apartment on De Tram carrying four or five live crabs bound together, and dangling from a cord held tightly in her small hand. She would be bubbling over with joy. Soon the plates would be stacked high with freshly cooked crab meat shelled and cooked to perfection. Her broad smile displayed her innocent happiness and warmth at being part of a family that loved her. We never considered her a peasant, and I deeply missed the young, naive little girl, and longed for her return from her village of My Lai. It would be six weeks before her return.

Susie and I slept close together this Thursday night, and we shared the dread of separating. We didn't discuss it, but there was a feeling of anxiety and sadness.

She walked with me to the main road the next morning, and stayed close until I caught a ride on the back of a Honda motorbike. It was a nightmare hitchhiking back and forth to work every day, and traveling Route 1 an average of a hundred plus miles each day. I had to give careful consideration to moving to Long Binh. I was between the devil and the deep blue sea.

It was after 0800 hours when I burst through the warehouse door, and Jack Pounders and Con were patiently waiting in Bruno's office. Bruno was unhappy. His eyes were fixed on the opposite wall and his fingers were methodically twisting one handlebar of his enormous mustache. It was one chilly atmosphere.

Chuck Bruno, sitting like a zombie in his swivel chair, finally broke the silence. "Bob, I'm not trying to be difficult, nor am I apologizing, but Pounders and I thought maybe you should consider living here at the compound."

"I've given it some thought, and it's risky to travel that damned highway. I think I'm pushing my luck, even though I wear this tiger claw around my neck that's been blessed by the Buddha."

"Tomorrow is Saturday, and Sunday is your day off," Jack said. "That'll give you time to get settled. There's a room at the end of the barracks that's quiet and close to the latrine and shower. O.K.?"

I wasn't happy, but I agreed with my three co-workers. "You guys win. I'll be settled in Sunday night. Can we arrange to haul several things to my girl's house in Saigon?" Pounders agreed to help Monday morning on the way to the engineering department in Saigon.

On Monday Con, Jack and I crowded together in the pickup and started on the daily jaunt to the city. Fighting between the Vietcong and Allied troops had simmered down, although there was some sniper fire. Jack instructed me on the pros and cons of expediting, and emphasized that my knowledge of materials as an asset. Con had a great sense of humor, and I felt he could be trusted. It was a good feeling.

That evening I slowly walked to the villa, and dreaded what was yet to come. University Village had become my home, and Susie was my right arm.

Jack, Dale and I enjoyed a drink together, and I called Susie into the living room. She sat on the arm of my chair, and I took her hand. "Fellahs, I'm moving to Long Binh Sunday, and Susie is going back to Saigon. RMK people thought I could better serve their interests if I lived in the company compound. I don't cherish the thought, but I can't fight city hall."

Nothing was said, so I excused myself. Susie followed me into the bedroom, and I held her body close for a long time. I looked down into her eyes. "Little one, I love you. We will be together again. I promise."

"Bob, we be together long time, and I will miss you, and maybe we be together again." Tears swelled in her black eyes.

"Susie, I will take the refrigerator, bed, and chest to your house Monday morning, and you keep. Tomorrow we'll get ready to leave."

We embraced again, and returned to the living room. "Jack, if Long Binh living doesn't agree with me I'd like to have my room back. Give me a month."

"Bo Priest and Mop want to stay here for a while, but he'll understand if you want to return. They're looking for another place to live in Thu Duc now that the Vietcong have moved on."

Susie packed everything, but I waited until Sunday morning to gather my personal effects. Monday I would take the heavy things to Saigon in the company truck.

Sunday afternoon I walked Susie to the main highway, and with suitcase in hand, she hailed a taxi. I waved goodbye, and somberly walked back to the villa.

Late Sunday afternoon Jack drove me to RMK's Long Binh compound, along with my suitcase and other personal belongings. We shook hands and I promised to visit Thu Duc on occasion. He drove away, and I walked to my new quarters in the barracks.

I was unpacking my clothes when someone knocked on the door. "Come in whoever you are!"

The door opened and my next door neighbor was standing there with a beer in his hand. "I'm Charlie Crow. You're Bob?"

"Yeah, I'm Bob Patterson, thanks for the beer. I'm settling in for the duration. Sit down."

"I work in warehousing. Word's out you're replacing Jack Pounders. Jack says expediting is a thankless job. Thinks his luck is running out. He's a damn good man."

"Yeah, Charlie, I get along fine with the big guy. I guess in three days I'm on my own." Charlie and I walked to the mess hall together. It was good food. Maybe I'd gain some much needed weight, as I'd lost quite a bit after my jeep accident.

We walked back to the barracks after dinner, and bid each other good night. I entered the near-empty room and slowly looked around. The room was small, but it had a ceiling light, and an army style bunk. A small desk stood in the corner with one drawer and a small table lamp. What more did I need? A ceiling fan would be nice.

Jack, Con and I made short work of loading the refrigerator, bed, dresser, and Susie's other personal belongings into the truck at Thu Duc, and we were off to Saigon. Con drove the pickup down the narrow alley to Susie's place, and off-loaded her goods quickly. She wanted to talk in private, so my friends waited in the truck.

"Bob, I think maybe my brother is killed by VC," Susie said, quietly. "I must go to Hue. I be gone maybe ten days. I don't know."

"I am terribly sorry, Susie. I'll miss you, and I'll worry. You must be careful." She looked so small to be traveling up Route 1 alone, and I felt utterly helpless.

I informed Jack of Susie's troubles, and told how she had lost her husband in the war. She was a brave woman. I would pray for her safety.

My mind tried to focus on what Pounders was teaching me about expediting, but it was difficult. Susie was constantly in my thoughts. God, how painfully I missed her.

Wednesday evening the office staff gathered around and bid Jack a pleasant farewell. He would spend a month in the States, and then return to marry his Vietnamese sweetheart. I envied him, and I thought about the completion of my contract, eighteen months away.

Expediting came easy for me, but the hard part was traveling Route 1. Con was an excellent driver, but they were damned uncomfortable trips. Long Binh was situated several hundred feet above sea level in rolling hills. Con felt secure until we reached the bottom lands and rice paddies where Vietcong snipers lay in wait, then fear would take over.

When we reached this lower terrain I would literally yelled at him. "De de mau, Con, de de mau! De mau len! Go fast Con, go fast." His eyes would widened, his foot would press down hard on the accelerator, and I hollered like a cowboy herding cows. We would relax once we passed through Gia Dinh into the outskirts of Saigon.

The war escalated, sniper fire increased, and our gunships and military jet aircraft became more active. When Con and I drove into the RMK Island to pick up materials, VC snipers pecked away from the jungle across the river. Every day we would watch American B-52 bombers high in the sky making their way up north above the DMZ to bomb the Ho Chi Minh Trail and Hanoi.

Early one morning Con and I were in the bottom land, and cruising at fifty miles an hour, when there was a loud explosion. The pickup windshield literally disintegrated, and Con screeched to a halt.

"My God, Con, don't stop here. De de mau!" We drove a mile down the road and stopped. We were both wearing dark glasses, and luckily neither was injured. We cleaned the glass off the seat, and continued on to the Island. We ordered a new windshield, borrowed a pickup and headed for Saigon. I never discovered what kind of explosion had nearly ended our lives. Was it a mortar? Grenade? Airburst? It didn't really matter.

It continued to be a strange day. Traffic was heavier than usual in downtown Saigon, and Con professionally weaved in and out of traffic. I hadn't been paying attention; I was thinking of Susie, and wasn't exactly sure where we were. All at once we became entangled in a traffic jam. We were wedged in tight, when a machine gun cut loose nearby, and people started running in all directions. Con started to bail out, and I grabbed hold of his shirt and hauled him back. "Damn you, Con, you aren't going anywhere. We're going to sit this one out together." American MPs with automatic rifles were running in the direction of the gunfire and within seconds they opened up. A few minutes later they dragged four bodies out of a building a short distance away, and traffic slowly started moving again. It was two hours before we arrived at RMK Engineering.

Con was silent until we were almost back to Long Binh. "Bob, I would quit job, but I have two baby san. This is bullshit." Con told Bruno and Charlie Crow about our experience, and his hands were shaking when he lit a cigarette. Bruno and Charlie didn't react; they'd never experienced anything like Con and I had been through.

Con and I would occasionally drive by Susie's house on Phan dinh Phung Street, and ask Waa, her neighbor, if there was any news of Susie. She would only shake her head.

Every day it was the same routine drive. It was to RMK Engineering on Duy Tan, the Island, and back to Long Binh. Sniper fire kept the job from becoming boring.

Three men that befriended me at the compound worked for RMK in electrical construction. There was Cuz Morgan, Ben Armstrong, and Cuz's son Bobby. Armstrong was a regular sort of man, and Bobby had just completed a tour of duty with the Army in Southeast Asia. After completing their tours of duty, some GIs had been granted discharges in Vietnam so they could remain in country and work for American companies.

Cuz controlled Ben and Bobby. He reminded me of the Godfather of the Mafia, and gave me the creeps. He had worked for RMK for a year, and had never been to Saigon. He continually asked questions about living conditions in the City and about the black market. I played dumb; I didn't trust him.

One evening in the mess hall Cuz approached me about moving to Thu Duc. He and his friends were aware that I had lived there. I was cool, and remarked it was an interesting thought, and promised to keep it in mind.

On the morning of March 6th I arrived at our warehouse office early to prepare for the day's business. I had considerable work stacked up and wanted to have a clean slate by Saturday. Con popped in the door and greeted me with a sheepish grin, his eyes were sparkling and I knew he was planning mischief. He was not only a con artist, but also a character.

"What the hell you up to this morning?"

"Bob, I have big surprise for leader Chuck Bruno. Bob, you watch, and I show you how I scare bossman."

Con took a piece of string about five feet long and stuck it to the ceiling with scotch tape, and then very carefully he removed a dead scorpion from a tissue. He scotch taped the ugly creature to the other end of the string, with the insect at Bruno's eye level. We retired to the outer office and waited in anticipation.

A short time later Bruno walked through the front door of the building and strolled into his office without greeting anyone. This was his daily ritual.

Con and I positioned ourselves to watch our leader's reaction. He sat down in the swivel chair without looking up, and started examining documents on the desk. We waited silently. After a few minutes he raised his head and his eyes focused on the creature, dangling at eye level. His eyes widened, his left hand reached up and started twisting a handlebar, and a smile formed on his thin lips.

"Con, come in here and get this creepy thing out of here." Con and I burst out laughing.

My Chinese friend aimed the truck for Saigon, while I thumbed through requisitions. We ran the highway gauntlet without mishap, and I ask Con to swing by Susie's house. A half block from her place I noticed a Vietnamese woman dressed in a long, white cotton dress with a black band on the upper arm. The black band signified a death in the family.

Con stopped the vehicle, and I ran up to her. "Susie, it that you?"

My little one turned and looked at me in astonishment. I took her hands in mine. She had been gone for ten days, and looked exhausted, thin, and drawn.

"Susie, I look for you every day, and worry about you. You are tired, and you must rest. I'll get room at Imperial Hotel for Saturday night, and we can talk. O.K.?"

She nodded. "Bob, I love you, but must go to see my baby san. I see you at Imperial on Saturday." She left quickly, and Con and I went on to RMK's engineering section. Saturday night seemed an eternity away.

After work Friday night I went by Bruno's room for a drink with him and Charlie Crow. After several stiff belts we began talking about our personal lives.

I told them about Susie's problems, and that I was meeting her Saturday night. These two yahoos wanted to meet Susie, but I knew their main objective was to have her find them girl friends. It made me feel like a pimp, and I didn't like the idea. I promised that when she felt better I would ask.

Con dropped me off at the Imperial late Saturday evening; Susie was waiting. We freshened up, and walked to the Rex BOQ for dinner. We didn't tarry, and after eating, returned to the hotel. We wanted to be together.

I asked Susie about her trip to Hue, and about her brother. "City of Hue long way from Saigon, and very close to DMZ where VC and Americans fight. Vietnamese bus take me long way, and American GI truck take me, and sometimes I walk. Take me three days to Hue, and I go to ARVN soldier, and he tell me where to find my brother. I find many American and Vietnamese soldiers, and they all dead in body bags. I look and look, and I find my brother, he dead four days. I die before I ever do again. I must forget. Bob, no talk again."

Susie and I rose early on Monday morning, and quickly showered and dressed. We walked to the street, and each hailed taxis to our respective destinations.

Con and I took care of business as usual, and after work Bruno, Charlie Crow and I met for our social hour. We slugged down several straight whiskeys and Bruno started pumping me. "Bob ol' buddy, will Susie get Charlie and me some broads in Saigon for the weekend? I'm getting horny as hell."

"Chuck, I'll ask her, but remember, I'm not a damn pimp. You must compensate the girls for their favors, and it's got to be accomplished in a discreet manner. Don't embarrass the ladies. You understand?"

"Bob, don't worry," Bruno assured me in his drunken stupor, "Ol' Charlie and me will pay boo coo. No sweat."

"Money isn't plentiful and the girls have to support their families." I said. 'You best treat these women with respect."

The following evening I was settled back on my bunk reading a magazine when Cuz, his son Bobby, and Armstrong walked through the door.

"Patterson, we been thinking," Cuz said, self-assuredly, "why don't the four of us get a villa, and we'll split the tab? You've mentioned that you thought barracks living is crap. Your girl can live with you, and we'll get dollies and set up housekeeping. What'd you think?"

"When do you want to move, Cuz?"

"The sooner the better. I'll give you money orders to change on the market, and we'll split the profit. It'll pay your rent and move your Susie."

The following morning I instructed Con to stop at RMK's rock quarry where Jack Hutson was working on the crusher. I asked if he knew of a villa for rent at University Village. He said to check with him that evening.

That evening in the mess hall I informed Cuz that Jack Hutson would be waiting for us at the Village. It was possible a villa might be available for immediate occupancy. Time was of the essence.

Jack was waiting, and we made the five minute walk to the vacant villa. The style was similar to Jack's except it was larger with each of the four bedrooms each having its own bath. The living room was spacious, and had a complete bar. The rent was three hundred MPCs a month.

Cuz said he would take it. I wasn't sure I wanted Cuz as a roommate, but at least I could get away from RMK's barracks.

Thursday morning March 14th, Con and I stopped by Susie's house. I told her to meet me the following evening in Thu Duc. I worried about my decision, but I wanted Susie and me to be together.

While having drinks at Bruno's quarters I felt uncomfortable. Chuck and Charlie knew something was wrong.

"Bob, I've known Cuz and Armstrong for two years, and these guys aren't regular construction people," Chuck said. "God only knows what they've been doing in Vietnam. Cuz boasted to me that money flowed like water, and that he was financially well-heeled. I didn't pry into his affairs, but I wouldn't rule out black market. Bob, he's involved in an international operation."

"Fellahs, maybe I was too hasty in my decision to move, but damn; I hate barracks living. I can operate from Thu Duc or Saigon as far as my job is concerned. I think I can handle Cuz, and I'll be cautious."

Cuz, Bobby, and Armstrong came into my room after dinner that evening while I was packing my gear. Cuz handed me six one hundred dollar money orders to change on the black market. Half the profit was to be mine. I told him that I would be at the villa tomorrow after work. I had planned to take everything with me in the pickup, and have Con drop me off at Thu Duc. Susie would meet me at the villa.

Cuz had made arrangements to have an RMK pickup at his disposal, and planned to be at the villa early in the evening. He said I could ride to Long Binh with him the following morning. I rejected the idea and told him Con would pick me up so we would go straight for RMK Engineering. This saved me a trip to Long Binh.

This disturbed Cuz because it meant he wouldn't have control. I ignored the threesome, and they finally got the message. As they left my room I assured them I'd be at University Village the following evening.

The next morning Con and I loaded my personal effects in the back of the pickup. I took Cuz's six money orders, plus two I had, and put them on my clipboard beneath my engineering requisitions. The pickup sped for Saigon, and our daily routine. I wouldn't change the money until the day's business was complete, and we were ready to leave Saigon for Thu Duc. There were several Army APOs along the route.

Con and I stopped at RMK's Island to pick up material destined for Long Binh. It was early afternoon, and we were ahead of schedule.

I thumbed through my notes and requisitions. Oh my God! They were gone! The eight-hundred dollar money orders were gone! My heart raced. "Con, go to the Island. De de mau!"

I had to retrace my steps. My mind rapidly traced every move I had made during the day. I couldn't remember setting the clipboard down. No way. I had been too aware of the money orders. Con was smart. I didn't tell him about the money orders. Could he have removed them from the clipboard without my knowledge? I didn't have an iota of proof.

When we arrived at the Island I stopped at the automotive spare parts warehouse. I looked everywhere, and shook my head in disbelief. I went back to the truck and told Con to continue to Long Binh.

Bruno and Charlie were in the office, and I didn't want to talk. I told them I was definitely staying at Thu Duc, and that Con would stop for me in the morning.

I didn't want to leave Long Binh, and I sure as hell didn't want to tell Cuz I'd lost his money orders. He and his boys wouldn't believe me.

Con and I made our trip to Saigon the following day, and I watched him closely for any sign of guilt. Nothing, absolutely nothing. Con was rigid as a statue, and displayed his usual poker face. If he had taken the money I'd never prove it in a thousand years. But there was no other explanation.

Con pulled the pickup in front of the villa at Thu Duc. Cuz's RMK truck was parked in the driveway, and Susie was sitting on the porch waiting for my arrival. I needed an excuse, and I felt guilty.

Susie ran out to greet me with a smile, hugs and kisses. I led her by the hand into the house, and nodded to Cuz and his friends as we walked through the main living room. Once inside the bedroom I whispered to Susie what had happened to the money, and that Cuz might not understand. I grasped the 32-20 revolver in my right hand and concealed it with a small leather folder I had carried into the villa. We walked out into the living room to face the inevitable.

Cuz wasn't a large man, and he wasn't physically strong. His wrinkled skin was a pasty white, and his hands were small with long skeletal fingers that reminded me of death.

Bobby and Armstrong were his protectors. Both were young, muscular, and experienced street fighters. It would be no contest.

"Bob, are you getting settled? Is this Susie?" Cuz asked.

"Yes." I answered, slowly. "Susie, this is Cuz, Bobby, and Armstrong. These are the men who will be living at the villa." Susie bowed politely.

"Patterson, did you change the money orders?" My stomach turned wrong side out.

"Cuz, I have bad news. Please hear me out. O.K.?"

The whey-faced weirdo stared straight through me. "What the hell you mean, Bob? You have bad news for me or for you?"

I could feel sweat on my forehead. "Cuz, this is hard to believe, but I lost the money orders off my clipboard. It doesn't make sense, but it's true. I never stole anything in my life." It grew quiet. My hand tightened around the revolver handle; sweat ran down my face.

Bobby snarled. "Patterson, you're a damn liar. I want those money orders or you're a dead man."

"Wait a minute, Bobby. Cool down. The world isn't coming to an end." I refused to be intimidated.

"Get with it Patterson," Cuz said, "Bobby means what he said.

You'll be a dead man. My son is one tough hombre, and he can break your skinny neck with one snap."

Bobby made his move. I pulled the revolver straight up and aimed it at his belly. Armstrong stepped in front of Bobby and wrestled him to the floor. They hit each other again and again. They were bleeding, and Cuz was waving his arms. I motioned for Susie to leave the room. The three stared in surprise at the gun in my hand pointed directly at Bobby.

Armstrong disgustedly pushed Bobby back, and wiped blood from a cut lip. "Bob, we didn't give you a chance to defend yourself. Why don't you put the gun down? I know you mean business. And Bobby, if I hadn't intervened, you'd be dead!"

"Thanks, Armstrong. I feel bad, but I didn't take the money. I'm not stupid. Leave Susie and me alone for a few minutes, and I'll make it up to you." I slowly lowered the gun barrel.

We walked into the bedroom. "Bob, why you have boo coo trouble?"

"Susie, I've got to come up with six hundred MPCs. I have three hundred."

She went to her suitcase and removed several bills, carefully counted out three hundred and handed them to me. I stuck the revolver into my belt, and walked back into the living room.

"Cuz, here are six hundred MPCs. If you would rather have money orders you'll have to wait."

Cuz counted out the cash. "Now what, Patterson?"

"Susie and I haven't unpacked. We'd better leave. This won't work out."

Susie and I walked out into the night, regretting my poor judgment about moving in with Cuz. We would spend the night at Jack's villa.

It was still early in the evening when we entered the living room of our old villa. Jack, Dale, and Bo were sitting in front of the television set, and Yvonne and Mop, Bo's girl friend, were jabbering away in the kitchen.

My three compatriots smiled. "Well, I'll be damned," Dale said, "isn't a little late to be out walking in the middle of VC country."

Susie and I gratefully plopped down onto the couch, and I took the 32-20 from out of my belt and gently laid it on the coffee table.

Jack's Texas drawl was unmistakable. "Bob, I thought you and Susie had snuggled in with Cuz and his boys. What's with the revolver?"

I explained about the money orders. "Bob, Cuz is a mean critter. Be careful. He'll get you from behind and cut your throat," Bo said.

"Bullshit. Cuz hasn't got the guts to do anything. He won't bother us." I looked at Hutson. "Jack, he's your neighbor. Lots of luck." I slugged down a cold beer.

The beer can opener was kept busy, and it was like old times. Now was a good time to ask Jack a question that had bugged me for months.

"Jack, why are there so many Texans in Vietnam? PA&E and RMK-BRJ are loaded with them. You're Texan, Chuck Bruno and Charlie Crow are Texan, Cuz, Bobby and Armstrong are all Texans. It goes on and on. Why?"

"Hell, Bob, didn't you know that Lyndon Baines and Lady Bird Johnson owned stock in Brown and Root Construction Company? It's headquartered in Houston. You're not that naive, Bob. I thought everybody knew about LBJ and his little ol' Lady Bird. They've got to make a living too, you know!" His small eyes narrowed and he grinned.

This was hard to swallow. The President of the United States owned stock in a company making hundreds of millions in Vietnam. It is a joint venture with Raymond-Morrison-Knudsen, a Boise, Idaho company.

I remembered that President John Kennedy had been attempting to scale down the war in Vietnam when he was assassinated. After Johnson became president he escalated the fighting, and committed more troops to Vietnam. Could owning stock in Brown and Root have any influence on LBJ's decisions? I knew it was a political war, but putting young American lives in jeopardy for personal monetary gain was unthinkable. How naive and gullible are we Americans? My body shivered with a blood curdling chill.

Susie stayed in the maid's quarters, and I slept on the couch in the living room. The next morning I intercepted Con before he went to Cuz's villa to get me.

At the office I explained to Bruno and Charlie what had happened, and that Susie and I would find an apartment in Saigon. Con could pick me up every morning, and business would go on as usual.

Furthermore, I explained, it would be easier to find girl friends for the Long Binh bachelors.

Susie and I stayed at Jack's villa for one more night. She had located a small apartment on Phan thanh Gian Street in Saigon. The rent was reasonable at seven thousand piasters per month. We could move the next day.

Jack told me that Vietcong had infiltrated back into the Thu Duc area. This was their third offensive, and they had assembled large numbers of troops. Jack had increased his fire power at the villa, and showed me their new weapons. In addition to the M-1 and M-2, Jack had commandeered an American M-16 and a Russian-made AK-47 automatic rifle. Several cases of ammunition were stacked in the room.

At 0100 hours flares illuminated the entire countryside, and machine gun and small arms fire erupted. The Vietcong were trying to hit the water supply tank again, and in the moonlight we could see bodies darting back and forth across the road just north of the villa.

By daylight the fighting had escalated considerably. Vietcong automatic rifle fire was much closer. Huey helicopters were humming overhead. The gun ships hovered, spit machine gun fire, gatling guns chattered, and rockets exploded. The onslaught was devastating, and it forced the local refugees to pour out of the jungle from all directions.

Susie and I prepared to leave for Saigon, even though Jack, Dale and Bo tried to talk us into staying until an all clear. But I'd had enough, and the women were frightened.

I disguised myself with dark glasses and a coolie hat, and with suitcases in hand, Susie and I walked to the roadway. We crawled into a bomb crater with hope a taxi or lambretta might come by that was attempting to make it to Saigon. The machine gun and automatic rifle fire was deafening, and we didn't know if it was coming from the enemy or allied troops.

I flagged down a lambretta, and we crowded into the vehicle among five Vietnamese refugees. The terrified driver gunned the underpowered motor as we sped through the middle of sheer hell towards Route 1.

As the lambretta reached Thu Duc and Route 1 junction, Susie leaned forward, and ordered the driver to turn right towards Saigon.

He violently shook his head. "Papa san, go Saigon! De de mau, Saigon!" He still refused to comply.

The frightened man attempted to turn left toward Long Binh, and I yelled, "the son-of-a-bitch is probably Vietcong." I pulled out the .25 automatic, and jacked a round into the chamber. I held the weapon in front of the papa san's face, and then pressed it to the back of his head. "Papa san, you go Saigon. Biet?" He shook his head up and down several times and turned right towards Saigon.

The going was tough. The driver had the throttle wide open, so it was difficult to steer the vehicle. Huge military trucks zoomed past inches from us, shaking the lambretta. I wondered if my time had come. The lambretta reached Gia Dinh Precinct, and papa san gradually slowed the vehicle to normal speed.

We crossed over the bridge into Saigon, and Susie told the driver to stop. I asked her to apologize to papa san, and I handed him three hundred piasters. His eyes lit up at the generous fare, and all was forgiven. We hailed a taxi to our new apartment on Phan thanh Gian.

While They Died

It was Sunday afternoon, March 17, 1968. Susie went to visit with her family, while I unpacked my suitcase. We would go to the Rex for dinner when she returned.

Our new apartment was small, but adequate under the circumstances. The single room contained a double bed, refrigerator, kerosine stove, and a shower with a built-in French style toilet. The toilet was not the modern flushing version, in fact, it was virtually indescribable. There was a wash basin, and a small mirror.

Business was booming at the Rex that evening, and being it was Sunday, many of the American officers were barbecuing their own steaks and baking potatoes. A Vietnamese band was raising the roof with hard rock music.

Susie didn't order dinner. She browsed the shops for treasures, and as always, came up with something nice. She was thrifty though, and carefully selected the less expensive ifitems. I ordered swiss steak and a tossed salad.

I was happy to be back in Saigon, even though it involved more traveling on Route 1 between Long Binh and Saigon. I felt safer. If the war should escalate again I could find refuge in Saigon.

The Rex was crowded on Sunday, so Susie and I shared our table with a U.S. infantry captain and major who had both just returned from fighting up north. I asked the men how things were going.

The major gritted his teeth. "Sir, the fighting is bad, and American casualties are heavy. Out there in the jungle it's impossible to tell who in the hell is the enemy. Women and children can kill you with grenades, and they set booby traps and bury land mines to blow you to hell. It's a bitch!"

The captain bit his lower lip. "We had one helluva tragedy in a small village northeast of here. An American combat unit led by a Lieutenant Calley went into the village of My Lai and massacred civilians. He and some of his men rounded up the villagers and ordered 347 of them shot. The village was thought to be a Vietcong stronghold, that may have cost many American casualties. We heard Calley had personally used a machine gun when some of his men refused to fire on the helpless civilians. Were they our enemy, or were they simple unarmed peasants? My God, this is a terrible tragedy." Both our guests were extremely emotional and tears filled their eyes. Susie and I were shocked, we excused ourselves and went back to our apartment.

Susie snuggled up close. "Bob, My Lai is where our maid Baby San and her family live. I think maybe Baby San no more. GIs kill boo coo people, and I very sorry for our little friend."

"Little one, I am sorry for Baby San. She was a very loving and caring person. The tragedy will be embarrassing to America. It was late and I had to work tomorrow, and Con didn't know where I had moved. I'd have to hitch hike to Long Binh.

Susie and I were becoming adjusted to our new home, and Con didn't mind picking me up every morning in Saigon. Fighting was sporadic along Route 1, mostly small arms fire. The VC loved to attack crowded Vietnamese buses, so occasionally we were forced to detour around an area were a rocket or mortar had slammed into a bus. Bodies would be strewn all over the place. It wasn't a pleasant sight. I'd have difficulty eating for several days.

On March 31st South Vietnam had received good and bad news. The bad news was that our President Lyndon B. Johnson stopped the bombing above the DMZ in hopes of de-escalating the fighting. It proved to be an opportunity for the enemy. The no-bomb order allowed the North Vietnamese to use the Ho Chi Minh Trail at will without interference from U.S. Air Force B-52 bombers. North Vietnamese troops and weapons could move unhindered down the trail into the South. The American politicians and the Pentagon screwed up royally on this one.

The good news was that LBJ had announced that he would not seek another term as President of the United States. Perhaps our next president would be more considerate of his fellow Americans. Greed and lust for power are a vicious combination, and it's unthinkable that monetary gain could take precedence over good judgment with our politicians and corporate generals. It was shocking to see American and allied soldiers, as well as Vietnamese civilians like Baby San dying uselessly, while the American rich reaped the harvest.

The month of March had come and gone, and April was rapidly slipping by, and the fighting had worsened in many provinces of Vietnam. Con and I were becoming more and more proficient. His driving skills and general alertness kept us in one piece, and my masterful expediting made us the talk of Long Binh. It also helped keep us in the good graces of our fearless leaders.

Living in Saigon was taking its toll. Long hours traveling Route 1 was stressful. Expediting materials to the job site was simple enough, but survival was becoming a high-odds gamble. The deck was stacked against me. I began to visualize a head-on collision with a GI six by six truck at seventy miles an hour or a Vietcong sniper's bullet finding its mark.

Drinking had become a nightly ritual to escape the realities of life. Susie and I began to see less of each other. At times she stayed with her family for days. I couldn't blame her for avoiding my presence. My behavior at times was intolerable. My income was far less than it had been at PA&E, and it was becoming increasingly difficult for me to support her family and my kids in the States. Inflation was spiraling upward, and of course, evenings spent in bars and restaurants had a staggering impact on my billfold.

One evening after work Susie came home with that sparkle in her eye. Now what was she up to? "Bob, Honey, my mama san and Susie do something to make money. We have Vietnamese friend with

American dollars, and she wants to own bar. Mama san and I work to bar. I will be big boss over Saigon tea girls, and teach them to dress and look pretty. Many GI come to bar and spend boo coo money. I no work to bar like tea girl."

I was impressed and excited. "Susie, where is the bar, and what will you name it?"

She had done her home work. She knew the American free enterprise system. "I will name Gala Bar. You go Tu Do Street to Ngo due Ky. Many people come all time and very busy bar."

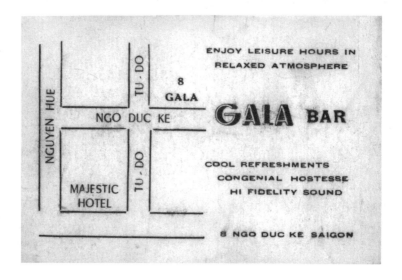

She handed me a well designed business card. On the left was a simple direction layout and at the top right said in small print, "Enjoy leisure hours in relaxed atmosphere". "Gala Bar" was centered on the card in bold letters. Small print under the business name read: "Cool refreshments, congenial hostesses, high fidelity sound". In very fine print at the bottom was the address, 8 Ngo due Ky. I was happy for my little entrepreneur.

She had good sound business ideas. "Bob, I give you boo coo cards, and you give to Americans, and they come to bar. Maybe you get American music records, and maybe you get whiskey and American beer for me. We make boo coo money."

Susie was sharp. I never imagined these thoughts existed in her pretty little head. Maybe ol' Bob should check out the black market for alcoholic beverages. Every bar in Saigon served American liquor and beer.

"Susie, when will you open the Gala for business?"

"Maybe open in fourteen days. Must get Saigon tea girls and whiskey and beer for bar. This was bar before, so no take long time. You help Susie?"

"Sure I help if you get me Saigon tea girl. O.K.?" She hit me with a pillow and wrestled me down on the bed. We both needed a new challenge, and now Susie could be self-supporting.

Saturday, May 5th was the Gala Bar's grand opening. I asked Bruno for the day off, and I got Bo Priest with his jeep to help transport American beer and whiskey I had acquired from various shady sources to the Gala. Several friends donated American records of popular times from the late 1940s through '60s, and Susie promised to keep the record player volume down so it could be enjoyed. Jack Hutson and Dale donated beer; Jack delivered it in person. Cooperation was fabulous, and Susie was ecstatic with the display of kindness extended by our friends.

Many friends were present for the opening. Lt. Hehn was in Saigon on leave from Da Nang, so he and Leo were there. Wendell Hestead and Tom were enjoying the affair, and Larry Potter, who was, surprisingly, still out of jail, sat at the bar sipping a whiskey-coke. There were dozens of people of a variety of races, and many I didn't recognize. Sax and Lon came through the front door and Susie beamed. They were favorites.

Curfew approached and friends departed. It had been a successful and rewarding event, and Susie and her business partners were most grateful.

Susie was occupied with her work, and I did everything to keep beer stocked in the bar's store room. I also located a source of supply for cigarettes.

My evenings and weekends were spent at the Gala, and my drinking became more frequent and heavier. My job at Long Binh was suffering, and I was depressed. I wasn't getting much attention from Susie, and

I was lonely.

On Monday evening, May 27th, the day before my birthday I was alone, wallowing in self pity and depression, and Susie had to work. I got dressed up, dashed down the stairs of the apartment and hopped into a taxi.

"Papa san, Fanette's Bar, Tran hung Dao. De de mau!"

I paid my fare and stepped to the curb. This was familiar territory. Neon signs glowed brightly, and traffic was speeding along the wide street. Cowboys stood in the shadows across the avenue at the entrance of De Tram Street.

I didn't miss the long walk down that alley to the apartment where Susie and I had lived, but I missed Baby San, and her warm smile and her simple lifestyle. I missed Sax and Lon.

The door of Fanette's bar closed behind me, and in the dimly lit room It was difficult to recognize the patrons and Saigon tea girls. I took a bar stool, ordered a whiskey-coke, and lit a cigarette. As my eyes adjusted to the darkness, I started making out familiar figures sitting at tables and standing at the bar. The girls were conning the GIs for drinks. Nothing had changed. Some of the girls noticed, and they greeted me. "Bob, how you? Long time no see. You buy me Saigon tea?"

Le Lynn was sitting at a table in a corner of the small room. With drink in hand I walked through the crowd. "Hello. Do you remember me?"

She answered in the familiar, low, sexy voice. "Bob, please you sit down. I miss you. You gone long time."

I called to the waitress for two cognacs. "Pretty one, we will drink together. I've thought about you, but I have been at Long Binh. I work for RMK-BRJ." We raised our glasses, and said in unison, "Chin chin, and good luck."

We drank and talked about the war. Her lifestyle was beginning to take its toll, and she looked tired. She folded her hands together to conceal the tremble. The alcohol seemed to help steady them.

"Bob, what you think about?"

"Le Lynn, Why you no have boo coo boy friends tonight?"

"Bob, I wait long time for you. Don't you know?"

"It's a good thought. Do you still live on De Tram Street with cowboys? Maybe you have American army general stay your house." I squeezed her hand.

I ordered two more cognacs. "Bob, thank you for drink. I no have boyfriend. I live alone, and I am free."

We made small talk and listened to music for two hours. Cognac flowed like water, and I hadn't eaten since early morning. Le Lynn was aware that I was drunk. "Bob, you come my house and eat, and we drink cognac together. Too late for taxi, and you drunk, so you have boo coo trouble. Curfew come soon. O.K., Bob?

"Sweetheart, I'm pretty drunk all right. We go your house, and I sober up."

I left a generous tip on the table and Le Lynn told the bartender she was leaving for the night. The patrons and the Saigon tea girls watched as we disappeared through the door. Traffic had ceased, and my friend took my arm to guide me across the empty street. Wow! I was cruising high.

The walk was good, and the night air was refreshing. Le Lynn helped me through the door of her cozy little house. I examined the room and was impressed with the expensive furniture, television set, and Sony tape recorder. There was a U.S. Army Colt .45 automatic half concealed under a pillow on the couch, and an army bayonet laid on the coffee table in plain sight. This was some gal.

"Bob, what you like to drink?"

"I will have cognac." She obliged, setting two drinks on the coffee table, and then moved close to my side. She leaned over and gently kissed me on the lips. Part of me wanted to run like hell. But there was no way I could escape, even if I'd wanted to. This was my birthday. Relax and enjoy, and what the hell, this is war.

"Le Lynn, I have wanted you for a long time, and I worry about you working at Fanettes."

She kissed me again. "Bob, I like you long time, but you have girl friend, and I like her. This not good for you and not good for me."

We went to her bedroom and undressed together. We made love, and then we lay close. I fell asleep in a drunken stupor.

At mid-morning I opened my eyes, and my head felt like it might roll under the bed. I didn't know where I was until Le Lynn entered the room. "Bob, you eat something?"

I shook my head, and reached for my pants laying on the floor. I walked to the bathroom, made myself decent, and went directly to the liquor cabinet. I needed a drink.

I poured a half glass of rot gut and gulped it down. It tasted horrible, but the warmth was gratifying as it settled in my innards. I was off to never never land, and hoped reality would never come back.

I poured another drink into the glass. Le Lynn sat opposite me and looked into my eyes. I raised my glass, and softly said, "Chin chin, and good luck."

"Bob, it is Sunday, but I must go work."

"Sure sweetheart. Bob will be gone in short order. Thanks for taking me into your house." I slugged down the drink and she walked me to the door.

She pecked me on the cheek and squeezed my hand. "You are good friend, and please you come again." I blew a kiss to her.

I didn't regret my affair with Le Lynn. This is war, and all is forgiven in war. I took the first available taxi back to the apartment.

Susie was at work, so I poured a drink of straight bourbon and slugged it down. I fumbled around in the refrigerator and found food. I broke off a large hunk of french bread and partially satisfied the empty cavity in my stomach. Then I went to sleep.

It was afternoon when I woke up. I leaped out of bed, popped a can of beer, and got in a cold shower. Thirty minutes later and I was in a taxi headed for the Gala Bar.

Susie was sitting at the rear of the dimly lit barroom. She completely ignored my entrance. I felt enormous guilt.

I sat down with two casual acquaintances of mine, ordered whiskey-cokes, and made casual conversation. The man's name was Henry Johnson, an Afro-American, employed by Page Communication. His companion was Marci, a French National and a longtime friend of Susie's.

Henry was six feet and a hundred eighty pounds. He was intelligent, soft spoken, and had been in country for about eighteen months. He worked in Page's office on Tran quang Khai Street in Saigon. He had a good job. American civilians envied Henry's success, and I admired him for his taste in women.

Marci was a native of Vietnam, born and raised in Saigon. Her father was a French National and her mother Vietnamese. She was small in stature and looked more caucasian than Asian. She had a beautiful smile, and a perfect figure. She had an unusually low voice, and spoke broken French. She and Henry made an excellent couple, and appeared to be very much in love.

I ordered several whiskey-cokes and had achieved my euphoria. I felt quick witted, and Henry and Marci were enjoying our visit. Susie, who had completely ignored me, finally came to the table. "Hello, Bob! When you come in? I no see."

I smiled sheepishly. "Oh, hi Susie. I knew you were busy, and didn't want to bother. Are you O.K.?"

Even in my current state I could see the pain I'd caused by my immaturity and stupidity. "I am O.K., Bob. You all right? No see you yesterday. You work Long Binh?"

"I'm sorry, Susie. I got boo coo drunk last night at Fanette's Bar. I couldn't get taxi after curfew." Looking her in the eye was impossible. It wasn't a matter of lying. It was a matter of not telling all the truth.

I bid Henry and Marci farewell and thanked them for an enjoyable evening. Susie walked me to the door of the Gala. "Bob, I stay with my baby san tonight. Maybe I see you sometime soon?"

My alcohol induced euphoria crashed, and I felt remorseful. I wanted another drink bad, and in the taxi back to the apartment I concentrated on how to make amends. I told myself Susie's wounds would heal, and in the meantime I must keep my cool. I paid the driver, and with a terrible sense of guilt, walked up the steep stairway. I was plagued by loneliness and regret.

I took my favorite bottle of booze from the cupboard and placed it to my lips. I drank until my body rejected the poison, and vomit spewed from my mouth. How could I work tomorrow?

A loud persistent pounding at the door awakened me, and I half fell out of bed onto the bare floor. "O.K.! O.K.! I'm coming!" I flung open the door. Con stood in the doorway grinning broadly.

"Chao Co, papa san. Morning is here today same same like

yesterday." He chuckled, and revealed his usual warped sense of humor. "Bob, what you do today? You go Long Binh and work, or you stay Saigon and have boo coo trouble with Bruno?" I felt and looked as if I was dying a slow, torturous death.

I pleaded with the driver. "Con, please go away and let me die in peace." He ignored my plea, and pushed me back into the room.

My eyes were betraying me. My watch said 0530 hours, and my numbed brain was searching for excuses. I dragged my body to the table where the bottle of booze was sitting, and half looked at Con. I drank, and then retched as my gut rejected the deadly venom. My eyes watered, and saliva ran down the corners of my mouth. I rushed to the toilet, and heaved violently.

"Con, you tell Bruno whatever, but there is no way in hell." I hesitated. "I can't make it to work. I'm sorry, Con. I'll see you same time tomorrow." He looked worried and I knew he was concerned for me. We'd been through a helluva lot together.

Early morning and no place to go. I hit the bed hard, and tumbled into a swirling turbulence. I blacked out for three hours. When I awoke, I desperately needed a drink. Susie kept several cases of American beer under the bed in reserve for the Gala. I pulled out a case, and opened a can to extinguish my thirst. A cold shower opened my swollen eyes and partially cleared my mind. A second beer helped calm my shaking hands. I dressed, and carefully walked down the stairs to the street.

I ordered the taxi and went to the American U.S.O. After I flashed my identification card to the old bewhiskered Indian security guard sitting in the doorway, I took a stool at the counter and ordered bacon and eggs and coffee. I managed to ingest the food, and ambled out into the sunlight, praying the food would remain intact in my gut and absorb the alcohol.

The Saigon River was buzzing with activity as I slowly meandered along. I walked and walked for hours, trying desperately to get well. I strolled back to Ngo duc Ky Street and the Gala bar.

It was early and the bar was nearly empty. Susie was sitting with a group of Saigon tea girls, who were waiting patiently for customers.

I sat at the bar, and ordered an American beer. Susie walked to the bar and stood close. "Bob, you O.K.?"

"Please sit down." I took her hand. "Maybe I work too much at Long Binh. Maybe I've lost it."

"Bob, I am afraid for you. Bruno make trouble for you. You no work, and he no like. Biet?"

"Yeah, I understand. Maybe I no work all week, and to hell with Bruno and RMK. I do number one job, and they know it." I was drunk.

"No matter Bob, I love you, and I am girl friend to you. Everything be O.K.?"

"Hell, Susie, you are my girl friend, and I love you. I drink for awhile, and then I go home." She squeezed my hand with approval.

The Gala started filling with people. Henry and Marci came in and took a table away from the crowd. I walked to their table, and they greeted me cheerfully. "Chao co. It's good to see you both again. Henry, you work today?"

"Some of Page Communication's people are leaving their jobs and returning to the World," he said. "The Vietcong are hitting damn hard with mortars and small arms fire at our installations everywhere in country. It's been continuous. It's a bitch."

"I know the feeling." I turned to his companion. "Marci, what do you think about the war?"

In her deep French accent Marci answered. "I live Saigon long time, and I love my country. Vietnam is first in my heart. All my life I watch the French pigs steal from my people. I watch the French beat my people and starve them. They work them in the fields and on the plantations like dogs, and the French bastards take everything for themselves."

She paused to take a drink of whiskey-coke, then she said bitterly, "Americans come, but they will go home, and North Vietnam will win the war. I am for Ho Chi Minh! He take his people's money to buy guns to fight for what he believe. Nguyen Cao Ky, South Vietnam's leader is corrupt. He take our money, but he no buy guns to fight. He take money and put in his pocket same as the American rich. Bob, you ask me and I tell you. I am for Ho Chi Minh!"

Marci breathed heavily and asked for another drink. She pointed her finger. "Remember this. South Vietnam's President Nguyen Van Thieu only think he big man, but he small man. Nguyen Cao Ky is not South Vietnam president, but he has great power. He is like general."

Marci laughed recklessly. "Nguyen Cao Ky rules the South, and he steal the people's money, and he put in his pocket. Maybe rich American steal your money too, Bob, and put in his pocket." Marci motioned to Susie, and she sat with us.

"Susie, do white mice policemen come to Gala Bar and take money?" Marci asked.

Susie looked around the room for possible Vietnamese police spies. Very softly she explained. "Saigon white mice come to Bar four times every month and take boo coo money from mama san and Susie. No matter how much Gala Bar make, police take half. If we no give to them, then mama san and Susie go to jail. Nguyen Cao Ky take boo coo money and put in his pocket. He do nothing for Vietnamese people. He lie, and he should die."

The waitress brought drinks, and I paid her. I gulped my drink and excused myself. I bid my friends and Susie farewell, and left the bar.

I took a taxi back to the apartment, and turned on the radio. I drank beer, and listened to Armed Forces news about the fighting. It was late, and I laid back on the bed, and felt the agonizing loneliness. I thought about my kids back in the States, and I longed for my Susie.

Con stopped at the apartment again Tuesday and Wednesday mornings, and I refused to accompany him to Long Binh. He said Bruno wasn't talking, but I knew it was the calm before the storm. He apologized that he would not be in Saigon Thursday, but he would come Friday morning for me. I promised I would be ready.

The following two days I spent at the Rex BOQ and Fanettes. I didn't drink heavily, and I took librium to stay calm. I dreaded the DTs.

Thursday night I went home early, and sipped beer. I listened to the radio and wondered what RMK's Bruno would do about my missing work for four days. Susie came to the apartment after closing the Gala, and I greeted her with open arms. I needed her.

We talked casually, and she knew I was troubled. "Bob, you go work tomorrow at Long Binh. If you no go, you have boo coo trouble."

"I know. Tomorrow I go Long Binh, and maybe everything be O.K. Susie, I am sorry."

It was long before dawn when Con pounded on the door. Much to his surprise I was dressed and ready. "Bob, you look number one. You good man to work, but when you drink you number ten thousand."

Susie laughed and kissed me goodbye. "Good luck to you, Bob. See you at Gala tonight."

I didn't discuss work on the way to Long Binh, but Con informed me that Charlie Crow had expedited while I was gone. I thanked him as the pickup glided to a stop in front of RMK's warehouse office. Time for reckoning had come.

I went directly to the mess hall for breakfast. I got a tray and walked through the line. Scrambled eggs, toast and coffee were always on the menu, and this morning I needed nourishment.

I saw Charlie and sat down at his table. I scooped eggs with my fork, but my shaking hand had trouble finding my mouth. My eyes were bloodshot and my face was flushed. Nobody paid much attention. Charlie had had the same experience, and I felt he was silently giving me his sympathy.

We walked to the warehouse together, and he stayed with me in Bruno's office. The big man was sitting in his usual rigid posture and twisting his mustache. I nodded a greeting, and he motioned for Charlie to leave the room.

"Patterson, have a nice vacation?"

"No, it was a hard trip. What's the verdict, Chuck?"

"Patterson, I was in Saigon yesterday and confronted Jake Harris about your absenteeism from the Job. As you well know, RMK frowns upon employees missing work without proper authority."

"I understand perfectly. I have no excuse whatsoever. I've done my job well, but I've fucked up.

He leaned back in his chair, still twisting the handlebar. "You're still on the payroll, and I want you to expedite until next week. Are you with me?"

"Sure I'm with you."

Bruno leaned forward. "Then you will transfer to Da Nang, and be assigned to our open storage warehousing facility." He hesitated. "Sound O.K., Patterson?"

"Bruno, I don't think you're telling me whole the story."

"Oh yes. There is one more thing. When scheduling can be arranged, you'll be flown to RMK's project located at Tan My. It's Hue's northeastern port, located about eight miles north of the city."

"Thanks, Chuck. Con and I are off to Saigon if that's all. I see there are a number of requisitions to be completed."

On the trip to Saigon I ask Con about Hue and Tan My. "Bob, you know the Vietcong boo coo fight at Hue with Americans and ARVNs. Maybe you should stay Saigon?"

"No stay Saigon. I will go Da Nang, but I think maybe I'm my own worst enemy. I raised havoc at PA&E, and now at RMK. Bruno has no love for me. My lousy attitude only expedites the process of elimination. It's either Tan My or back to the World."

After work Friday evening Con dropped me off at the Gala. The Bar was humming with customers, and I was happy for Susie and her mama san. Their success would make my departure easier.

Susie was her usual self. "Hello, Bob. You go to table, and when not busy I come to you." She was one happy little entrepreneur, and nobody was more deserving.

I ordered straight coke. I needed to stay sober, at least until I was settled at Da Nang. There could be a rough road ahead.

Susie stopped by the table. "Bob, no drink whiskey tonight? That is good. I see you Saturday after work, and Sunday maybe we go to Rex. I stay with my baby san tonight. O.K.?" I pecked her on the cheek, and went home.

On Sunday afternoon Susie and I joined Sax and Lon at the Rex for dinner. I only drank two beers all afternoon, and told Sax of my transfer to Da Nang and Tan My. He shook his head.

"Bob, there has been a lot of fighting up north at Khe Sanh and Hue. You're nuts for going to Tan My." Susie agreed with Sax.

"I can only wait and see. If the situation worsens I'll come back to Saigon. No big deal."

Sax wished me good luck as we shook hands. Lon cautioned me to be careful, and we parted company. They were my best friends. I bought

Susie a pair of earrings, and we went to the apartment.

We stayed together for the next three nights. Few words were spoken, and we didn't stray far from each other. I would take Gala business cards to Da Nang and distribute them to Americans. It would help Susie's business.

Wednesday morning Con picked me up at the apartment, and we drove to RMK's office on Duy Tan Street. Several employees loaded gear into the back of a GI six by six truck and we drove to Tan Son Nhut Airport. At dawn we boarded a World War II vintage DC-3 airplane for the flight north.

While They Died

The aircraft leveled off at its designated altitude, and the pilot announced, "Men, this is a relatively short trip to Da Nang. We will be cruising at an altitude of three thousand feet over the South China Sea, three miles off the Vietnam coast. Flying over land attracts enemy rockets and small arms fire, but since the U.S. Air Force has air supremacy we shouldn't encounter enemy fighters. Please keep your seat belts fastened. Thank you."

The twenty-five RMK employees relaxed, and casual conversations broke the silence. The humming of the two propeller-driven motors was all too familiar to my ears and somewhat nostalgic. I had flown in DC-3s with Johnson Flying Service in Idaho. They were also used extensively by Wein Airlines and Interior Airways in Fairbanks and Barrow, Alaska. I had flown in this type of aircraft many times under extreme and adverse weather conditions, and never had a more reliable plane been built.

The coastline with its endless snow-white beach and blue ocean attached to green velvet jungle was beautiful, and it would have been enjoyable to travel this fascinating country in peacetime.

Time passed and again the pilot announced over the intercom. "Fellahs, check your seat belts. I'm on the final approach to the United

States Marine Airstrip, Da Nang, Vietnam. Good luck to all."

An RMK-BRJ bus was waiting at the edge of the runway to provide transportation to the company's westside camp located about two miles from the South China Sea.

The company housing complex was situated at the foot of a lofty mountain covered with dense foliage. It was a typical construction camp with two story barracks, latrines, showers, and a mess hall. RMK had even provided entertainment. There was a club, complete with bar and gambling tables.

The camp definitely wasn't strategically situated though. The Vietcong had a bird's-eye view from the top of the mountain directly above the camp. Hell, the enemy knew when we went to the latrine. It was an exceptionally hazardous location, and moving about in the open could prove fatal. We were fortunate the Vietcong were lousy marksmen.

The Americans had named a mountain directly to our north Monkey Mountain, and one to the south Marble Mountain. They were appropriately named because of numerous little monkeys in the area, and, according to the experts, Marble mountain was solid granite. The two were separated by Da Nang Harbor, bulging with a variety of sea going craft. The water was cluttered with everything from Chinese sampans to U.S. Navy destroyers.

It was Saturday, mid-June 1968, when I arrived at Da Nang. The weekend allowed time to get settled in my quarters on the second floor of the barrack, and familiarize myself with the surrounding area.

My quarters were located on the second floor at the end of the barracks. There was a pleasant breeze blowing alternately from the north and east which provided considerable relief from the intense heat.

I had settled in when my next door neighbor came over and introduced himself. "I'm Jack White from Boise, Idaho."

"I'll be damned. I'm Bob Patterson from Boise, Idaho."

Jack invited me into his room for a beer. He had a huge ice chest in the room, and it was filled to the brim with ice and American beer.

"Bob, this door is always open, so anytime you want a beer just help yourself. Of course, when you get your monthly ration you can replenish the stock. Agreed?"

I thanked him for his hospitality, and we started to talk about home. "Where did you live in Boise?"

"I own a home on Mountain View Drive, not far from North Cole Road, Bob."

"Hell, Jack, I lived on West Clement just off Mountain View. It's a damn small world."

White was a heavy duty mechanic superintendent, and had worked for RMK in several countries. He had owned a rock crusher in the States, but went bankrupt because of under financing and under bidding contracts. Big construction companies were rough competition. He couldn't compete.

Jack was blue eyed and blond haired, and about six feet tall. He was slender and wiry, but his hands were huge. Several fingers and knuckles on both hands had been broken working on heavy equipment.

I explained that due to my building materials background, I was being assigned to identify materials that were without federal stock numbers.

It was great to have an Idahoan for a friend. He could keep me informed of general activities. We drank several beers, then had dinner at the mess hall. It had been a long day. Sleep came easily.

After breakfast Sunday morning Jack arranged to get a company vehicle, so several RMK employees drove to the South China Sea for a swim. This was great. The sand was the whitest I had ever seen, and the water was deep blue and remarkably clear. The magnificent white-capped waves lazily rolled in one after another.

We took turns guarding our valuables at the pickup while the others enjoyed the swim. Many small Vietnamese children were lurking in the shadows, and any clothes and valuables would instantly disappear if left unattended. I didn't think about my forthcoming trip to Tan My.

Monday morning arrived, and after a hearty breakfast, several employees crawled into the back of a company pickup, and we were off to work. Within ten minutes the vehicle stopped just short of the

U.S. Marine Air Base at RMK's eastside warehousing complex. The supervisor in charge assigned me to one of the warehouses that included a desk, one forklift, and one Vietnamese driver.

My job was to open crates that had no identification, record the contents, re-seal same, and on and on. It was an easy task, and to a certain degree I was my own boss. I worked at my own leisure.

After becoming acquainted with some of the employees, and satisfying them I was a regular guy, they invited me to have beer at a U.S. Army Green Beret combat unit's base camp. The camp was located two miles south of RMK's east side complex, at the foot of Marble Mountain.

Marble Mountain contained numerous caves, and the Vietcong had built strong fortifications hidden from view. They periodically, lobbed mortars down into the camp. Nobody knew why the camp was situated in such a vulnerable area.

I enjoyed drinking beer and visiting with the troops, and I wondered how many would be wounded or killed. I shuddered at the thought, but American corporate generals weren't concerned. They were too busy stuffing Vietnam War profits into their pockets.

Every morning on the route to work, the pickup truck passed close to the American military mortuary at Da Nang. The area stank of formaldehyde. The metal building that contained the embalming apparatus was huge, and at one end were several truck bays. Their doors were usually open to allow the stench of the formaldehyde to escape. Inside the building were rows of metal racks. Each rack was designed to hold a body. On every trip by the mortuary we would count the body bags containing American GIs. Armed Forces Radio always reported light casualties, but we knew different.

Sea Land Services, Inc. had the contract to transport the bodies, and their eighteen wheeler refrigerated trucks stood by to take GI remains to the airport for the trip back to the World. I wondered just how many mortuaries the U.S. Government had in Vietnam.

One of my friends at Da Nang had access to a motorcycle. We'd get about half crocked at RMK's club and then head for the city of Da Nang. It really wasn't that exciting, and it couldn't compare to Saigon, but it was a change of scenery. The Chicago and the New

York bars were the social centers for the Americans civilian and GIs alike. The tea girls were everywhere, and I'm confident a lot of money changed hands. I missed Susie terribly, and alcohol was my way of coping with the loneliness.

Monday morning was always welcome, because my work helped keep my mind occupied. I gave every RMK employee a Gala Bar business card with hopes they would patronize Susie's bar when they were visiting Saigon. It was important to keep her business flourishing.

Late Thursday afternoon while I was typing a letter home to my kids, the office manager came into the warehouse with the news of the day. I had been at Da Nang for four weeks, and I thought maybe I would be permanently assigned to the area.

Gibson, the office manager, put his hand on my shoulder. "Bob, I am truly sorry, but come Monday morning there will be a plane scheduled to fly you to Tan My. It isn't necessary for you to work at the warehouse anymore, and you're still on the payroll. Do whatever you choose until Monday." He turned and left. The news sounded like a death sentence.

After finishing my letter I dropped it by the company post office, and returned to my quarters. I went to Jack's room, popped a cold beer, and walked out onto the balcony. I leaned over the rail and reminisced about the good times. I suddenly realized that between now and Monday it would be necessary to make a major decision. Do I journey to Tan My or Saigon?

Jack White joined me after work, and I told him the news. No one in RMK's area wanted to advise me, and I couldn't get information about conditions at Tan My. I knew there was fighting, but how fierce, and what were my chances of survival if American troops pulled out of the area?

On Saturday afternoon I went to a U.S. Marine PX and picked up my beer and whisky ration. The guys at Tan My would probably appreciate a drink, and I may as well go in style. I returned to my room and opened a fifth of bourbon and proceded to get drunk. Jack joined me, and before long we had consumed the fifth of booze.

On Sunday I went swimming in the South China Sea with my friends for the last time. I was drinking heavily, but exercise and food kept me in line. I had made good friends in the past weeks, and at the company club that evening everybody wanted to buy drinks for me. We closed up the joint.

Monday morning and "D" Day arrived. I ate breakfast, returned to my room, and lay back on the bed. I had the feeling that my luck was about to run out.

I had been lucky to survive the many hours I'd spent dodging bullets while traveling Route 1 between Saigon and Long Binh. And now Tan My. The fighting around Hue was heavy, and I would be eight miles further to the north. Neither I nor RMK-BRJ had anything to gain by my presence in that hellhole.

A while later Gibson came into my room. "Patterson, your plane's ready to depart for Tan My. I'll drive you to the runway."

I sat on the edge of the bed. "Gib, you've got the wrong plane, I want the one going to Saigon!"

"Are you kidding, Bob? Do you know what this means?"

"Yeah, Gib, it means I'll probably lose my job, but that's better than losing my ass."

"O.K. Bob. The DC-3 for Saigon will depart later this afternoon. I'll pick you up and drive you to the airstrip. Sorry."

"Thanks, Gib. There's no animosity. It isn't your decision. I'm not a coward, but I have a gut feeling." He departed with a handshake.

The plane was on schedule, baggage was loaded, and about thirty passengers boarded for the trip to Saigon. I was feeling depressed until some guy pulled out a well concealed jug, took a long blast of rot gut, and handed me the bottle. I was surprised. Having alcohol on an aircraft was absolutely against company regulations.

"Hell, my friend, the world isn't coming to the end," he said.

I took a huge gulp of poison. "Thanks, I needed that. I refused an assignment to go north for RMK, and I think they'll fire me."

"Where were they sending you?"

"Tan My," I said in an embarrassingly low tone, my eyes never leaving the floorboards of the aircraft.

My newly found friend hollered loud and clear. "Shit! That's probably the best decision you've ever made. I work for Alaska Barge, and after six months in that hellhole I told them to shove it."

"May I have another drink?" I took a deep sigh, and followed with a hefty guzzle of rot gut. Saigon Airport came into sight, and soon my friend and I got off the DC-3. The plane was on the ground, but we were still at about thirty thousand feet. I really had a buzz.

Had I made the right decision? My friend and I parted company, and I hailed a taxi for the Royal Hotel. I'd spend the night there, and go directly to RMK's office first thing tomorrow morning.

I walked into the hotel, and Benny greeted me with open arms. I signed the register, and we briefly visited. It was good to be back in Saigon.

I slowly walked to the Gala Bar, opened the door and nonchalantly took a stool at the bar. The bartender brought me a whiskey-coke, and Susie walked over to sit beside me.

"Bob, I know you come back to Saigon. I miss you every day, and I think you have trouble. Vietcong everywhere in Vietnam. You stay here?"

I took her hand and explained. "Susie, I no go Tan My. Boo coo fight. I go to RMK tomorrow morning, and maybe I lose job. Choi oi!"

"Bob, you work for anybody. Many jobs in Saigon. No sweat."

I told her where to join me after the bar closed. I had another whiskey-coke, and returned to the Royal. Benny and I reminisced about old times, and I went to the bar for a night cap. Susie joined me there.

We embraced tightly, and enjoyed warmth and security in each other's arms. Her body next to mine assured me that I could face tomorrow's uncertainty.

Tuesday morning I enjoyed the short walk up Tu Do Street to RMK's office on Duy Tan. The coolness of the early morning air was pleasant, and the streets were not yet congested with traffic.

Bob Hyenberg, the personnel manager, watched me as I passed by the front desk, and headed up the stairs to the second floor. I tapped on Jake Harris's door and entered.

"Patterson, I've been expecting your arrival," Harris said. "Gibson radioed from Da Nang that you decided to return to Saigon rather than accept an assignment at our Tan My installation. He informed me your work had been satisfactory, and he was sorry that you were leaving."

"Jake, I'm not chickenshit for not accepting a transfer to Tan My, and I have no excuses. I have a gut feeling that I've been pushing my luck."

Harris didn't hesitate. "Patterson, I have no alternative but to terminate you. Here is an envelope containing your severance pay and a letter addressed to you from the States. Sorry." He stood and shook my hand, and I nodded politely.

I asked the receptionist at the front desk to see Bob Hyenberg. "Please you sit down, he very busy man." I'd been this route before, and waiting had become a way of life.

I opened the manila envelope containing my check and the letter. The check was for an even thousand dollars, survival money. It might be a long haul between pay checks.

The letter was from the Idaho First National Bank, Fairview Branch, Boise, Idaho. It briefly stated that my ex-wife was delinquent on the house payment and a two hundred thirty-one dollar remittance was necessary or foreclosure was imminent. I'd make it a point to have money in the mail.

The receptionist led the way to His Majesty's office. The personnel manager appeared to be enjoying himself. "Patterson! My God, I thought you were up north at Da Nang."

"You knew before I got off the plane in Saigon that I refused an assignment to Tan My."

"Sit down. What can I do for you?"

"Harris just informed me that I was terminated for refusing an assignment. All I need from you is a release on my contract so I can pursue other endeavors."

"No way, Patterson. You bypassed me in the first place. It'll be a cold day in hell before you'll get a release. Your performance with RMK has nothing to do with your present situation."

"Look, Bob, I've got five kids to support back in the States. This isn't any skin off your nose. Think about it, O.K.?"

A lady came over to the desk from across the room. She was about five-four, quiet spoken, attractive, and in her midthirties. "Excuse me, but I overheard the conversation. I'm Mrs. Bob Hyenberg."

I stood and acknowledged her presence. "How do you do, Mrs. Hyenberg,"

"Bob, Mr. Patterson is right. Why not give him a release? He needs the work, and we're just Americans over here trying to do a job."

Hyenberg retaliated without hesitation. "This guy can go to hell." My heart sank, but I managed to keep my cool.

"Mrs. Hyenberg, thank you for your concern, and Bob, please think about it. I'll be back in a few days."

"One other thing," Hyenberg said, quietly, "turn in your defense card and company identification cards. You're not entitled to those credentials when you're not employed."

"Bob, my ID cards were stolen at the hotel last night." He knew I was lying, but the cards were important for survival.

"Patterson, if you're caught using those cards I'll personally see that you're expelled from Vietnam."

"Mrs. Hyenberg, thanks again for your concern and understanding, and Bob, I'll see you in a few days. Please think it over. That release on my contract is very important."

The USO was humming with activity. There were as many American civilians as GIs taking advantage of the service. In addition to excellent American food, table tennis, pool, soft couches and lounge chairs, there was a telephone service on the second floor. All Americans, civilian and military, had access to the privilege.

After lunch at the USO, I strolled down Tu Do Street toward the Gala. Business was slow in the early afternoon so Susie and I took a table at the rear of the bar.

She had located an apartment on Tran que Cap Street not far from her home on Phan dinh Phung. The rent was eight thousand piasters, and it had two rooms with toilet and shower.

"Susie, RMK is reluctant to give me a release on my contract. I will know in a few days. I can play the black market until my ID cards expire, and there is a remote possibility I can find job. I will go to Thu Duc until the apartment is available."

"No worry, Bob, we do O.K. Say hello to Jack and Dale at Thu Duc." I left the bar and hailed a taxi for the trip to the country.

Jack and Dale arrived at the villa just after dark. We talked about Da Nang, and they asked me to stay a few days. Both had worked for RMK, and agreed Hyenberg was a horse's ass.

Lynn Berksnyder and Tina came by for a beer. Lynn offered to buy my 32-20 revolver for two hundred, but I refused. "Patterson, when you get hungry enough you'll sell. I want that gun for Tina." I didn't answer, but I could see the vultures circling overhead.

The next day Bo Priest and I went to APOs for money orders to change on the black market. He had been making a living off the market for a year, so I listened when he offered advice.

"Bob, now that you're unemployed black marketeering will become a way of life. When you go to APOs to get money orders wear dark glasses. Let your beard grow for several weeks, and grow a mustache. Change clothes often, and wear a hard hat one time and an army fatigue cap the next. Don't change money at the same APO, move from one to another. Saigon is loaded with army APOs. Be creative. O.K.?"

"Thanks, Bo. I'll be the man with a thousand faces. I'll become another Lon Chaney."

"One more thing. Sometimes GIs will purchase money orders for you. Give them twenty bucks for their time, but you're taking a risk. GIs are getting wise about changing money orders on the market. When they have a fist full of your MPCs sometimes they will go in one door of the APO and exit by another door. Goodbye money."

That evening Wendell Hestead and Tom, his girl friend, paid a visit. We talked about Idaho and the hot summer they were having in the States. Wendell missed his home town of Burley, and I longed for the mountains of Idaho. He told me there was always room at his villa if I needed a place to stay. I had friends, but I also had pride.

It was June and I hadn't written to the family for a month, nor had I sent money. I couldn't afford to exhaust all my resources, as it would be difficult to recoup.

I told Jack and Dale that I would take the bedroom off the maid's quarters, and Susie would spend nights with me. They were accommodating.

The third morning Susie and I bid Jack and Dale farewell. Both agreed to patronize the Gala Bar on occasions. The Bar always had American beer and quality scotch and whiskey available to friends.

Susie and I hired a taxi to drive us to our new home, and as usual, enjoyed the beautiful countryside on the way to Saigon. We turned off Route 1 into Gia Dinh Precinct.

Susie smiled and squeezed my hand. "Little one, why are you looking so smug?" I asked.

"I think about something, but no tell you. You get mad," she answered.

"No get mad. What you say?"

"I say to you, Chuck Bruno come to Gala Bar to see me same day you go to Da Nang, and he boo coo drunk. He tell me he move to Saigon and get apartment. He give me money to stay with him."

"What did you say to him?"

"I tell him I'm Bob's girl friend, and I no could live with him for anything. He leave Bar and no come back."

"Susie, maybe Bruno got me transferred to Da Nang so he could have you. He isn't beyond it, and he knows how to pull the right strings."

Susie and I got out of the taxi at the corner of Le van Duyet and Tran Qui Cap, and I paid the driver. We entered a tailor shop and I was introduced to An Binh, the owner.

The attractive, middle aged lady was polite and greeted me in Vietnamese. Susie told her I would be living in the upstairs apartment, and I would be in and out daily. We would pay seven thousand piasters rent each month. An Binh bowed, and returned to her sewing machine.

Susie and I walked up a single flight of stairs, and I unlocked the door. It was a two room apartment with a bathroom complete with sink, toilet and shower. The front had one double bed and a small chest of drawers with an old refrigerator in one corner. The other room was furnished with a gas range, a cupboard and table with four chairs.

The place was immaculate, and Susie had our personal effects in order. It was liveable, but the traffic noise was deafening. It would take some getting used to. I pointed to the street and shook my head.

Susie shrugged and laughed. "Home sweet home!"

We rose early the next morning, and Susie fixed coffee. I mentioned the importance of contacting Vietnamese immigration since I didn't have a sponsor, and I must go to RMK's office about my contract release. Susie would go to immigration because she had contacts there.

The huge government complex was overstaffed with employees, but long lines of people needing assistance proved their inefficiency. Susie's reputation as a popular entertainer meant she was well known to many people, and it paid off. All Vietnamese knew "Zoom", the famous singer and dancer.

Susie and I walked past the lines of people and straight into a small room occupied by an officer in the familiar white uniform.

"Lt. Bac, hello to you. Remember Susie?" She said.

"Come in." The Lieutenant beamed. "Susie, I have not seen you for long time. I hear about your success. You sing very well."

"Lt. Bac, this is Bob Patterson, my good American friend. He want to talk."

The officer gestured to be seated. "Sir, how can I be of assistance?"

"Lt. Bac, I have just recently become unemployed. Do I need special papers to stay in Vietnam until I find a job.?"

"Mr. Patterson, what is the time frame?"

"I hope to work soon. I'm trying to get a release on my contract from RMK."

Lt. Bac looked at Susie and then turned to me. "Mr. Patterson, you are South Vietnam's special guest. Please don't worry. You have reported the situation and I can see no problem. Check with me occasionally and inform me of your status."

Susie and I politely acknowledged the kind words. Bac and I shook hands and we left the building. "Susie, you are truly remarkable, and again I thank you from the bottom of my heart."

The little one and I went our separate ways. She took a taxi to the Gala, and I hoofed it to RMK's office. I enjoyed the walk and I definitely needed the exercise.

I greeted the receptionist, and asked to see Hyenberg. I took a seat in the waiting room, and casually watched people come and go. I hadn't noticed before just how large an area the complex covered.

The huge construction company employed thousands of people in dozens of locations throughout Vietnam. RMK must have had tremendous political clout in the U.S.A. to have such a large contract.

I had recently read an article in a leading magazine about RMK-BRJ's accomplishments in Southeast Asia. Overall costs of the construction firm totaled more than $800,000,000 since the contract was awarded by the Navy in 1962. More than 270 projects had already been completed. RMK-BRJ was, at present, engaged in 600 projects at nearly 40 locations and was operating at a rate of more than $30,000,000 of work-in-place a month. This figure would increase to approximately $40,000,000 a month.

RMK-BRJ employed a work force that exceeded 50,000. This included 40,000 Vietnamese, some 18,000 Americans, and 6,000 third-country nationals, including 2,300 Koreans and 3,100 Filipinos. More than $105,000,000 in equipment was now employed in the total program and constituted probably the largest spread ever assembled by a civilian contractor.

RMK-BRJ was only one of 231 companies employed in Southeast Asia. The total dollar volume was in the billions. And thousands of young American kids were dying to accomplish this feat.

The little receptionist beckoned to me. "Sir, please come. Mr. Hyenberg see you now."

The office manager leaned back in his chair. "Patterson, you just don't give up do you?"

"No sir, Mr. Hyenberg. All I ask is a release on my contract."

Mrs. Hyenberg had seen me come into the building, and followed me into the office. "Bob, why the hell don't you give the guy a break. It's no skin off your butt," she said, disgustedly.

"No way. This guy didn't accept a transfer to Tan My, and I'm seeing he's out of the country."

Once again Mrs. Hyenberg pleaded. "Bob's got a family to support in the States, and he needs an income. Sign the release, and let it be."

"Bob, please give me a release. I'll pay you if that's what you want."

"I don't want your money. Leave my office before I call security."

"Thanks for your compassion, Mrs. Hyenberg. You're a gracious lady."

It was good to step out into the sunlight. I slowly walked toward the Gala Bar, and thought how easy it would have been for Bob to sign the release.

The Gala was jumping with customers, and the bar's Saigon tea girls were working in harmony to entertain the GIs and civilians. Susie was an excellent instructor, and the girls excelled. I was happy for her success.

Susie joined me at the bar, and moved close to my side. It was a relief to be rid of Hyenberg, but I would probably approach him again.

"Bob, you no do good at RMK office. Be happy, and everything be O.K."

"Susie, I've been in Vietnam for over a year, and I am wiser and more cautious. We will be all right." I patted her leg.

After finishing my beer I stopped by the USO for a hamburger and milk shake, and then took a taxi to the apartment. I had to do some soul searching and plan my strategy. My ID cards would expire in less than sixty days. No identification meant no access to APOs for money orders, or entrance into any U.S. Military installation, that included the REX Hotel.

Susie arrived just before curfew, and we retired early. The entrepreneur had things to do before going to work in the morning, and I didn't want to interfere with her business. Money didn't come easily for the Vietnamese people, and she had her children to raise and educate. Most of all, she was happy with her success.

Susie was up early in the morning and put on coffee. She quickly showered and dressed and we drank coffee together. The deafening traffic noise hadn't commenced.

An hour later two young women arrived at the apartment. Susie and the two women stayed in the other room. I heard them chattering for at least an hour. Susie appeared to do most of the talking. I was completely ignored.

Curiosity got the best of me. I peeked into the room. All three were squatted on their haunches, with the girls facing Susie. She was carefully applying their make-up, and at the same time instructing them how to solicit for Saigon tea at the Gala.

They didn't resemble the two charming young girls that had entered the apartment. Now they possessed a striking air of sophistication and grace. Each girl was busy stroking the other's lustrous, long black hair with a brush. Susie did her job well, and she was wise to never leave Bob alone with either beauty.

The two young women left the apartment, and the entrepreneur explained that for some time she would be training young girls in the art of survival. It was good business for the Gala Bar.

"Bob, must hurry to work, and please come to bar today. O.K.?" It was a swift kiss, and a cheery goodbye.

Without a release on my contract with RMK-BRJ it seemed futile to look for a job with another contractor in Vietnam. But I scanned my list of contractors for one that might ignore my predicament. The American contractors had an agreement with each other not to hire anyone without a release. This eliminated job-hopping, and kept undesirables from being rehired in country.

There was John Harrison at Alaska Barge. He'd seemed willing to hire me last year. I also knew Henry Johnson with Page Communication; he might help, but their starting wage was only eight hundred a month. Could I afford to be selective? Philco-Ford's salary was low, so they were a last resort. I'd check out several companies before I'd give up.

It was afternoon when I left the apartment and took a taxi to the USO for lunch. I didn't have to show my ID card to the bewhiskered Indian security guard as I entered. He recognized me, and I greeted him. When my ID card expires I won't have any trouble getting in the USO. The food is good, cheap, and they have telephone service in case of an emergency.

After lunch and coffee I strolled down Tu Do Street toward the Gala Bar. Tu Do was always bustling with activity. Literally thousands of people of many nationalities took advantage of black market goods displayed on the famous street. You could purchase anything from American soap and Johnnie Walker Black Label Scotch to any of a variety of choice prostitutes. It was unbelievable.

While They Died

The war was accelerating by leaps and bounds, and the State Department and Pentagon in our nation's capitol were still misleading the U.S. taxpayers. American troop involvement in South Vietnam stood at five hundred-fifty thousand, and our generals were confident we would win.

Susie didn't want to talk about the war, but she sometimes asked a simple question. "Bob, what do America do? They stay Vietnam? They go home?"

I had difficulty looking her in the eye. I didn't know what America would do. I hoped they would stay and finish what they had started. They promised they would help South Vietnam, but I had a gut feeling we would lose, and the Americans would leave. Politicians don't win wars—they cover up their tracks.

Susie took a taxi to the Gala, and I walked to the USO to have breakfast. I wanted to kill time, and I needed to gather my thoughts. Hyenberg wasn't going to give me a release on my contract, and I had been procrastinating about contacting other companies about a job.

It was mid-afternoon when I walked into the Gala, and all the employees greeted me. My frequent visits to the bar made me feel like I worked there. I was generous about buying Saigon tea, and if they were running short on beer or booze, I could always find a source to replenish the stock. The Vietnamese people were appreciative. They were simple, but they had values. I couldn't let them down.

Jack and Bo came to the Gala from Thu Duc late afternoon and we drank beer together. I asked Bo if we could change money at Long Binh, because I had been using the APOs in Saigon to the limit. I'd used every disguise imaginable, and most of the APO clerks knew me anyway. Hell, it was becoming a joke.

Bo cautioned me that if one GI out there blew the whistle I'd be out of the country. He welcomed me to come to Thu Duc anytime and we would go to Long Binh.

My two friends departed, and I passed time by playing gin rummy with Susie. The Vietnamese loved to gamble, but were terrible losers. Many times I would let them win just to stay in their good graces.

By evening the bar was full of patrons, both civilian and military. I was getting drunk, and a young GI sitting next to me was out of beer, so I got him a refill.

"Thank you, Sir, I appreciate it," he said.

"Don't worry about it. The drinks are on me tonight."

"Sir, I hear you loud and clear. Thanks again."

The kid smiled, and I couldn't believe how young he looked. I'll bet he shaved once a week whether he needed it or not.

"What's your name, and where's your outfit?"

"I'm Ronnie Jones, and I'm stationed at Long Binh. I'm on R and R. You know, rest and relaxation."

The military usually sent GIs on leave outside Vietnam to choice locations. They might go to Guam, Thailand, the Philippines, or Japan, and Army Special Services provided women, wine and song. I didn't question why he was in Saigon for R and R, as I only wanted him to have a good time.

Ronnie met Susie, and I told him about our companionship. He wished us the best, and I wished him good luck. Susie and I left at closing time and went directly home.

The following morning we had coffee before she left for work. "Bob, you look for work today, or maybe you change money?"

I brushed off the question. "Hell, Susie, everything is O.K. I've got people to see. I'll look tomorrow or whenever."

I got to the Gala about noon. I needed a beer to put out the fire. I'd consumed more booze the night before than I realized. My young friend Ronnie was there, so I took a stool next to him at the bar. I ordered two beers, and we touched glasses.

Ronnie seemed like a nice kid. He was quiet and reserved. He told me he was nineteen and from Ohio.

We were now sitting shoulder to shoulder, and becoming more intimate. I was beginning to relax, and I was always the good guy after a few beers.

"Bob, I've got to ask you something."

"Sure, Ronnie, what's on your mind."

"Sir, Ah—ah—I'm on R and R, and I'm broke flat as hell, and I don't have anyplace to stay for the next week. Could you loan me a hundred MPCs until payday? I'll get paid then, and I can settle up."

I took a deep breath. "Look, Ronnie, I'll do better than that. I'll give you the hundred, if you can buy some money orders for me at an Army APO." I didn't tell him about making a profit on the market.

"Sure, Bob, I can do that. When do you want them?"

"I'll give you three hundred right now. You keep a hundred, and get me two hundred in money orders. Can you swing that?"

"No problem, Bob. I'll go right this minute."

I excused myself, and motioned to Susie to meet me in the storage room. I asked for three hundred in MPCs to give to Ronnie to get money orders.

Susie got her satchel, pulled out a large roll of bills, and counted out the MPCs. "Bob, you don't know GI very long and you drink boo coo beer. Maybe you wait."

"I'm O.K., and this kid's on R and R. He's harmless, and he needs a father for a few days." I pecked her on the cheek, and slapped her on the butt. "Never fear my dear—when good ol' Bob is here."

Ronnie glanced around the room as I stuffed the three hundred MPCs into his fatigue pant's pocket. "Bob, I've got things to do, and I'll get the money orders at Long Binh. See you at 1200 hours tomorrow. Don't worry." The kid quickly disappeared out the door. After he was gone, I started to worry.

Damn. I hardly knew the guy. My teeth clenched together. I felt sick in my gut, and I pictured three hundred dollars vanishing into thin air. The sauce has gotten to my feeble mind. I've gone dinky dao. Did the GI really sucker ol' Bob?

Susie and I sat at a table, and I was quiet as a stone statue. My heart was beating like hell. I hated to think of losing that kind of money, particularly when I was unemployed.

"Bob, maybe you make mistake."

"Damn, I don't know. Ronnie said he will be here tomorrow with the money orders. Tomorrow may never come. Choi oi."

We took a taxi home, and Susie held my hand tightly. She would stand by me regardless of the outcome. I'd used poor judgment before when money was involved in the black market, but I had always come out all right.

The bartender at the Gala had just finished putting the money in the cash drawer to start the day's business. I ordered a beer.

It was precisely 1200 hours when Ronnie came bounding in the door of the bar. Damn, was I happy to see him. Susie came over and we greeted our faithful friend. He slipped me the two hundred dollar money orders.

"Bartender, Give my GI friend a cold beer."

"Bob, it's been a long night. Where can I take a shower and change my fatigues?"

"Susie, can Ronnie use our apartment?"

"No sweat, Bob. You do whatever," she answered.

"Ronnie, here's my key ring. You go to the tailor shop and ask for An Binh. She owns the apartment above the business, and say you're a friend of Bob. You'll find clean towels, my razor and soap. Take your time, and I'll be right here."

Soon after Ronnie left the bar I told Susie I was going to Johnnie's bookstore to change the money orders into MPCs. I walked out of the bar and turned right on Tu Do Street. The bookstore was a five minute stroll, and I was in no hurry today.

Johnnie gave me a hundred ninety for each money order. It netted me one hundred eighty dollars. Not a bad day's work. My young friend and I were going to experience a flourishing relationship.

It was nearly closing time before Ronnie came by the Gala with my key ring. He apologized for the delay, and said he'd see me tomorrow. I mentioned perhaps he could get more money orders.

"Give me the MPCs and I'll have them in two days. "We went to the supply room, and I carefully counted out two hundred MPCs. He put the military script deep into his pocket, and we shook hands.

It was getting late, and I wanted to stop at the USO for a sandwich. Susie would follow later. It had been a long and prosperous day.

When I got to the apartment I unlocked my clothes closet to make sure everything was intact. I occasionally went through this routine just to make sure.

The only thing unusual was the .25 Browning clip was laying on the bottom shelf. The gun was in its usual place on the top shelf. I couldn't remember removing the clip, and Susie would only have touched the gun in an emergency. It was strange, but sometimes strange things happened to me after a night at the Gala Bar.

The following morning I asked Susie about the clip laying on the bottom shelf of the closet. She hadn't touched the gun. She thought maybe I moved it while I was drunk.

Ronnie came to the Gala the second day with two money orders. He slipped the certificates into my hand, and I ordered a beer. I gave him twenty-five dollars in MPCs as his reward.

"Bob, if you come to Long Binh tomorrow, I can change four to six hundred MPCs for you. I have a couple friends that will help with the deal if you give us fifty dollars in return. These guys can use a few bucks. Fair enough?"

"O.K., Ronnie, I'll meet you at 0900 hours at Long Binh."

Charlie at the Continental changed my money orders for one ninety five each, that netted one-eighty profit. I told Susie I would spend the night at Thu Duc, and Bo and I would travel to Long Binh to change money.

Bo and Mop lived on the outskirts of Thu Duc in a small house. The accommodations weren't first class, but they were free, and Mop, like most Asians, was an immaculate housekeeper. She didn't speak English, but our pig Latin got us by.

Bo and I visited while Mop fixed fried chicken. I hadn't thought about bringing American beer, so we bought some bomi bom at a roadside stand.

When we arrived at Long Binh Ronnie was waiting at a table outside a military PX. I introduced Bo, and slipped four hundred MPCs into Ronnie's bulky fatigue pocket. He said to wait.

My GI friend had been gone two hours. "Bob, kiss your four hundred goodbye," Bo said. "That guy is smooth, and he clipped you."

My heart sank. "Who can you trust these days? I've been so good to this boy."

"Honest Bob is just trying to make a living playing the market. The CID frowns upon this activity, or didn't you know?" Priest turned away and laughed heartily.

I hated to be out four hundred, but it was funny as hell. "Honest Bob just trying to make a living."

We climbed into the jeep and Bo turned the ignition key. "Hold it Bo! There's Ronnie coming out of that barracks."

"By damn, Patterson, you've been living the good life. I thought it was goodbye to your hard earned money."

Ronnie was out of breath. "I thought you had left. I had a helluva time trying to find my friends. I don't know where they could be. I'm sorry, Bob. Here's your four hundred MPCs. No money orders."

"Don't worry about it, Ronnie. Get in, and we'll go to Saigon."

When we reached the outskirts of the city Ronnie went his way. Bo spent the night with Susie and me, and I gave him a case of American beer to take home. Our apartment looked like a liquor warehouse from what I had accumulated by devious means.

Three days passed and no Ronnie. Maybe his R and R was over, and he was back with his outfit. I still had some money, and I would be able to change on the market for a while.

On the fourth day Ronnie showed up at the Gala. "Hi, Bob, good to see you. I've been out in the boondocks, and wasn't able to contact you."

"Thought maybe your R and R was over, and you were long gone."

"Still want me to get money orders, Bob? Same deal?"

"Sure thing. Did you find your two friends?"

"Yeah, they'll be in Saigon tomorrow, and we can get you six hundred in money orders if you like."

"O.K., Ronnie, tomorrow is fine. Come early to the apartment."

He wanted to shower and change, so I gave him the key ring, and he was off to the apartment. He'd drop the keys off before closing time.

After this next transaction I'd send money to my kids. Something always occurred to brighten the day when the chips were down.

When Susie came home that evening I told her of the plan, and that I'd put up four hundred MPCs. She was welcome to throw in two hundred, and I would get money orders for her. We would make a few easy bucks.

The following morning Susie gave me the two hundred, and I put it in my shirt pocket. I put four hundred in my pants. I never carried all my money in the same pocket, not in Saigon with pickpockets lurking in every cranny.

Ronnie and his two friends arrived at 0900 hours. Ronnie came into the room, and the other two stood in the doorway.

"Susie, you go see your baby san, and Ronnie and I will work things out." The GIs let her through the doorway.

My GI friend and I stood toe to toe. His eyes narrowed and a smirk appeared on the boyish face. We moved toward the clothes cabinet at the same time. He got the jump and reached the .25 Browning first. He pulled the clip off the shelf, slammed it into the butt of the gun, and jacked a bullet into the chamber. In desperation I grabbed his arm, hoping to free the firearm.

One of his friends hit me in the ribs, and the force of the blow sent me reeling to the floor. I got up quickly only to take a fist to the side of my head. These men were young and they were big and they were determined.

The two buddies pushed me back onto the bed, and Ronnie pointed the gun at my chest. "Cough up the money, Patterson, or die. I don't give a shit either way." Ronnie didn't appear the young innocent boy anymore.

My shaking hand reached into my pants pocket, and I threw the roll of four hundred MPCs to the bottom of the bed. Ronnie picked up the bills, and leveled the gun at my head. One of his friends grabbed his arm. "Don't shoot the bastard. Breaking out of that stockade at Long Binh has us in enough trouble. Let's get the hell out of here."

Ronnie had cased the apartment, and knew exactly where everything was. He took the .25 Browning and two boxes of ammo and left.

I lit a cigarette with a trembling hand, and poured a cup of coffee. I sat at the table, and slowly inhaled the smoke. I didn't want to believe Ronnie had set me up. But I suddenly realized his fatigue jacket didn't have his name tag. I remember it appeared to have been ripped off. The threads were still intact on the jacket; it had evidently been removed when he entered the stockade. One other thing should have made me suspicious. He'd said he was on R and R, and was stationed at Long Binh. He would have taken R & R leave outside the country. He was thorough, and he was no amateur. I suddenly realized how gullible I had been. Being alive was the only consolation.

Jack Hutson had told me at the Gala a couple weeks back about a prisoner breakout at the Long Binh stockade. The black prisoners had rioted and killed several white boys, and some whites had escaped to save their skins. Most hadn't been captured, but the military police were in no hurry. There was no way in hell the prisoners were going to escape from Vietnam.

I slowly walked to Susie's house. She and her baby sans and mama san were sitting on a mat in the small living quarters. Susie had known trouble was brewing before she ever left the apartment, and I could tell she was worried and frightened.

"Bob, you have trouble with GIs. I'm happy you tell me to leave. I afraid maybe they kill you."

"Susie, I lost my four hundred MPC notes, but here is your money. It's all here. I am sorry."

"Bob, you keep money to change on black market, and in two days you have boo coo money. No sweat." She squeezed my hand.

"Susie, one thing I don't understand. Ronnie knew about the .25 Browning automatic, but where is the 32-20 revolver?"

"Oh, Bob, I put in other room behind box where I keep food. I think you have trouble. I say many times you good man, but when you drink you dinky dao."

I didn't leave the apartment that day. I was shaken, and knew I was lucky to be alive. Tomorrow I'd go to Long Binh and change money. I wasn't finished yet, but I was teetering on the edge.

The next day I met with Bo. "Bob, there's a bright side to the story about your GI friend. I talked to two American MPs at Thu Duc last night. The three young escapees were caught just north of the Newport Bridge on Route 1."

"What the hell happened, Bo?"

"Easy Bob. These three GIs were army deserters out of the Long Binh Stockade. After they robbed you they commandeered a taxi. For some reason they wanted to go to Long Binh. A local business man saw the three escapees shanghai the taxi and alerted the white mice. They radioed the Vietnamese MPs at Newport, and the MPs set up a road block."

"Sounds like a real shoot 'em up bang Hollywood movie."

"Yeah Bob. When Ronnie and his friends saw the road block they forced the taxi driver to skirt around it. Ronnie leaned out the window and started firing the .25 auto. Can you imagine shooting that pea shooter at MPs armed with M-16 automatic rifles? Ronnie had automatic weapons with him, and used the .25 auto. That doesn't make a lot of sense."

"I can't believe it, Bo. They must have been desperate, or wanted to commit suicide."

"The MPs opened fire when the taxi didn't stop. The taxi driver, Ronnie, and one of his friends were killed. The other was unharmed. There were twenty seven bullet holes in the taxi."

"How are you sure it was Ronnie and his buddies?"

"A Vietnamese MP captain told the American MPs that he confiscated a small nickel-plated, pearl-handled .25 Browning automatic. That's how I'm sure it was Ronnie."

"Thanks for the information. You just made my day."

The days passed, and Ronnie haunted my thoughts. The three young GI deserters had been desperate, and I can understand why they escaped from the stockade. Their lives had been in jeopardy. The blacks were armed with knives, and several whites had been killed. Ronnie and his friends panicked. They had run for their lives, but their efforts were in vain.

I wish Ronnie had leveled with me about his situation. Perhaps I could have talked to the U.S. Army Provost Marshall. At least he would be alive.

One Saturday night in mid-July I partied far beyond any sane limits at the Gala Bar. Sunday morning my head felt like it was about to shatter. I hoped to die and be released from such torturous misery. Susie hadn't stayed the night, and I couldn't remember how I got to the apartment. I lay motionless, and afraid to even chance blinking my bloodshot eyes. It was miraculous I still breathed.

A thunderous pounding at the door nearly caused my head to explode. I leaped up, and charged forward. I had to stop that intolerable racket.

I flung open the door, and bellowed, "Who the hell are you, and why are you killing me with this infernal racket?"

The would-be tormentor standing at the door was a six foot, sandy haired, blue eyed U.S. Army staff sergeant in badly wrinkled and soiled fatigues.

Grinning like a Cheshire cat the voice announced: "General Patterson, I am Sergeant John Scott O'Leary at your service...better known as Scotty."

"What can I do for you, Sarge? I can't do much for myself right now with this terrible hangover."

"Bob, don't you remember me? You and I drank much cognac and whiskey-coke at the Gala last night. You really don't remember?"

"I'm sorry my friend. I can't recall much of anything. I do know Susie didn't come home last night. Can you shed some light for me?"

Scotty raised his eyebrows in disbelief. "Bob, you really must have been out on your feet. We had a blast. You bought drinks for the house, and you tried to make a couple of Susie's Saigon tea girls. Me and everybody else thought you were the life of the party."

"Great balls of fire! I'll bet Susie will never speak to me again. The life of the party, you say?"

"Susie thought you were hilarious. She was happy that you were having a good time. She is a very lovely and understanding lady, and you're the envy of every American in Saigon. Believe me."

"Thanks, Scotty. I can't see why she stays with me. I don't mean to cause trouble, but it's always just a jump away. Do you know how I got to the apartment?"

"Susie and I helped you into a taxi, and she told the driver to make sure you got into the apartment. Scotty shook his head. "Those Vietnamese rangers in the Gala were mad as hell."

"Sarge, what happened? The VN rangers have been friends for a long time."

"Well, Bob, you were pretty drunk, and we had pulled several tables together. There must have been fifteen of us laughing and raising hell in a general way. You were wisecracking and buying drinks like crazy." Scotty hesitated. "Out of the blue you yelled, 'To hell with the VN rangers. The American soldiers are tired of fighting your damn battles. You guys are yellow. Why don't you fight like men?' There was dead silence, and I mean dead."

"Oh, my God! I didn't think I could get that drunk. I have the highest regard for the Vietnamese rangers. They are first class soldiers, well trained, disciplined, fearless, and exceedingly patriotic. I owe each and every one an apology."

"Look, Bob, the rangers are in the Gala right now, and they're waiting for you. They are all carrying forty-fives. Susie suggested I take you to Thu Duc for a few days. I've got a jeep outside on the street. I'm off limits in Saigon, and I've got to get to Long Binh or my stripes are gone. I could be in trouble right now."

Chapter Eighteen

"O.K., Scotty. I'll shower and dress, and we'll be out of here."

We tossed a case of beer in the back of the jeep, and Scotty drove slowly toward Route 1. He didn't want to attract an MP's attention, and get a free military escort to Long Binh.

He pulled into Jack's driveway, put the case of beer under his arm, and we walked inside. Yvonne met me in the doorway and she obviously wanted to pick a fight. "Bob, what you want here?"

"Hi, Yvonne ol' girl. Good to see you. This is Scotty, and he was kind enough to drop me off on his way to Long Binh. I'll be here a few days."

"You no live here anymore, and you make trouble with me. You tell Jack I lie and I steal his ring and money when he drunk."

"Forget it, Yvonne. I've got enough trouble without your bullshit. Leave us alone, and I'll explain to Jack when he comes home." How Hutson could tolerate this creature was beyond my imagination.

Scotty opened a beer, but I declined. I felt terrible. We talked casually for a couple of hours, and we decided I should probably move my personal effects out of the apartment on Tran que Cap. I was pushing my luck, and it might be some time before the VN rangers simmered down.

"Scotty, how am I going to get my things out of Saigon? I shouldn't go there, and Susie is busy at the Gala."

"Bob, don't worry. It's still early in the day, and I can rush back to your apartment in the jeep. No sweat."

"It's risky for you, and besides it's off limits. You know the consequences if the MPs get wise."

"I'll drop by the Gala before going to the apartment, and tell Susie of the plan. She'll come to Thu Duc to see you."

"Damn, Scotty, be careful, and I thank you. You can put my personals in the large wooden box that's stored under the stairway, and stuff the overflow in the old suitcase under the bed. My 32-20 revolver and the ammo is in the kitchen area hidden under the utensils. I'll be right here." I walked with him to the jeep, and wished him the best.

It was dark when Jack got home from RMK's rock quarry, and Dale came in shortly thereafter from Long Binh. Each greeted me cordially, and with beer can lids popping, I proceeded telling about my escapade with the VN rangers. They laughed and laughed, but I didn't share their humor.

My concern for Scotty was growing by leaps and bounds, as it was late. I hoped he stayed at the apartment until tomorrow.

Jack and Dale left for work in the early morning, and I passed time by reading and sipping coffee. I didn't feel well. It wasn't the hangover; I was very tired, and I had a fever and diarrhea. I vomited, and had a terrible thirst. A rash broke out on my upper body, and my eyes and urine were dark red.

I retired to the bedroom off the maid's quarters where it was quiet, and slept for several hours. Scotty woke me in the late afternoon.

"Bob, I'm sorry for the delay, but the MPs arrested me just after I picked up your stuff. I had just pulled onto Route 1, and I was pushing hard. The siren caught my attention, and I knew it was trouble. The MPs escorted me to Long Binh, and confiscated your wooden box and the 32-20 revolver. I am truly sorry."

"Scotty, how did you get here?"

"The Provost Marshall gave me a citation, and I will have to go before a court marshall. It won't be too serious. I'll probably lose the rocker under my sergeant stripes, but no big deal. I'm still allowed to drive until the military hearing."

"How do I get my things from Long Binh?"

"Jack or Dale won't have any trouble getting your personals, but the military will keep the firearm. Of course, you know it's against regulations for a civilian to carry a gun."

"Scotty, I don't blame you, but the gun belonged to my dad, and it's been in the family since the 1930s. This is bad news."

Scotty left for Long Binh, and Jack came to the villa early from work. I explained about Scotty's misfortune, and about the wooden box and the revolver. He would pick the box up the next day after work.

Jack had been studying me since coming home, and he gave me a terrifying jolt. "Bob, I think you've got hepatitis."

A shock wave streaked through my body. "My God, how can you tell?"

"I've had hepatitis, and you've got all the symptoms. Your eyes in particular are a dead giveaway. They are red as hell, your face is flushed, and you have a fever. I hope it isn't the infectious kind. Everybody in the household will be in jeopardy."

"What should I do Jack? I'm not employed, and a military doctor won't see me since I don't have a current ID card. I need help."

"Bob, stay here for a couple of days, and if you don't get better, I'll have to ask you to leave. In the meantime I'll have Yvonne sterilize everything you touch."

"Thanks, Jack. I'll be particularly careful, and I'll use the same eating tools." I excused myself, and retired to the room at the rear of the villa.

I slept for nearly two days, my thirst for water was endless and the dysentery worsened. I vomited repeatedly and my body was burning hot.

Bo Priest came to visit when Jack told of my plight. "How are you doing, Bob?"

"Lousy, Bo. I can't stay awake, and I'm getting weak. I have dysentery, and it hurts to urinate. I need a doctor."

"Bob, I'm taking you to my place, and Mop can tend to you. Yvonne would let you lay here and die. I'll help you into the shower. It'll be good for you, and we'll get some clean clothes."

Bo helped me into his small house, and I laid on the couch until Mop could make up the bed. I immediately fell into a deep sleep, and she only awakened me long enough to give me water.

Two weeks passed, and I didn't get any better. I called for Mop, and I tried to make her understand that I needed a doctor. "Mop, I need doctor. Biet?" She shook her head sadly. "Mop, I need bac si. Bac si help Bob. Biet?"

She smiled and nodded. "Bac si! Bac si! Biet."

She helped me out of bed, and dressed me. I barely had legs to stand on. She took my arm and steadied me, and we slowly walked down a well worn path through the thick jungle. We stopped to rest, and she repeated several times, "Bac si. Bac si."

We entered a clearing where a small house stood, and two small boys were playing at the edge of the jungle. Mop knocked gently on the door, and we entered. She was tired from supporting my weight, but smiled and helped me into a chair.

The room was small, and smelled of medicine. It was neat and well kept, and I was confident Mop had brought me to see a professional medical doctor.

An Asian woman appeared from another room dressed in white slacks and a doctor's smock. She smiled and acknowledged my presence. "Ma'am, do you speak English?" She answered in French.

She took my temperature and listened to my heart and lungs. She tapped all over, checked my reflexes, and very professionally looked into my ears, and throat, and examined my eyes.

She handed me a specimen bottle and pointed to a door. I nodded with a smile and left the room. I returned with the bottle, and she looked at it carefully. Mop and the bac si talked momentarily, and each took an arm and led me to a counter. They placed my hands on the counter, and Mop proceeded to take down my pants. The bac si went to a cabinet, removed a syringe, and filled it with a clear liquid.

I felt very vulnerable and weak. I needed help. Was she Vietcong, or was she a friend of the family? It was too late to worry. She hit me in both cheeks of my butt, and it was over. I pulled up my pants, and Mop helped me back to the chair.

I took several piasters out of my pocket. "Mama san, how much?" Mop took five hundred piasters from my hand, and gave it to the bac si. My friend steadied me, and we walked back through the jungle toward her house.

The two shots in the butt helped. I started regaining my energy, and my appetite was better. I surmised the syringe probably contained vitamin B-12. Soon I could exercise lightly by walking up and down the road in front of the house, and I was progressively getting stronger each day.

Mop guarded me like an angel from heaven, and took me to the bac si every two weeks as regular as clockwork. The bac si gave me a shot in the butt on every visit, and I developed everlasting trust in the sweet lady. We had developed a mutual admiration, and I didn't want it to end. I wished we could communicate, but it was out of the question. She spoke no English, and I knew only limited Vietnamese.

I was quite sure she was a French national.

It was September, and the time had come for me to spread my wings. I made a special trip into the jungle to bid my favorite bac si farewell, to thank her for tender loving care, and for saving my life.

It had been months since I had written to the States. I deeply missed my family, but they wouldn't understand. I wished I could work like other Americans in Southeast Asia.

I had lost considerable weight which altered my features. Changing money would be easy, since nobody would recognize me with a hard hat and dark glasses. The RMK ID card would soon expire, and I needed to keep money in reserve.

My biggest loss over the months wasn't only money. I had lost both the Browning automatic and my 32-20 Colt revolver. I felt naked without a firearm at my disposal.

Bo took me to the Route 1 junction, and we bid each other farewell. "Bo, come to the Gala, and keep in touch. I'm forever indebted to you and Mop. I'll never forget you." We gripped hands, and I waved goodbye. The jeep disappeared down the road.

I hitched a ride to downtown Saigon, and took a taxi to the Tourist Hotel on Hong Thap Tu. I hurried past the security guards and walked through the lobby to the desk. The clerk cheerfully greeted me. "Mr. Patterson, good to see you. Been long time."

"It has been a while," I replied. I signed into an empty room on the fifth floor. I picked up my suitcase, and walked to the elevator.

As the key turned in the lock of the door, and I entered my new home, I considered myself fortunate to be in Saigon rather than laying in the jungle with hepatitis. There was always a brighter side.

The cool water from the shower poured down on my head and over my battered body. It was heaven, and I thanked God to be alive.

I slipped on shorts, and laid on the bed staring up at the ceiling of the bare room. I thought of my past experiences in Vietnam, about my present situation, and what might be in store. My future was shaky. I was on a slippery course down a steep and never-ending hill.

Alcohol was beginning to control my life. I was depressed and self-destructive, and the situation would worsen if I didn't change my lifestyle.

My thoughts suddenly focused on my visa. I had overstayed in the country. My visa had expired, and knew of no way to extend it. It was early afternoon, and I had to see my friend at Vietnamese Immigration.

In less than fifteen minutes the taxi pulled to the curb on Vo Tanh Street. The government service building was crowded even worse than my last trip with Susie, and again it reminded me of the U.S. Government.

Lieutenant Bac was absolutely smothered in paperwork. He motioned for me to sit, and continued fumbling through files. "Lt. Bac, I was here a couple months ago with Susie, the popular singer and dancer. Do you remember?"

"Mr. Patterson, have you found employment?" I couldn't believe he remembered my name.

"Lieutenant, I have been staying with a friend at Thu Duc for some time. I have been quite sick with hepatitis, and under the circumstances I haven't looked for work. But it was necessary to see you, and report my misfortune."

I handed the officer my passport. "Mr. Patterson, you been overstayed for quite some time. I understand your problems, so please continue to check with my office from time to time. You have lost weight, and you look tired. But you are still a special guest." He returned my passport, and resumed his endless task with stacks of paper work..

"Thanks, Lieutenant, I won't bother you. I'll see you soon." I humbly bowed, and disappeared into the street.

The taxi sped toward Ngo duc Ke Street and the Gala Bar. I had missed Susie, but was aware her flourishing business provided ample income to support her family.

Lights had been turned low to create an exotic atmosphere, and the music was playing a 1960's American song.

The bartender greeted me. "Hello, Bob. Can I get you something?"

"Sure, papa San. Give me American beer." My eyes peered through the dark room for Vietnamese rangers. I hoped the soldiers were forgiving, and thanked God the place was empty.

Susie came to the bar and sat down. "Hello, Bob. Bo tell me you boo coo sick, and I think maybe you come to see Susie. I am happy you are all right."

I put my arm around her waist and pulled her close. "I missed you, and I am sorry about trouble with rangers."

"Rangers not mad. Lt. Hehn come to bar, and tell them to leave Bob alone. They understand Hehn, and they will not hurt you." She rested her head on my shoulder.

"I am staying at Tourist Hotel, and I want you to come tonight."

"Bob, I come to you tonight, and I stay with you." I brushed her lips with mine and left the bar.

The USO was buzzing with GIs and civilians, and I enjoyed a chili-dog and a vanilla milk shake. It was so good to have American food, and it was great to see the activities of the bustling city.

It was after dark when Susie entered the hotel room, and we embraced and I kissed her mouth. We undressed, and I held her tight, and I wished that morning would never come. It was a passion that would not die. It would last forever.

Morning did come, and we showered together, like in days past when we lived on De Tram Street. We dressed, and sat on the bed to have a serious talk.

"Susie, I don't know what I am going to do. Work will not come easy, and we can not stay together. You have good job, and you can take care of your baby sans. I need money for the black market, and I hope everything be O.K. Do you understand?" We sat in silence.

"Bob, you do what you think. I will stay at my house, and I wait for you, and I come to you anytime. Bob, I love you."

"Susie, I will always love you, and I will come to Gala to see you." She handed me two hundred MPCs, and told me to make money on the black market. I thanked her, and promised to pay her back. She left the room; a lump rose in my throat, and I was alone.

The Tourist dining room was empty. I ordered ham and scrambled eggs and french bread, and I drank coffee, and stared out the large picture window at well groomed plants and shrubs and the neatly trimmed lawn. I was deep in thought.

"If it isn't Bob Patterson! What are you doing here at the Tourist? I heard you were up north at Da Nang." There was a tremendous slap on the back.

"My God, George Lachapelle. I thought you had gone back to the States." I jumped up and extended my hand.

We talked at length about our days together at PA&E, and what had transpired. I told him about losing my job with RMK-BRJ. He had just signed a contract with Alaska Barge. I envied him, and I told of my misfortune of not getting a release on my contract.

"Bob, what are you going to do? No contractor will touch you with a ten foot pole."

"It looks bad, and my ID cards will expire soon. That means no black market, and no income. I've checked out several companies, but they turn their heads. I told Susie this morning that we would have to separate."

"Bob, let's walk down Tu Do, and we'll have a few drinks on me. I'm flush and we can talk."

"It's better than brooding here at the hotel. Let's hit it." One last binge for ol' time's sake.

George and I didn't stop raising hell until curfew. Then we caught a taxi back to the Tourist. He had a fifth of rot gut, and we drank until it was gone. He passed out on the bed, and I curled up in a corner. Just like old home week.

The next morning was the usual punishing hangover and grueling agony. We walked to the USO and managed to keep down tomato juice and toast. Then it was back to the booze. In the afternoon George picked up three fifths of whiskey at the army post exchange, and brought it back to the Tourist. We didn't stop to eat. I drank until my body refused anymore punishment. I vomited, and went to my room and slept.

This nightmare continued for a solid week. But it was finally time to face the inevitable. I went to George's room and he was still out cold.

I shook him gently. "Lachapelle, it's Bob. I'll go downstairs and get beer and tomato juice."

He opened his eyes slowly. "Oh my God, I'm dying."

"Stay here, and I'll be right back."

I returned with the necessary ingredients to start the long road to recovery. I plunked down two six packs of American beer and a gallon of tomato juice. "The time has come to face reality."

"Bob, don't fret, you'll be well healed in a couple of days."

"Thanks. I promised myself I would quit the booze."

"I know the feeling, Bob. I've got to get my butt to Alaska Barge's office this afternoon. I'm shipping out for someplace up north. I can make big money, and can't afford to screw up."

George loaned me two hundred. I'd see him when he returned from up river. We shook hands, and parted. I went back to my room with a six pack and started easing off the hangover. I didn't need the DTs.

The Tourist Hotel management was getting concerned about my bill. My excessive drinking made me a high risk, and they were aware of my financial status. I assured them not to worry. I'd always come through in the past.

The six pack of beer helped me to recover, and the USO's milk shakes and American food eased the pain. I'd survive.

The closest APO was in the PX not far from the Continental Hotel, so I purchased two hundred dollar money orders. Cheap Charlie at the Hotel got me one ninety five in MPCs, and I was swinging high.

Next stop was an APO on Tran hung Dao, and then it was to the Cholon PX. I changed at Johnnie's Bookstore, and walked to the Gala.

I had accumulated three hundred eighty MPCs, and still had two hundred in money orders. I ordered beer and took a table. Susie joined me, and without speaking I counted out two hundred MPCs.

"Bob, I hear you very sick from whiskey." She slapped me on the arm and laughed.

The Tourist Hotel manager smiled as I reeled off fifty MPCs for my room rent. Once again I was a guest in good standing. I went to my room and recounted my profits.

It was Saturday, and Sax and Lon would be home. I took a shower and changed clothes, and within minutes the taxi was speeding up Hai ba Trung Street. I paid the driver, and walked through the maze of buildings.

Lon opened the door, and yelled to Sax. "Bob come to see you."

"My friend, it's been a long time. Where the hell have you been?"

"It's a long story, Sax. I was laid up in the jungle outside of Thu Duc with hepatitis for over two months. Then George Lachapelle and I had a week long blast, I'm still shaky. Helluva party."

He got glasses, and poured whiskey-cokes. "I talked to Susie at the Gala, and RMK won't work with you on the release. I'm sorry. It doesn't look good for you. What about money, and your visa?"

"Lieutenant Bac at Vietnamese Immigration, an admirer of Susie's, is protecting me on the visa, and I'm changing money on the black market. It's risky as hell, but I have no alternative."

"Dammit, Bob, I knew when you moved to Thu Duc with Hutson, things would change for you. Those people aren't your type, and you've let yourself down."

Sax and I went to the International House for a good steak. The place was humming, and the noisy slot machines reminded me of Reno. Soon we were sipping whiskey-coke.

We sat at the bar, and talked about the war, and about America. We ordered t-bone steaks, and we gorged ourselves. Sax and I were friends, but we didn't have much in common anymore. Time had passed, and Susie and I weren't together, and I sensed a cool atmosphere.

A taxi dropped me off at the Tourist, and Sax went on his merry way. I had gotten myself into a dreadful predicament, and tough times lay ahead.

Chapter Nineteen

More bad tidings. My RMK identification card had expired, my total net worth was one hundred fifty MPCs, and my living costs would devour that in short order.

Susie could get me an apartment, but that was out of the question because I wasn't in a position to repay her, and I was losing the incentive to look for work.

I ran across Chuck Bruno, and surprisingly enough, we had lunch together. We passed the afternoon by talking about the war, and discussed my tour at Long Binh. I mentioned Bob Hyenberg and RMK-BRJ, but he immediately changed the subject. He had heard of my decision not to go to Tan My.

It was mid-September, and I longed to write my family, and explain the situation. I wasn't going to be employed by an American contractor, because of Hyenberg's refusal to cancel my contract, and my likelihood for hire with a private sales company was nil. I had no contacts with private business.

Most American companies in Vietnam had contracts with the United States Government. But there were a few American companies doing business in the private sector with Vietnamese citizens. Also, other counties did business in the private sector.

Clothing manufacturers were flourising in export, as were rice exporters. Vietnam was the third largest rice exporter in the world. But my expertise was in lumber manufacture, sales of building materials, and hardware merchandise. I could adjust to other types of sales, but what? Susie knew nothing about sales, and had no contacts with business people in these particular fields.

I had bypassed the Gala for two weeks, but yearned to see Susie. We still loved one another, but absence created a certain coolness. I wasn't employed, and it was embarrassing, and my drinking caused me to be irritable.

It was late afternoon when I walked through the door of the bar. I ordered cognac, and the bartender reluctantly placed it on the bar. Susie and the Saigon tea girls were happy to see me, and my friends still seemed to respect me. They were sorry about my predicament, and I hoped they didn't pity me.

Susie and I sat together. "Bob, please don't drink whiskey. You get sick, and you lose money. Listen to me."

"I'm all right. I wanted to see you and make sure everything is O.K." I was blunt, and I avoided looking at her. I called to the bartender. "Give me a double cognac." Susie moved to a table, and left me to my misery.

Every time I ordered another cognac the bartender cringed. I drank and drank until I achieved oblivion, and staggered from the bar. Susie followed me into the street. I turned and looked at her. I wanted to ask for her help.

I wandered from bar to bar. The hours passed, and Saigon tea girls asked for drinks, and I drunkenly obliged. The world whirled round and round, and I was falling into a black hole.

My eyes opened and followed the contours of the room. My room? I realized I was at the Tourist Hotel. Thank God. There was a six pack of American beer on the small table, and I slowly stumbled toward it. I popped a can and drank recklessly. It was warm and nauseating, and I lit a cigarette, sucked in smoke and drank. I opened another beer. I tried to recollect the night before, but to no avail. Where had I been?

I showered, and I drank another beer. I shaved and dressed. I found two quarts of Black Velvet in a sack by the bed with my pants crumpled on top, as if trying to conceal its presence. Someone must have given me the whiskey, but who? I was in a room filled with mysteries, like a James Bond movie.

I removed my billfold from my pant's pocket, and slowly spread it open like a poker hand. It was empty. I vaguely remember Saigon tea girls at a bar. I was broke. Oh Susie, why didn't I listen?

My Idaho First Bank account was closed, but I had my checkbook. Do I dare write a rubber check? Why not? This is war. I will find a job somewhere and pay back the money. My head was thumping, and I took a long blast of rot gut. I felt like I was losing my mind.

I continued to drink for four days. Thé booze was gone. I slowly sipped beer, hoping to delay the DTs. I managed to shower and dress. I didn't shave, hoping nobody would recognize the pitiful derelict I had become. Who really gave a damn about the sinful and the wicked? I laughed devilishly at myself.

I wanted to breathe clean air. I walked to the Gala Bar. It was early in the day, and it hadn't started filling with patrons. It was quiet. Susie took a stool at my side and squeezed my hand tightly. I knew she could feel my violent tremors. She had seen me drunk, and was aware of my obnoxious behavior. I weakly smiled and acknowledged her presence. "Bob, Honey, you O.K.? You no look good. Maybe you go see bac si."

I leaned close and whispered into her ear. "I've been better, and I need a beer. Will you loan me piasters?"

"Bob, I give you anything. I love you too much." She walked to the back room, and returned with money. Her small, dainty hand carefully tucked the roll of bills into my shirt pocket.

I dreaded the Dts, but I knew I had to face the inescapable. We silently sat together, and held hands tightly. The bar began to fill with patrons, and Susie excused herself.

My friend Sax approached through the darkness of the room, took my arm, and led me to a table. "Bob, you look like hell. How you making it?"

"Terrible, damn it. I've been drunk for at least two weeks. I'm going to blow up like a bomb."

"Shit, Patterson. Get your head out of your ass!" Sax frowned with concern.

My mind was wandering, and my eyes were seeing funny little people. "Sax, I've been to the States, and visited with my family. How about that?"

"You've been to the States, huh? And how did you get there and back to Saigon?"

"Hell, any damn fool knows that one. I flew on an RMK jet, just me alone with the pilot. Sax, it was beautiful. And I visited with my family."

"Bob, you're hallucinating. You need help. Look, I'm your friend, and I'll take you back to the Tourist. O.K.? You really should go to the States and seek medical help. You look malnourished. When did you last eat?"

I didn't hear my friend, and I didn't want to hear. I was trying to focus my eyes, and saliva was trickling down the corners of my mouth. I was trembling, and I couldn't hold the beer in my hand.

Sax called Susie to the table. "I'm taking Bob home. Don't worry about him." She wiped my mouth, and kissed my cheek.

"Thank you," she said, "you are good friend. Maybe tomorrow Bob sober up." She shook her head.

The taxi stopped at the Tourist, and Sax wished me good luck. He shoved fifty MPCs into my pocket, and laughed as the driver roared away. Sax knew I'd be all right. He'd had drinking problems of his own in days past, and was aware of the Dts, and the violent tremors, and hallucinations.

An alcoholic's pain and suffering is like a pregnant woman during child birth. She endures excruciating pain, but after the birth she doesn't remember the event. Therefore, she is prepared for another child birth in the furure. An alcoholic experiences the same thing, so is prepared for another drunk in the immediate future! It is a vicious cycle. Once the alcoholic takes the first drink, he becomes helpless over alcohol, and his life becomes unmanageable. He has to learn NOT to take the first drink to keep his sobriety.

I staggered in through the lobby and pushed the elevator button. I leaned against the wall. People were watching me, but I really didn't care.

I laid down on the bed. The room kept going around. The ceiling fan sounded like a C-130 cargo plane preparing for take-off. I closed my eyes, and I could see little people huddled in a corner. They pointed their fingers at me and giggled like small children. I opened my eyes; the room was spinning faster and faster, and the little people vanished. I closed my eyes, and the little people reappeared. It was for real, and it wouldn't stop. Darkness.

Morning came, and I dressed. I went to the dining room, and drank coffee and ate toast. Tonight my wife Georgina would be at the "I" House for dinner. I mustn't forget. I walked the five flights of stairs to my room, and I desperately longed for sobriety. I asked God for His help.

Later I stood on the balcony, and I saw my brother and my mother sitting in a limousine on the street below. I frantically yelled and waved, but they didn't see me. I ran down the stairway, and darted across the lobby into the entryway. I raced to the street, but it was too late. The limousine was gone. I thought they didn't want to see me, that my drunkenness would have embarrassed them.

I bought six beers from a vendor, and returned to my room. It was very strange. Why were my brother and mother in Saigon? Was I going insane? They didn't love me anymore. I lay back on the bed and closed my eyes. The little people appeared. They were pointing and giggling.

Later that night I showered and shaved, and dressed in a white shirt and tie, and put on my favorite blue suit. Georgina was to meet me for dinner, and I didn't want to be late. The desk clerk gawked as I stumbled past him, and walked to the curb.

I stopped a young Vietnamese riding a Honda, and asked if he would take me to the International House. He obliged and I got on the seat behind, and we hastily roared away in the darkness.

I gave the youth two hundred piasters, and strolled into the "I" House. I walked up the stairs to the formal dining room, and the hostess seated me at a small table. I ordered a whiskey-coke, and waited for Georgina...and waited...and waited. Finally, I ordered steak, and ate in solitude. I was lonely, and I was disappointed. Why hadn't

Georgina come to dine with me? It had been so long.

Back in the Tourist Hotel I sipped beer late into the night. I was scared. I was caught up in a dreadful dream. It was time to face reality, and decide my destiny. Had I been hallucinating? I couldn't tell what was real. I closed my eyes, and the little people were in the corner of the room, and they were giggling and they were staring. I wasn't afraid. They wouldn't harm me.

In the morning I opened a beer and gingerly sipped, and my hands slowly steadied. I walked to the USO. It was humming with activity, and the old bewhiskered Indian didn't ask for my ID. I had bacon and eggs and coffee. I was on the brink of saneness.

Later I strolled out into the bright sunlight, and walked down by the Saigon River. I went to a pharmacy and got librium. The drug would calm my stomach and shaking hands. I was thankful the Vietnam Government didn't control prescription drugs like the U.S. Government and the American Drug manufacturing companies.

My total finances mounted to exactly fifty MPCs, thanks to Sax's generosity. I decided to write a bogus check. Then I would find a job and pay it back. Susie and I would be together.

Two grimey Indian-born natives were running a black market operation not far from Johnnie's Book Store. They fronted their operation with a tailor shop, and it was obvious that making clothes was incidental compared to the money market. My conscience would be clean if I didn't repay the bastards. They'd ripped off a lot of American soldiers, and I'd teach them a lesson they'd never forget.

I browsed the shop for several minutes, and one of the Indians approached. He excitedly rubbed his hands together.

"May I help you, sir?"

"I need money. You can help me?"

"Oh yes, sir. Indeed I can help you."

"Can we be alone? I will write a personal check."

"We can go into my humble office. Please follow me."

The office was filthy, with papers and bolts of cloth strewn everywhere. He sat in a chair behind an ancient desk, and I sat on a wobbly stool facing him. I wanted to make the transaction and get the hell out of there. It was dark, and curfew wasn't far away.

"Sir, how much do you desire?"

"Three hundred MPCs will hold me for a few days."

He nodded his approval. We both knew my check would bring about three hundred dollars profit on the market. I removed my checkbook from my hip pocket, and hurriedly made it out for three hundred dollars.

Without hesitation the Indian's greasy hand peeled off the notes. He examined the check, and I quickly departed. Cold chills ran down my spine.

I had time for a couple drinks, so I turned into the nearest bar on Tu Do. I was drunk and it was dark by the time I walked up the street toward Hung thap Tu and home sweet home. With curfew only moments away I quickened my step, and I stumbled several times. My condition was obvious to anyone who was watching.

A hedge bordered the sidewalk on my left. It had bothered me in the past, because it seemed like an excellent hiding place for muggers. Aware of my vulneralitity, I picked up my pace, desperately peering into the darkness.

Suddenly, two strong hands clamped around my arm, and I was jerked through the thick shrubbery. Fists came from every direction. A heavy thud on the back of my head quickly ended the assault, and I was in my ever-famous never never land.

It was long after curfew when I dragged myself into the Tourist Hotel lobby. The desk clerk rushed over, and helped me to the elevator. He helped me to my room, and called to the house boy for assistance.

They helped me get my shirt off, and helped me into bed. The desk clerk used a cool washcloth to carefully removed the dirt and blood from my face and head, then he pulled the sheet over my body. The ceiling fan turned quietly, and the light clicked off. I fell asleep.

It wasn't really necessary to check my finances. My billfold was untouched, but my pockets had been picked clean of money. This had to be work of the Indians. Now what?

For two days I remained in my room, and had the house boy get food and beer for me. Since my hotel bill had been recently paid I had no trouble putting my expenses on a tab. I would see my Indian friends again.

The third morning I felt a little better, but I resembled a boxer who had managed to stay three rounds with the champ. I had cuts and bruises and a badly swollen black eye. I could hide some of the damage with dark glasses. The time had come to visit the tailor shop.

I entered the tailor shop, and Ol' Greasy, my favorite Indian, approached with his obnoxious and ever present smile. Rubbing his hands together he excitedly asked my favor.

"Oh, Mr. Patterson, you are back so soon? May I interest you in new suit this beautiful morning, or perhaps a professionally tailored sport coat with pleats and epaulets?"

"Let's go into your office and talk."

"As you command, sir."

Greasy sat behind the desk, and I perched on the rickety stool facing him. He was crouched, ready to spring to make another kill, and I detected pleasure on the disgusting man's face.

I purposely removed the dark glasses to reveal the beating I had received from his henchmen. "Mr. Patterson, you are badly beaten, and I am so sorry. What has happened to my friend?"

"I got beat up on my way to the Tourist Hotel after I left here. My money is gone. I need another three hundred."

"I am happy to help you again, sir."

This was absurd, but I had no alterative. My only satisfaction was my sure knowledge that the check would bounce straight in the air. I quickly wrote the check, and I handed it to the Indian.

He turned and reached into a small safe on the floor, and counted out three hundred MPC notes, and then quickly laid the money on the desk. I double checked the amount, and without speaking turned and left his filthy wallow. I felt the same chill I'd experienced before, and I shivered.

The USO was only five minutes away, and I quickened my steps. The Indians knew I was staying at the Tourist Hotel, and outsmarting the greasy bastards would be difficult. Paranoia took root in my mind.

The USO's chili dogs and milk shakes were out of this world. I spent a few hours talking to the American soldiers and just watching the young people playing cards, shooting pool, and writing home to the World.

After lunch I walked along the Saigon River, and thought about home and of Georgina and my kids. I wondered if I would find work. I was concerned about the Indians, and the rubber checks. My predicament was festering, and a band-aid remedy wouldn't heal my problems.

It was late afternoon, when I strolled down Ngo Duc Ke Street, and soon I was in sight of the Gala. I was reluctant to enter, but my desire to see Susie outweighed my reluctance.

Susie was happy to see me, and she beamed. "Bob, Honey, it is good to see you. You be O.K.?"

"I'm fine, Susie. I have trouble, but nothing to talk about." In the darkness of the room she couldn't make out the evidence of my encounter with the thugs.

The bartender served a whiskey-coke and a Saigon tea, and I grasped the glass. "Chin chin, Susie. I love you forever. Good luck to you."

"Chin chin to you, Bob. Good luck to you." She smiled, and laid her head on my shoulder.

It wasn't necessary to discuss my plight. We knew that our dreams were shattered. My mistakes had been costly, I was neglecting my family, and Susie and I had nothing left but sweet memories.

The Vietcong were relentless. Deadly enemy mortars exploded night after night in Saigon proper, and were causing many civilian casualties.

U.S. troops were becoming more and more demoralized. Some American leaders wanted to quietly bow out of a bad situation, and try to save face.

It was obvious it was a no-win war. The American soldiers were asking themselves, "Why fight and get killed or wounded in a war, which might soon be ended by withdrawal or peace? Who wants to be the last man killed in this fiasco?" In a combat situation, when a soldier's will to fight falters, his morale soon follows.

Vietnamese citizens frequently asked the same simple question. "What do America do? They stay Vietnam, or they go home?" It was embarrassing, and I couldn't look into their eyes and tell the truth. Were the Americans going to put their tails between their legs and run?

Susie and I sat close to each other, our thoughts focused on the happy times at our apartment on De Tram Street, and the good times in our villa at Thu Duc. I wouldn't continue to burden her with my problems. I only wished for her and her baby sans' happiness of a good life in their beloved land.

At dusk I bid Susie and the Gala farewell, and took a taxi to the Tourist. I didn't want to risk walking up Tu Do and Hung thap Tu Streets with three hundred MPC notes in my pocket. I would exercise extreme caution in the days to come.

I entered my room and quickly secured the door from the inside. The old style locking mechanism was in dire need of a replacement, but at least, it offered some protection.

The two house boys stationed at the end of the halls on each floor could be bribed to open the door for a paltry fee, and security wasn't their main objective. Prostitution was their more lucrative source of income.

Stress from the day's activities had taken its toll, and I was exhausted. I lay back on the bed, and labored to gather my wits. Sleep overtook my thoughts, and I completely relaxed for the first time in weeks.

I dreamed of my youth, and the happy days. I was in the mountains of Idaho, fishing my favorite stream, catching small brook trout, and cooking over the open campfire. I dreamed of my good days with Boise-Cascade Corporation and of my lovely family. The dream was interrupted by a heavy hand pushing down hard on my face, and cold steel pressed tightly against my throat.

A voice whispered to me in broken English. "Do not breathe, or I cut your throat." My eyes opened, and I saw the thin silhouette of a figure hastily searching through my pants, and then impatiently casting them aside. Two male voices spoke in French, then a hand raised my head, and another hand grasped the roll of bills from beneath the pillow. The knife remained at my throat, and I could taste blood from my lips. The hand crunched down again and again on my head, and I dared not move. The two figures quickly crept out of the room and vanished. I didn't try to follow. It would have been suicide.

I walked to the bathroom to tend my wounds. I was cut on the side of my face, and my nose was bleeding. I used a wet towel to stop the bleeding, and I went back to the bed. No need to look for my money. I knew everything was gone. I counted my blessings, and tomorrow was another day.

The Indians had played their hand. Wait until my rubber checks are returned. The bastards will go berserk. I was amused, but I was in deep, deep trouble again.

The next morning I borrowed twenty-five MPCs. I completely bypassed Tu Do Street, and went to a local restaurant off Hai ba Trung.

I had breakfast and coffee, and killed time by walking aimlessly about the crowded streets. Deep down inside my mind I couldn't accept the idea that I was ignoring reality again. Drinking only prolonged the agony that I couldn't find a job. Without a release on my contract from RMK-BRJ my situation was hopeless. If I was half way smart I'd try to find a way to go back to the World. That too, was a helluva challenge.

Late afternoon I went to the Gala, and took a stool at the far end of the bar. Susie casually strolled by and gently squeezed my arm. I ordered American beer, and slowly gazed around the room. I didn't have any enthusiasm, and I didn't give a particular damn. I left early in the evening, and took a taxi to the Tourist.

The next week I stayed close to the hotel, and passed time by reading and talking to other guests about the war. There was little else to discuss.

Newcomers staying at the Tourist complained about the loud and frightening noise of the incoming enemy mortars. We seasoned veterans usually slept through entire bombardments, and laughed when it was discussed by the wide-eyed neophytes.

The hotel manager was getting worried again about my room rent, but I always shrugged it off as incidental. So far it was working. I made the long walk to Vietnamese Immigration on Vo Tanh Street, and talked to Lieutenant Bac about my visa. He had no desire to trouble me.

Everything was on an even keel until my old friend Jack Hutson came to visit one Sunday afternoon. He brought along a couple fifths of my favorite whiskey, and we each took a bottle firmly by the neck and retired to the hotel patio. One of the house boys brought coke and ice and glasses, and we sat back to sip whiskey-coke and carry on casual conversation.

As the afternoon progressed, we became boisterous, and the hotel manager began to complain. We laughed it off, and apologized for our drunkenness.

I told Jack about my financial situation, and my growing hotel bill. "Hell, Bob ol' buddy, don't worry about a thing. Come out to Jack's villa at Thu Duc and spend a few days. We'll change money on the market, and settle up with the hotel. How does that sound ol' buddy?"

"It sounds like heaven, Jack. I'll run up stairs to my room, and throw a few things in my suitcase."

I dashed through the lobby to the elevator. In short order I returned to the patio carrying my suitcase. Hutson stood on wobbly legs, and sheepishly grinned. I grabbed his arm, and we made for the street where his Toyota was parked. I realized he was pretty drunk, and wondered aloud if I wanted to ride to Thu Duc through Route 1 traffic. He laughed it off. "Shit, don't worry about a thing."

The hotel manager ran up and took hold of my arm. "Mr. Patterson, sir, you are leaving, and you have not paid the room bill. You owe me two hundred thousand piasters."

"Papa san, don't worry. I'm going to stay with my friend for a few days, and I will be back to pay you."

"Please, Mr. Patterson. I want my money, and then you go to friend's house."

Jack fixed things good and proper. He pulled a short-barreled .38 derringer from his pocket, and held it to the manager's head. "Shut up you son-of-a-bitch or I'll blow your brains out. Do you understand English?" My heart sank. I didn't want to believe what my friend was doing.

American MPs screeched to a halt from one direction, and Vietnamese white mice approached from another. An American MP corporal confronted Jack and me.

The corporal shook his head. "We got a call that an American civilian was about to kill a Vietnamese civilian. Did I hear right? Fellahs, what seems to be the trouble?"

I was starting to explain when Jack sped away in his Toyota. "My God, there goes my alibi in that car!"

"Mister, you've got some explaining to do," the MP said, "and you better start now, and you better talk straight and fast! Understand?"

"Corporal, please believe me. I'm an American civilian staying here at the Tourist; my friend was visiting me from Thu Duc. We had a few drinks, and I was going to visit at his villa. The manager thought I was skipping out on my bill. Most of my clothes are still in my room."

The hotel manager stepped up within a foot of my nose. "This man lie. He leave, and no come back. He owe me money, and I want now."

"I don't have the money, but I can get it."

A Vietnamese police captain waded into the debate. "I will take this American to our precinct, and we will get the truth. This is not a matter for the U.S. Military Police. Is this understood?"

The American MP shrugged and looked me straight in the eye. "Mr. Patterson, I am sorry, but there's nothing I can do. This is within the jurisdiction of the Vietnamese Government. You must go with him."

"Look fellahs, if I go to a Vietnamese jail I'll never be found! I've heard there are over eighty precincts in Saigon alone. Please, you can't do this to me."

The two American MPs got in their jeep and left, and the four white mice and I got into another jeep. The vehicle raced toward an unknown destination. I had no idea whatsoever where they were taking me or what my fate would be.

The four policemen sat silently in a strict disciplined military manner, their shoulders back, chin in, garrison hat balanced squarely on the head with the brightly polished bill one inch above the eyes. The butts of American M-16 rifles were resting on the floor with the stock between their knees, and the barrel pointed skyward.

Wedged between my captors, it seemed an eternity before the jeep slid to a halt. I was half pushed, half dragged out of the vehicle, and two police walked in front and two behind. Their rifles were held at high port, ready to fire on command.

I was paraded into the precinct and ordered to sit at a desk at the rear of the room. I glanced around the large room. There were ten white-uniformed policemen sitting at desks with typewriters and telephones supplied for each individual.

The Tourist Hotel manager arrived in a private car. The captain and three police officers sat in desks on each side. At precisely the same moment and in unison each white mouse started tapping a pencil on top of his desk. Tap...tap...tap....

The hotel manager silently observed the action with interest. The tapping must have gone on for twenty minutes. I had to do something. I faced the captain in charge. "Sir, may I use your telephone?" His eyes never left mine, as he acknowledged with a slight nod.

I placed the telephone receiver to my ear. It rang and rang and rang. A small, soft, sweet oriental voice said, "Numba please. Numba please. Numba please."

"Hello, operator, operator."

"Sir, may I help you please? May I help you?", the polite, soft voice answered.

"Please get me the United States Embassy."

The voice hesitated and then answered. "Yes, sir. One moment please."

It was Sunday night, and I wondered if there would be an answer. The phone rang, and I waited. It rang again, and again, and I waited. Finally a deep male's voice boomed, "This is Sergeant Conroy, Sergeant of the guard, United States Embassy. May I help you."

"Sergeant, please listen closely. My name is Bob Patterson. I'm an American civilian, and I'm calling from a Saigon prison precinct. I am here for questioning about an incident at the Tourist Hotel I swear I am innocent. The number on this telephone is 128515. Sergeant, do you read me?"

"Sir, I read you loud and clear. Now listen. You need help. I'll call the officer of the day, and I'll get back to you in fifteen minutes. O.K.?" The phone clicked.

The Vietnamese captain had monitored the call, but remained

motionless, and was apparently unimpressed. He kept looking into my eyes, and his compatriots kept tapping their intimidating message. Tap...tap...tap....

I was gaining confidence, and I glared back at the officer. The sergeant at the Embassy would return my call, and I would get out of this mess. The pencil tapping stopped. Thank God.

I was sitting close to the rear door of the office and I could hear laughter. I turned, the door was partially open, and I could see round tables and beer bottles and people. I stood, turned my back on my captors, and slowly moved toward the door.

"Sir, you can not leave." the officer said, quietly.

"Captain, I'm going to the beer garden. Would you like a beer? I'll bring you one."

"I am on duty, and can't drink." He was surprised, he was caught completely off guard, and he was embarrassed.

Each of the policemen unholstered a 45 cal. revolver, but I didn't stop. I had to call their bluff. I had a weird sensation in my back, and envisioned a 45 slug slamming into me. Two of the police followed closely behind. We sat at a table and they smiled, approvingly.

I ordered a bomi bom beer, and drank it, and I ordered another. After finishing the second we walked back into the precinct office and waited. The telephone didn't ring. The officer and the hotel manager quietly talked in Vietnamese.

The manager rose, and advanced to the desk where I was sitting. "Mr. Patterson, I will not put you in prison if you promise to give money for your room."

"Yes, Sir, you have my word." I sighed deeply, and bowed to the captain and the other policemen. I slowly backed toward the front door, and gratefully stepped into the freedom of the cool night air.

It was after curfew, and there was no moon. It was pitch black. Where was I? And where in the hell was I going? Not a taxi in sight. I stood in the street and wondered what to do.

An off-duty policeman slowly approached on a motor bike, and I raise my hand. "How much to take me to Newport docks? I am going to Thu Duc."

"You go into Vietcong country. I take you to the docks, but no farther. I want five hundred piaster."

"Let's go, papa san. Here's your money." I didn't hesitate to straddle the back seat.

It was scary traveling on the back of a Honda after curfew in the darkness. This was no-man's land, and there were no rules. My Vietnamese driver and I would be easy targets. I could sense hostile eyes following our every move. The small Honda motorcycle hummed along the highway at forty miles an hour, and I thought we would surely become airborne.

The vehicle stopped at Newport, just short of the bridge spanning the Saigon River. I thanked my savior, and walked to an area where GI six by six trucks were moving slowly along in a convoy.

The last truck came in sight and I yelled up to the young driver. "Are you going up Route 1 toward Thu Duc?"

The driver hollered down to me. "Yes, Sir. Need a lift?"

"Yeah, can I come aboard?"

He stopped, and I ran around to the other side of the truck. A young man riding shot gun jumped out carrying an M-16, and I crawled in the middle.

The convoy gained speed as it maneuvered over the Newport Bridge, and we entered Vietcong country. The driver said they would be stopping at an army mess hall for chow if I cared to join them. I was hungry as hell, and didn't hesitate.

There were many GIs eating at the mess hall, but the room was surprisingly quiet. Each young American's thoughts were thousands of miles away, and they longed to be with their families. There was a warmth and togetherness among these young warriors. There was a feeling of patriotism, yet there was an undercurrent of resentment. They reminded me of cattle in a feed lot, waiting their turn to go to slaughter.

My two GI friends informed me their convoy was detouring around Thu Duc because of reports of enemy troop activity. It would be more practical for me to stay at the mess hall until daylight. I poured another cup of coffee and sat at a table occupied by several American MPs. I soberly stared across the room.

An MP colonel shook my arm. "Sir, the world isn't coming to an end. You're in deep thought."

"Colonel, I'm debating whether to journey to Thu Duc tonight, or wait for morning. It's damn important that I see a man. The bastard ran out on me today in Saigon, and I have some getting even to do."

"My sergeant and I are headed up Route 1 to Long Binh. We'll drop you off at Thu Duc junction, but you shouldn't be out there alone. That area is crawling with Vietcong. How about it?" The colonel waited.

"O.K. Sir, but don't drive onto the Thu Duc road. The VC will spot those eagles on your shoulders at five hundred yards, even in the dark."

The only sound was the jeep's engine, and the passing of an occasional army truck. The colonel, the sergeant and I peered into the darkness trying to detect anything that might move. The jeep pulled to the side of the road at the Thu Duc junction.

The colonel turned his head toward me. "Mr. Patterson, you don't have to walk into that nightmare. We'll take you on up the line to our outfit to spend the night."

"No sweat, Colonel. I've walked into the villa many times before in the dead of night, and I've still got my scalp."

"O.K., Patterson. You've either got guts or you're crazy." We shook hands, and my two compatriots wished me good luck.

The jeep vanished into the night, and I hesitated before starting into no-man's land. I took a deep breath and walked briskly, swinging my arms and taking long steps. Jungle birds broke the silence with chatter, but nothing moved. I had been blessed by the Buddha, and no harm could come to me. I still wore Susie's tiger claw around my neck.

I could see Jack's villa silhouetted against the skyline. I opened the gate, and quietly walked to the door, eased it open, and tiptoed toward his bedroom. Slowly I turned the door knob, groped along the wall with my hand, and switched on the light.

Jack and Yvonne sat up in bed like scared rabbits. Jack was surprised, and Yvonne was speechless. I laughed until tears ran down my face. Jack must have thought I was a raving maniac. This trip was worth a million bucks.

Jack broke the silence with his famous Texas drawl. "Patterson, how in the hell did you get here?"

"I hitchhiked all the way from a Vietnamese jail. You son-of-a-bitch, you owe me. You're going to pay the price. Remember the times Susie and I bailed you out of trouble?"

I stood over the bed looking down at him. I was furious, and my fists were clenched. I wanted him to give me one reason why he'd left me holding the bag. I slowly backed off, and waited for a response. His hands and his knees were shaking, and sweat was running off his face.

"Bob, I'm sorry. What do you want from me?"

"Jack, I want two hundred thousand piasters for the Tourist Hotel, and I need at least a hundred MPCs to see me through some rough times. Early tomorrow morning you and I are going to Saigon. Do I make myself clear?"

He stammered, and he was breathing hard. "S-Sure enough, Bob. We'll take care of it at first light."

"I need sleep. I'll take a couple winks on the couch."

Yvonne fixed breakfast, and we ate in silence. Afterward Jack and I went to his bedroom, and he grabbed a huge roll of bills from a small strong box. He counted out one hundred MPCs and handed them to me. Then he stuffed two hundred thousand piasters into his pocket. The Toyota Corona backed out the driveway, and we roared toward Saigon. Our eyes never met.

Chapter Twenty

The Toyota stopped at the curb, and I waited until Jack got out of the driver's side. Together we slowly walked up the steps and through the lobby of the Tourist Hotel.

The hotel manager greeted us, and shook my hand. It dumbfounded me how he could be so cordial after accusing me of trying to give him the shaft. "Mr. Patterson, I am very happy you are all right. It has been most unfortunate, and I am so sorry. Please forgive me."

Jack peeled off two hundred thousand piasters onto the counter, and the little man counted carefully. He turned, and disappeared into another room, and returned with a paid receipt. "Thank you, Mr. Patterson, and please honor me as a guest in our humble hotel. Your room and your personal belongings are in order."

I walked to the curb with Jack, and we stood silently trying to think of words. I extended my hand. "Jack, I'm sorry it caused bad relations. Time will heal."

Jack hesitantly clasped my hand and smiled weakly. "Bob, good luck, and no hard feelings." He promptly sped off in the Corona, and I turned back into the hotel, knowing that trust and friendship were gone forever.

I took the elevator to the fifth floor and walked to my room. It was spotless, just as the manager had stated. The two house boys were also courteous, and told me to call in case of need. Helluva change from days past. It does make a difference when the rent is paid.

October in Southeast Asia was totally different than the Northwest United States. Back home the trees and foliage were turning color, there was a coolness in the air, and the mountain tops sported a touch of white. Geese were flying south in their awesome "V" formation. Soon they would forage in winter paradise in Mexico and South America. Hunters were scouring the wilderness for big game, and high country dwellers were preparing their homes for deep snow and sub-zero temperatures. Fire wood was stacked in neat rows, ready to combat the wind and savage cold.

Vietnam was always the same, summer and winter, except for the rain. It was the dry season or the rainy season, and it was hot, and the humidity was ever present.

Yesterday's harrowing experience was still foremost in my mind, but at least, I was flush with a hundred MPCs in my pocket. I showered quickly, changed my clothes, and within minutes was strolling down Tu Do Street toward the Gala Bar. When I reached the Continental Hotel I detoured off the main drag, as I had no desire to come face to face with the two Indians who wanted my scalp.

By now the Idaho First National Bank had returned my checks for three hundred dollars each, and the Indians would be on the warpath. I'm sure they would overlook the fact that they replenished their coffers with their own money, and made a profit on the market with my personal checks. Of course, I broke even too, but I took the hard knocks.

The Gala bartender greeted me cordially, and placed a whiskey-coke on the bar. Susie was busy, but eased by my stool. "Hello, Bob. I must talk to you. You stay here, and I tell you something." I smiled, and took a big gulp of rot gut.

The man sitting next to me got my attention. "Is Susie a friend of yours?"

"Yeah, she and I are friends," I answered, casually. "I've known Susie for about a year and a half. Why?"

"My name is Bob Pearson, and I'm a civil servant for the U.S.

Taxpayer." He thrust a small, clammy hand in my direction.

"Bob Patterson," I muttered.

Pearson sighed deeply. "That Susie is the sweetest little bundle of joy in all of Saigon. I'd like to eat crackers in bed with her anytime."

He asked the bartender for two more drinks, and insisted on paying. I didn't argue under the circumstances. After several rounds we exchanged our life histories.

The fifty year old was a retired chief petty officer, and was double dipping by working for the government in civil service. He was ready to retire from his job and move to Florida. His financial entitlement was staggering, and I envied him for his success. Bob was no dummy, and we talked until the bar closed. He had covered most of the expenses, so I wasn't under financial pressure.

We were both three sheets to the wind, and feeling cheerful in general. I told Susie I'd see her early the next afternoon, and we could talk. I wanted her to come and spend the night, but first, I must find employment.

The following morning the Gala was quiet, but it was early, and the bartender was still preparing the necessities for the daily activities. He was cutting lemons and onions and whatever, and Susie was inspecting her Saigon tea girls. The little lovelies were an important part of Susie's business.

I ordered a beer, and when Susie finished her task with the girls, she casually slid onto a stool at my side. She took my hand, and looked up into my eyes for several moments.

"Bob, Honey, I hear about you write bad checks to Indians. If you no pay back they kill you. I mean for sure. Do you biet?"

"Susie, I understand. The Indians steal American GI's money, and they beat me up and steal from me. They can go to hell."

"Bob, remember you have no gun, and Indians have many friends, and I say they kill you. You must very soon leave Vietnam."

Bob Pearson took a stool next to me on the other side, and nodded. "Good morning, Bob and Susie."

We greeted our new acquaintance, and I ordered him a beer. Little Susie and I lowered our voices, and continued our serious conversation about my survival. My problems seemed to be an every day occurrence, and I was pushing my luck. This wasn't worth dying for.

"Susie, I don't have enough money to buy a plane ticket to America." I was noticeably uneasy. "If I had an ID card I could make eight hundred in one day, and be out of here. Don't worry. I'll be careful." I smiled and patted her knee.

"Honey, I am afraid for you. Please get money and go to America. If you don't go, you die for sure. I will miss you, but if you go to America, then I not worry about you." She smiled and excused herself. "I have work to do, and I must make money to care for my baby sans."

I thought about my baby sans back in the States. I rationalized about leaving the orient. Maybe I could better help my family in the good ol' U.S.A. I believed Susie about the Indians killing me. I was aware of their nasty and brutal tactics.

Pearson thanked me for the beer, and we sat silently and didn't share our private thoughts. My head was spinning with ideas, but nothing seemed to jell. I was between the devil and the deep blue sea.

"Bob, you and Susie are more than friends," Bob said. "I couldn't help but see your love for each other, and Susie's concern for you. Please don't hesitate to ask if I can possibly be of assistance."

"Thanks, Bob. But putting it bluntly, I don't have a job, I'm overstayed three months on my visa, I owe two Indians six hundred dollars in U.S. green, and Susie just told me the bastards are going to kill me. Other than that, I'm getting along just great." I managed a faint chuckle while Pearson's mouth dropped in complete surprise.

We drank several beers. Susie dropped by occasionally and stood close at my side. I knew she was concerned for my safety, and we both realized the risks. It was plain and simple, either leave Vietnam or die.

"Pearson, I'm hungry as hell. Let's go to the USO for a hamburger. I don't want to get drunk today." He agreed, and I told Susie I would come back again tomorrow morning. We would play gin rummy, and talk about our times together.

After lunch I left Bob, and walked to the Tourist Hotel. I avoided Tu Do Street, and my eyes were continuously searching every nook and cranny for Indians, and I was getting very paranoid.

I walked across the lobby of the hotel, and the manager confronted me about my ever increasing bill. I promised to get current within the week, and he agreed. He probably knew of the Indian's plot to end my career, and that's why he was anxious to be reimbursed. I didn't blame him.

It was best for me not to leave the hotel, so I passed the time drinking coffee in the hotel restaurant, and talking about the war with the PA&E employees who resided there.

The war was still raging at Long Binh, and Huey gunships were engaged in fighting much closer to Saigon. Artillery and mortar shells were more prevalent on the outskirts of the city. American GIs' morale was at a low ebb. They wondered what they were fighting for.

Susie was patiently waiting for my arrival at the Gala. It was early, and the bar wasn't open for business. We didn't talk, but it was evident my departure was near. We casually played gin rummy, and the time passed quickly.

Bob Pearson came into the bar in the early afternoon, and we took a table. Each ordered a beer, and watched the lovelies charm the patrons. It was a floor show. Saigon tea girls accounted for about half the bar's revenue. It was all part of the Saigon circus.

Pearson and I gulped several beers. He wanted me to see his apartment, and show me how government employees fared in Southeast Asia. I bid Susie a warm goodbye, and told her not to worry.

The taxi took Bob and me to an expensive apartment complex. I couldn't believe how well government people lived, all at the expense of the American taxpayer. I was really impressed. The maid was just finishing the daily cleaning and politely bowed out of the room.

Pearson went to the refrigerator and returned with two beers. He tuned the small radio to a Vietnamese station of exotic music, and we settled back into comfortable chairs in the living room.

"Bob, I've been thinking how to help you get out of your dilemma. Are you interested?"

"Yes, I'm interested. I've racked my brain for a solution, but I'm a complete blank."

"Here's my plan. I told you I was going back to the States this week. My passport is in order, my shot record is current, I have a plane ticket and confirmed reservations. I'll be on a flight in two days. O.K so far, Bob?"

"Yeah, but what's this got to do with me? It's your ticket home."

"Now hear this, as we say in the Navy. We look enough alike to be brothers, and our physical stats are identical. I won't need my U.S. Government ID card, but I'm not giving it to you. I'm going to place it on the bookcase in the corner, and I'm going to leave the room for a couple minutes. When I return it will probably be gone."

"I copy O.K. I'll try not to stumble on my way to the bookcase." We both laughed, and Pearson conducted his disappearing act.

He was gone for a short time, and then entered the room. "Bob, do you suddenly see a brighter future ahead?"

"Amen, I don't know what to say."

"Bob, can you find a couple hundred MPCs to get you started on the black market?"

"No problem. Susie will help me, and I can reimburse her. I'll repay the Tourist within a couple days, and believe me Bob, I am forever grateful."

We shook hands, and raised our beer for a toast. "Chin Chin, Bob. Good luck"

"Chin Chin Bob, and good luck to you. Maybe someday we'll meet again." I walked the mile to the Tourist Hotel, and went to my room. Tomorrow will be a brighter day.

I donned my favorite disguise, a hard hat and dark glasses, and slowly walked toward the USO. A hearty breakfast was in order, and then off to a hard day working the black market.

I walked into the Gala and took a table. "Good morning to you Bob," Susie said. "You look happy today, and why are you happy?"

I moved close to her. "Susie, the man I drank with last two days is going to America. He gave me ID card to get money orders, and I can get plane ticket, and I will leave Vietnam."

"Bob, I am happy. Wait here, and I come back.

She returned and snuggled close. "Here is two hundred MPCs for you to change. You pay me later."

"Thanks, Susie. I will pay you tomorrow. I must go now." I brushed her cheek with my lips.

I quickly walked to the APO just off Tu Do Street, and bought money orders. Then I went directly to Cheap Charlie at the Continental Hotel. The money orders brought one hundred-ninety on the market. Then I rushed to an APO on Tran hung Dao, and then to the Cholon PX. By late afternoon I had accumulated a thousand dollars profit. I felt like John D. Rockefeller. I was wheeling and dealing. Who said there's no such thing as a fast buck?

I didn't stop at any of my favorite bars along the way to the Tourist Hotel. I stopped at the French restaurant for Chinese soup, and went directly to my room. I shoved the roll of MPCs into my shaving kit, and settled in for the night. I wasn't about to screw up, and lose my hard earned loot.

After completing my morning ritual I had breakfast at the hotel, and returned to my room. I wanted to pay Susie first, and then I would check out plane fare and reservations for my journey. I put my money in three different pockets, and my passport and shot immunization record in the other shirt pocket. I might need the documents at CAT Travel Agency.

I took every imaginable detour to avoid my Indian friends, but I doubted if they would attack in broad daylight. I walked briskly, and stayed fully alert. It was a beautiful morning, and a soft cool breeze was blowing into my face. I thought a change of luck was imminent.

I walked straight to a back table at the Gala, and presently Susie sat at my side. I placed two hundred fifty MPCs into the palm of her small hand. "Thank you for love and kindness. You keep the extra fifty, and I owe you more than money could ever buy." I kissed her on the cheek.

"Bob, please, you be careful. Indians everywhere in Saigon. Do not walk alone, and you take taxi." She went behind the bar to wait on customers, and I waved as I left the bar.

CAT Travel Agency was only a short distance from the Gala, and it wasn't long before I was talking to my friend Annie about reservations. She was a lovely lady and very accommodating. "Bob, long time no see. How can I help you?"

"Annie, I need price on a one-way ticket to Boise, Idaho, U.S.A., and time schedule."

She thumbed through a huge catalog. "Your one-way ticket will be five hundred-fifty MPCs, and I need one day's notice for reservation. Pan American has several daily flights. You are not coming back to Vietnam?"

"Annie, I would like to stay in Vietnam, but I must leave for personal reasons. I love the Vietnamese people, and you have been very kind to me."

Annie asked the same simple question I'd been asked again and again. "What do America do? They promise to stay in Vietnam, but I think they go home. The communists will kill us, and the Russians will come. Bob, you are friend. What you say?"

"Annie, I honestly don't have the answer. The Vietcong will probably win the war, and the Americans will leave. I am sorry, and I wish I could tell you something." I sadly shook my head.

It was mid-afternoon, and I wanted a stiff belt of whiskey. It was so hard to look these people in the eye, and tell them the Americans would leave them high and dry. It's not the fault of the American soldiers. They are brave men and they are patriots. The American industrialists and the crooked politicians were the culprits. At times it was hard to admit I was an American, although I loved my country and respected my flag.

I longed for a drink. Minh's Bar was on Tu Do Street, and it was located near the Saigon River. The street was not heavily traveled, and it was secluded and safe. I didn't have to worry about getting my throat cut, and I would upset Susie if I went to the Gala and drank hard liquor.

I walked through the door of the bar. "Hello, Minh. Give me whiskey-coke."

"One whiskey-coke for my friend. Bob, how you been?"

"Everything O.K. I think maybe I go back to America. RMK refuses to give me a release on my contract, so I don't really have a choice. I will leave in a few days, and I wanted to see you."

"Bob, it is nice of you. We have drink together for old times at Minh's Bar."

We touched glassed. "Chin Chin, Minh. Good luck to you."

"Chin Chin, Bob. Good luck to you."

We dispensed with the formalities, and got down to some serious drinking. Minh wouldn't allow me to buy drinks, and I had ample whiskey-cokes stacked up on the bar. We laughed, and talked about Jack and his escapade last Christmas. It was down the hatch, and away we go. I could lick the whole damn world.

It was dusk, and Minh was worried about my safety. Drunk Americans were easy prey. "Bob, I send for taxi, and you go home. Curfew come soon."

"Minh, it has been great fun, and you are good friend. I will miss you." I stumbled as she helped me into the taxi.

"Driver, go Tourist Hotel, Hung thap Tu. De de mau! And away we go!" I was at thirty thousand and climbing.

It was almost dark, and the taxi chugged up Tu Do. I was lonely. I missed Susie and the villa at Thu Duc, and I missed Long Binh, and I missed Sax and Lon, and I missed the warm, white sandy beaches of Da Nang. Tomorrow I must make plans to leave.

The taxi driver went whizzing past Hung thap Tu, and in my drunkenness I yelled, "Papa san, you son-of-a-bitch! Go back to Tourist. You dinky Dao!" He kept going. I reached over the front seat, and with both hands I grabbed the bastard by the throat. "I said Hung thap Tu—Tourist Hotel. De de mau! De de mau! You Vietcong bastard. I'm not as drunk as you think, you thieving SOB!" He abruptly turned the small vehicle around in the street, and stopped fifty yards from the hotel entrance.

I climbed out on wobbly legs, and threw three hundred piasters in the front seat of the taxi. "You son-of-a-bitch. Three hundred's all you get, and that's too damn much. You should be shot." I turned, and walked toward the Tourist. I was mad and I was drunk. The taxi driver sat motionless in the front seat.

I hadn't gone twenty steps, when the taxi door slammed, and I turned. The driver was bearing down fast with a tire iron held above his head, and I saw murder in hateful eyes.

My reflexes were slow, but I raised my left arm to cushion a hefty blow from the weapon. Blood spurted from a large gash, and it flowed down my arm and hand. I caught his arm, and tried to wrestle away the iron, but he twisted free. I hit him in the vitals, and he flinched.

I hit him in the face, and my ring crumpled on my finger. I hit him again with all my strength.

I sank to my knees from a blow to the head. My adversary grunted as he dealt me a near fatal blow to the back of the neck. My face crunched as it slapped the concrete sidewalk. The world went black. Oh, my God!

Bright lights made it difficult for me to make out the form looking down at me. The staff sergeant's voice softly explained, "Sir, you're going to be all right. You're in the emergency room at the U.S. Army 17th Field Hospital on Tran hung Dao. Do you hear me? Can you see?"

My eyes blinked repeatedly, and I was having trouble focusing, and my head throbbed. "What the hell happened. Did I win the battle, or did I lose the war?" The bright lights were turned down, and I could see the doctor and the staff sergeant.

The doctor explained. "Sir, witnesses said a taxi driver beat the hell out of you with a tire iron, but he managed to get away. We've stitched up the back of your head and neck and a nasty gash on your left forearm. You're a very lucky man. You'll be all right in a few days."

"Thanks, Doc," I sighed, deeply. "I appreciate you." I was suddenly sick, sober and sorry.

"Sir," the doctor asked, "may I get your name for the record. You didn't have anything in your pockets except a handkerchief."

"My name is Bob Patterson, and evidently the driver stripped me of eight hundred MPCs and my passport. Helluva deal. Don't you think, Doc?"

"It happens every day to the GIs. You civilians are usually pretty lucky. Maybe you live a mite too recklessly." He smiled, politely.

I slowly pulled myself into a sitting position and moved my neck. My arms and legs seemed to function. My head ached and my neck was sore as hell, but I was alive.

"I'm O.K., Doc. What day is it?"

"Well Bob, it's October 25. Does that make sense to you."

"Sure as hell does make sense. Is there someone that will take me to the Tourist Hotel on Hung thap Tu?"

The staff sergeant volunteered his services, and helped me to my feet. "Come along slowly Mr. Patterson, and we'll walk out to my jeep."

I slowly walked through the hotel lobby, past a wide-eyed hotel manager, and pushed the elevator door back. I unlocked the door to my room, and immediately eased my body onto the bed. I slept the clock around.

My entire body ached, but I managed to sit, and then I stood on shaky legs. The shower felt wonderful, and I let the warm water flow over my head and down my scarred and broken torso. My mind flashed back to the 93rd Evac Hospital at Long Binh, and the agonizing pain caused by the jeep accident. My body shuddered.

I sat on the bed's edge and thought of my devastating predicament. No passport and no money. This meant I had no identification, and I couldn't even prove my nationality. There was but one alternative. Call my brother back in the States. Oh my God! What a horrible thought.

It was 0930 hours when I entered the USO, and I suddenly realized I had no money whatsoever. The good ol' USO didn't charge for coffee and cookies, and I was famished. I ate cookies feverishly, and ignored several GIs gawking at me.

I walked to the second floor of the USO, and asked an American hostess how to make a collect call to the States. She handed me a form to fill out and pointed to a basket marked "collect calls". I was advised it would take approximately four hours to complete the call.

The form was simple enough. Herman Patterson, LaGrande, Oregon. Street address unknown, telephone number unknown. The hostess said not to worry, that the information was readily available, and she advised to me to be patient.

I read magazines for awhile, then I excused myself, and went to the cafeteria for more coffee and cookies. Living on coffee and cookies at an American USO in Southeast Asia. That would undoubtedly qualify for a place in The Guinness Book of World Records.

The operator finally announced my name over the intercom. "Mr. Patterson, please enter telephone booth number nine. Your party is on the line."

"Hello, Herman," I bellowed, "is that you?"

A disgusted and unbelieving voice answered. "Yes. Bob, what the hell you want this time of day?"

"What time is it in America?"

"Dammit, it's two o'clock in the morning. Where are you?"

"Hell, Herman, I'm in Saigon, Vietnam. And I need some help damn fast."

"Well, Bob, tell me what it is, and let's get off the damn phone. It's going to cost me a fortune."

"Herman, this is serious. I got mugged, and lost my life savings and my passport. Other than that, everything's just fine. Do you hear me?"

"Bob, let me think, and that isn't easy at this hour." He sighed deeply. "Call me back tomorrow at this same ungodly hour, and I'll try to have some answers."

"O.K. Herm, I'll do what you say. But don't let me down. Good night." I hung up the receiver and left the USO.

I walked the back streets to the Tourist, and settled in for a long wait. The restaurant manager brought me coffee, and I told her she'd have to wait for money. She shrugged and walked into the kitchen. I made it a point not to disturb the hotel manager, as he might decide to send me to prison for ignoring my delinquent bill. Paranoia had become my middle name.

The next day at precisely 1200 hours I made out another application for a collect phone call to America, and patiently waited my turn. The anxiety was building, but so far so good. Not much more could happen to ol' Bob. Think positive.

I dreaded leaving Vietnam, and I hadn't fulfilled my mission to help my Vietnamese friends. But at least, I'd gotten better working conditions for the local and third nationals at Long Binh. I would miss Susie painfully, but I would cherish our memorable times together.

It had been three hours, and the hostess called my name. I quickly entered the phone booth. "Hello, Herman, this is Bob. Can you hear me?"

"Yeah, Bob, I hear you loud and clear. Dammit, now listen to me."

"I'm listening, Herman. How does it look?"

"Bob, I talked to the U.S. State Department, and on November

2nd you have an appointment with Mr. Paul B. McCarty, the Consul General at the U.S. Consulate. Do you follow me?"

"Yes, Herman. Please go on."

"Now listen, Bob. McCarty will issue you a new passport, and I've instructed the State Department to give you two thousand dollars. I am including a one-way Pan American plane ticket that will be waiting for you at the Consulate. Just be patient and hold on."

"Thanks, Herman. I copy your message, and I'll be back in the World in short order. Thanks again. Give my best to your family. Goodbye."

It would be three days before I can see McCarty, and get my passport. I can hold on, and for now I'll have a delicious breakfast of cookies and coffee. I didn't want to think about ham and eggs.

If I get two thousand dollars from the State Department I doubt if good ol' Bob will return to America. I made a fiendish cackle and rubbed my hands together.

Most of the next three days I spent at the Gala Bar, playing gin rummy with Susie or one of the Saigon tea girls. I never mentioned being mugged and losing my money and passport. I had caused enough anguish, and it was time to straighten out my life.

Henry Johnson, my black friend with Page Communication, came to the bar and I had a couple of beers with him. I privately explained about my misfortune, and that I was waiting to see the U.S. Consul.

I asked Henry if he would take me to Bo Priest's villa at Thu Duc. I wanted to see Priest, and give my best to him and Mop. My friend didn't hesitate, and within minutes we were traveling in a taxi toward Thu Duc.

When we arrived at our destination Henry told the driver to wait. Mop answered the door, and a huge smile crossed her face. "Bo, va day! Bob come."

We waited, but Priest didn't come to the door. Mop waved to us to enter. Bo was propped up in bed with pillows to his back, and clad only in a pair of shorts. He was skin and bones, and his thin face exposed cheek bones and hollow eyes. His small, thin legs were dwarfed by huge knee joints, and the knuckles in his toes were swollen twice their normal size. The man was literally dying from malnutrition, and God only knows from what else.

Bo managed a smile through snaggled teeth, and Henry and I tried to hide our shock. "Bo, Henry and I just dropped by to say goodbye, and I'm leaving for America in a few days. Is there anything we can get for you?"

"Yeah, Bob, go find a vendor and get me some bomi bom beer. I would sure as hell drink a beer with you."

"It is done." Henry gave me piasters, and I left to find the beer. I couldn't believe my eyes. I returned with several beers. They would probably be his last.

I took Bo's frail hand into mine. "Hang in there, my friend. Thanks for your everlasting friendship." Henry and I returned to Saigon in silence.

The next morning I walked to the U.S. Consulate on Thong Nhut Boulevard and confronted the Consul's secretary. "My name is Bob Patterson, and I have an appointment with Mr. McCarty."

"Mr. Patterson, come with me please. Mr. McCarty wait for you."

The Consul General stood, and shook my hand. He looked at me rather skeptically, and I really couldn't blame him. Henry and I had closed up the Gala, and my skimpy diet had left me with a rather pitiful, haggard appearance. He asked me to take a seat.

"Patterson, I'm a busy man, so I will make this short. Fill out this form, and briefly explain how you lost your passport."

I explained how the taxi driver had attacked me, and relieved me of my passport and life savings. McCarty scanned the paper, and reached into a drawer of the luxurious walnut desk. He examined a passport, and told me to fill it out with my name, birth date, and all the other essential information. He scribbled his signature, and ordered me to sign. My hand was shaking terribly, but I managed to scrawl my name on the designated line. I smiled, and he shook his head in disgust.

"Patterson, you owe the U.S. Government twelve MPCs for the passport, and the Consulate will need two pictures before I can release it to you. I am also holding a one-way plane ticket. I'll date the passport when it's presented to you." He had me in a very difficult situation.

"I haven't got five dong, Mr. McCarty! That taxi driver took every damn cent I had. My brother told me the U.S. State Department was instructed to give me two thousand dollars. Where in the hell is it?"

"Simmer down, Patterson. Remember you're the one in trouble. I've heard nothing about giving you money."

"I'll be back with the twelve MPCs, McCarty." I dejectedly went back to the hotel.

Later in the day I took my detoured route off Tu Do to the USO and had cookies and coffee, and passed the day reading a well-worn Reader's Digest. I returned to the Tourist before dark, and the restaurant manager gave me food. I thanked her, and immediately went to my room.

Two days later I ran across Chuck Bruno and he offered to buy lunch. We walked to the USO. My old bewhiskered Indian friend asked Bruno for his ID card, and we walked through the door. I ordered two chili dogs and a double vanilla milk shake. Bruno slowly ate a hamburger, and then sat back in his chair and twisted his mustache, quite amused as I devoured my food.

"Bob, what have you been up to? The CIA's been to Long Binh inquiring about your whereabouts. Charlie and I didn't say anything, but we were curious."

"Chuck, it's probably about my expired visa or maybe the State Department is trying to verify that I had my passport stolen. Believe me, it's been one helluva mess. I'll be leaving Vietnam in a few days." Bruno shoved twenty MPCs into my shirt pocket, and quickly left before I could thank him. Maybe this guy was all right.

My thoughts centered on getting money for my passport, and I refused to ask Susie. No way. I slowly walked in the hot sun to the hotel thirty minutes away. I must figure a way to get out of this nightmare. Suddenly a hand grabbed my arm and spun me around. "You Bob Patterson?"

I pulled away. "Yeah, I'm Patterson. What's your problem?"

"I'm Jacobs, Criminal Investigation Division, United States Army." He flashed credentials.

The CID agent stood in my path. "Patterson, I've been watching you, and it's my understanding you don't have a visa, and you're overstayed in the country. Is that right?"

"Hell yes it's right, but what business is it of yours? You're not my keeper."

He moved close into my face. "Patterson, either get your passport straightened out or the CID will arrest you. Do you read me?"

"I read you, and now you hear this. You didn't pay my way to Vietnam, the U.S. Government didn't pay my way, nor did any U.S. company pay my way to Vietnam. I paid my way to this country, and if anybody asks me to leave, it'll be Vietnamese Immigration. Go get fucked, and leave me alone." He turned and left without a word.

I woke in the night; sweat drenched my body. My nerves were unraveling; my hands trembled and my legs were weak. My belly ached, and I was hallucinating. The strange little people kept appearing when I closed my eyes, and I had nightmares about Indians taking my scalp.

It was November 17th, and I still hadn't gotten my passport. When I managed to get money I spent it on food and booze. I went to the Gala and visited with Susie.

"Bob, you let me help you," she said. "You are sick, and the Indians will come for you. They very mad. Please. I help you?"

"Susie, we've been through this time and time again, and the answer is no. I want to leave Saigon with you loving me, and not hating me. I am sorry, but I must go to my room." She was crying when I left the bar, and I was miserable.

I laid on the bed and stared at the ceiling fan going around and around, and I closed my eyes, and I saw the friendly little people, and they were pointing at me and giggling. I heard somebody laughing crazily. I laboriously opened my eyes, and a face was peering down at me, and only inches away. I frantically leaped out of bed, and fell hard to the floor. The hideous laugh caused chills to run down my spine, and I slowly raised my head to face my end. Another nightmare? A deep voice boomed. "Bob! Dammit! Wake up!"

My heart was thumping in my chest, and I couldn't believe it. I stuttered, "C-C-Chuck? Chuck Alexander? Is that you?"

"Hell yes it's me. What did you think I was, a ghost?" I joined his laughter, and I became hysterical, and I wept.

I wiped my eyes. "Where you been, Chuck? I haven't seen you for six months."

"My job takes me all over Southeast Asia. I'm with CID, Army Intelligence. You look terrible. What's happened to you?"

"Ah shit, Chuck. RMK wouldn't give me a release on my contract, so I can't get any work. I went on a running drunk, and a taxi driver relieved me of my life savings and my passport. I wrote two hot checks to a couple of greasy Indians, and they're hell bent to kill me. I owe the Tourist Hotel sixty thousand piasters in back rent. The U.S. Consul is holding a plane ticket and my passport, and I haven't got twelve MPCs to get them. Can you top that?" I sat on the floor and shook my head, and my crazy friend damn near laughed himself into a frenzy.

"Bob, tomorrow we'll get you straightened out at the Consulate, but right now we're going to eat. I'm going to buy you the biggest steak the International House has to offer, and then we'll go to the Gala Bar and see Susie. How's that sound, my friend? And don't worry about the Indians. This .45 Army Colt will change their lives." My friend helped me to my feet, and pushed me into the shower.

I shaved, put on clean clothes, and we took the elevator to the lobby. He took my arm, and we walked into the hotel manager's office. He paid my debt, that totaled sixty five thousand piasters.

After a much needed meal at the "I" House, Chuck and I strolled into the Gala. Susie came running over. "How are you, Chuck. I happy to see you. You put Bob under your wing, and take care!"

We took a table and the waitress brought whiskey-cokes, and we settled in for a relaxing evening. I was ecstatic, and I wasn't afraid, and I had a friend, and I loved Susie. It was great to be alive.

Chuck gave me money, and I got a room at the Royal Hotel. Susie and I stayed together, wished that someday the war would end, and we could find happiness. It was a memorable night, and I could never repay this sweet, brave, and lovely little bundle of love. She would remain in my heart forever.

I met Chuck at the USO the following morning, and we had breakfast. I had two photos made, and we went together to the U.S. Consulate.

The receptionist told the Consul General on the intercom that I was in the waiting room. Presently McCarty appeared with a politician's smile plastered on his face. We walked into his office, and he beckoned us to sit.

"Mr. Patterson, I see you have finally decided to retrieve your passport."

He rummaged through a stack of documents, and presently picked out my passport. I handed him the two photos and twelve MPCs. He stamped the book, and handed it to me. I thumbed through the pages, and shook my head. It indicated the issue date November 18, 1968. It was the right date, but he'd included limitations that weren't to my liking.

On page five it stated: "Extensions, amendments, limitations. Embassy of the United States of American at Saigon, Vietnam. LIMITATIONS: This passport expires March 17, 1969, and shall not be extended without the express authorization of the Department of State. Signed, Paul B. McCarty, Consul of the United States of America".

"Mr. McCarty, you only gave me a four month's extension on my passport. I may decide to go to another country other than America, and this limitation could cause me difficulty. I demand a full five year extension. Isn't that legal?"

McCarty stammered, "Y-Yes, Mr Patterson."

"Dammit, McCarty, then stamp it right, and I'll be on my way. Someday I'll find out what happened to the two thousand bucks I was to receive from the State Department."

I was hostile, and Alexander casually flashed his credentials. Why was the U.S. Government always interfering with my private life? They had no jurisdiction over me.

The passport was restamped: "Embassy of the United States of America at Saigon, Vietnam. Extended Nov. 18, 1968 — Expires Nov. 17, 1973. Signed, Paul B. McCarty, Consul of the United States of America".

The Consul General gave me the one-way plane ticket to Boise, Idaho. My brother Herman had written *non-negotiable* across the face. "Chuck, I don't think Brother Herman trusts me."

We departed the Consulate, and got a taxi for the trip to CAT Travel Agency. I waited for Annie to free herself with a customer, and I asked for reservations to Boise, Idaho, U.S.A.

After a lengthy conversation on the teletype Annie returned to the counter with the conformation. "Mr. Patterson, you are on Pan American's flight 808, departing Saigon at 1400 hours, November 23rd. Good luck to you."

Chuck had several day's leave, so we spent time wandering from bar to bar, and eating exotic foods. My capacity for alcohol had reached its limit, and I really didn't enjoy myself.

My departure day arrived, and the moment I most dreaded. I told Chuck I wanted to be alone with Susie, and he understood. I took a taxi to the Gala, and slowly opened the door. Susie was waiting for my arrival, and motioned for me to follow.

We took a table at the rear of the bar, and I held her hands tightly in mine. Tears swelled in our eyes, and I was trying so hard to be casual.

We expressed our undying love for one another. It would last forever. I was regretful of my mistakes and misfortunes, but I was satisfied with our relationship.

"Susie, I love you, and I will think of you every day."

"Bob, I love you, and I wish you good luck from the bottom of my heart." She hesitated. "Bob, every day tell America about South Vietnam. Tell your people that Vietnamese are human beings same same Americans. Tell them to stop killing Vietnamese mama sans and baby sans and old papa sans. Tell them to stop burning our villages, and destroying our rice paddies with the wicked orange cloud. Please tell America we need their help. Your President promise he would help Vietnam, not kill our people. We want to be free country."

I held her tight, and sighed deeply. "I promise, and I will pray for you and your baby sans." I kissed Susie, and we reluctantly walked toward the exit. I opened the door, and hesitated. Our eyes met for the last time, and then she disappeared into the darkness of the bar. I walked out into the street.

A taxi pulled to the curb, and I paid the driver. Chuck was waiting for me in the hotel lobby and I looked at my watch. "We've got plenty of time. I'll pack my things."

I showered, and packed my personal effects. I put on my blue suit, and slipped on my dress shoes. I was dressed exactly the same as when I entered the country. My appearance had been altered somewhat. I had lost considerable weight, and added scars to my face made me look older.

I picked up the suitcase, and we took the elevator to the lobby of the hotel. The desk clerk waved goodbye.

I gritted my teeth as the taxi sped towards Tan Son Nhut International Airport. It was a most difficult departure from a city I had learned to love.

I went through Vietnamese customs, and declared twelve MPCs for eleven dollars in U.S. greenbacks. No more military script, piasters or black market.

Chuck and I exchanged farewells, and he melted into the crowd. I walked into the airport bar and ordered an American beer.

I hadn't noticed the man sitting on the next stool. We glanced at each other, and I blurted out, "My God, Bernie Gough."

"My God, Bob Patterson. Two Boiseans meet again. Where you headed, Bob?"

"I'm headed back to the States, reluctantly that is."

"I'm headed back too. What flight you on?"

"I'm on Pan Am's flight 808 to Boise, via San Francisco. How about you?"

"I'm on Thai Airlines going to Bangkok. It's a detour." He chuckled. "Change your ticket, and come with me."

"I'd like to, Bernie. But financially I'm in terrible shape. Thanks."

"Don't worry, I'm flush, and you can pay me back when you get on your feet. Bob, come on."

"Damn, I need a break. O.K. you're on. Let's exchange this damn ticket."

It was November 23, 1968, and the Thai Airline Boeing 707 roared down the runway, and lifted off into the sky blue yonder. I had an overwhelming feeling of relief. The aircraft banked sharply to the right, as if the pilot knew I wanted one last look at that doomed city. I had a full view of Saigon. I visualized Susie tending to her Saigon tea girls, and managing her bar. I whispered, "Farewell Sweet Susie." It had been an unforgettable experience, and I would remember Saigon and Susie forever.

Bernie and I spent nine days in Bangkok before we left for America. When the United Airline 727 touched down at the Boise Airport we looked at each other.

"Bernie, there isn't any sense talking about Vietnam—nobody's going to believe us. Why were we there—and what was gained?"

There are two winners and two losers in the Vietnam war. The two winners are the North Vietnamese communists, and greedy American corporations and crooked politicians who reaped enormous profits.

The losers are the seventeen million South Vietnamese people that lost their freedom to communism and faced extreme poverty, and the fifty-eight thousand young American soldiers who gave their lives in vain. There are three million North Vietnamese soldiers and civilians not accounted for, and still missing.

This war was "The Great American Fiasco" that the people of this nation should never be privileged to forget.

Is it possible the United States is not a democracy? It is probably the most sophisticated oligarchy in history; it is flexible and well designed. A government in which the power is vested in a few. A government by which a small group exercises control, especially for corrupt and selfish purposes.

The End

While They Died

List of U.S. Contractors Operating in Vietnam for the United States Government

1. Adrian Wilson & Association (OICC)
   65 Bis Mac Dinh Chi, Saigon

2. Air America Inc. (USAID)
   P.O. Box 1248, Saigon

3. Airlift International Inc. (USAF)
   P.O. Box 10816
   APO 96307

4. Aju Construction Co., Ltd. (OICC)
   314/4 Phan Thanh Gian, Saigon

5. Alaska Barge & Transport Inc. (USNAVY)
   24-A Chi Lang, Gia Dinh

6. Allied Advance Corp. (USARMY)
   110 Cao Thang, Da Nang

7. American Express International Banking Corp.
   (USARMY)
   APO 96291

8. A & M Enterprises, Inc. (USAID)
   511 Bis Vo Nguy, Phu Nhuan

9. American Vietnamese Architects & Engineers
   (OICC)
   40 Hong Thap Tu, Saigon

10. American Motor Corp. (USARMY)
    Nha Trang Area Exchange
    APO 96240

11. American Medical Assoc. (USAID)
    217 Hong Bang, Cholon

12. American Power Jet Co. (USARMY)
    APO 96307

13. American Trade Development Co. (USAID)
    7 Nguyen Tri Phuong, Cholon

14. Amtraco Construction Corp. (USNAVY)
    44/8 Ngo Duc Ke, Saigon

15. A.P. Norman Corp. (USNAVY)
    c/o Oriental Hotel
    36 Le Loe, Saigon

16. Applied Technical Services Inc. (USARMY)
    524 Thanh Thai, Cholon

17. Applied Technology/Div. of Itek Corp (USAF)
    Box 7102, APO 96307

18. Asia Napping Inc. (OICC)
    207 Hien Vuong, Saigon

19. Asia Pacific Fargo (OICC)
    40-B Dang Dung, Saigon

20. Asian International Laboratories, Inc. (USAID)

21. Associated American Engineering Overseas,
    Inc. (OICC)
    28 Le Quy Don, Saigon

22. Atlantic Towing Ltd. (OICC)
    66 Tu Do, Saigon

23. AVCO/Lycoming Division (USARMY)
    34th Gen. Spt. Gp. (AMS)
    APO 96309

24. Bank of America (Military Banking Facility)
    26-36 Phan Van Dat
    Box 30, APO 96243

25. Bekins Airvan Company (USAF)
    26-28 Ham Nghi, Saigon

26. Bell Helicopter Co. (USARMY)
    251/6 Cach Mang, Saigon

27. Bendix Field Engineering Corp. (USAF)
    A-2 Lu Gia, Phu Tho

28. Booz Alen Applied Research Inc.
    4-B Ben Bach Dang, Saigon

29. Boo Hung Sa (USARMY)
    8 Tran Quy Khoach
    Tan Dinh, Saigon

30. Brandford Tailors (USARMY)
    20 Phju Kiet, Saigon

31. Braniff International (USAF)
    616th MASS (MAC) Tan Son Nhut

32. Canadian Marconi Co. (USARMY)
    34th General Support Group (AM&S)
    APO 96307

33. Caribe Diamond Works (USARMY)
    c/o Cholon Main Exchange
    APO 96243

34. Central Navigation & Trading Co.
    29 Yen Do, Saigon

35. Certeza Cko. (OICC)
    30 Nguyen Cu Trinh, Saigon

36. Chase Manhattan Bank (Military Banking
    Facility)
    Box 20, APO 96243

37. Chilyang Shipping Co. (OICC)
    110 Hai Ba Trung, Saigon

38. China Air Lines (USEMBASSY)

39. Chrysler Motor (USARMY)
    c/o Cholon Main Exchange
    APO 96243

40. Chuong IL Express (USARMY)
    349 Tran Quy Cap, Saigon

41. Climate International Co. (RMK)
    2 Truong Quoc Dung, Saigon

42. Collins Radio Co. (OICC)
    c/o RMK/BRJ
    12 Thong Nhut, Saigon

43. Columbia Export Packers, Inc. (USARMY)
    12 Cong Ly, Saigon

44. Columbia Scientific Corp. (OICC)
    RMK/BRJ District V - Code 010.5
    APO 96143

45. Commowealth Associates Inc. (USAID)
    c/o USAID ENG/EP
    Saigon

46. Commowealth Services, Inc. (USAID)
    c/o Majestic Hotel
    Saigon

47. Compania De Vanegacion Arrojo S.A. (OICC)
    278-A Cong Ly, Saigon

48. Computer Sciences Corp. (USARMY)
    179 Gia Long, Saigon

49. Connell Brothers Co. (USAF)

50. Continental Air Lines Inc. (USAF)
    616th MA Spt Sqn, APO 96307

51. Continental Air Services Inc. (OICC)
    c/o Air Vietnam
    P.O. Box 1541, Saigon

52. Control Data Corp. (OICC)
    d176 Hai Ba Trung, Saigon

53. Cook & McFarland Inc. (USARMY)
    227 Phan Thanh Gian, Saigon

54. Dae Lim Industrial Co., Ltd. (OICC)
    116 Tran Quy Cap, Saigon

55. Daniel, Mann, Johnson & Mendenhall (USAF)
    3 Ho Van Nga, Saigon

56. Data Systems Div. (USARMY)
    Litton Systems Inc.
    Litton Industries
    Hq, ACTIV, APO 96386

57. Dayele Yanghaeng Co., Ltd. (USARMY)
    93-Ter Hung Vuong, Thi Nghe

58. Decca Navigator System, Inc. (USARMY)
    P.O. Box P-12, Saigon

59. Degill Corp. (USAID)
    93-95 Ham Ngni, Saigon

60. Dillingham Overseas (OICC)
    c/o Dredge L.B. Dilingham, RVN

61. Dynalectron Corp. (USAF)
    c/o USAF, APO 96307

62. Eastern Construction Co., Inc. (USAID)
    204 Su Van Hanh, Saigon

63. Education Consultants, Ltd. (USAID)
    203 Vo Tanh Noi Dai,
    Tan Son Hoa, Gia Dinh

64. Electronic Specialty Co. (USAF)
    6 Huynh Quang Tien, Saigon

65. Elliget Enterprises Inc. (USARMY)
    60 Duy Tan, Saigon

66. Engbuild International Inc. (USARMY)
    227 Phan Thanh Gian
    Saigon

67. Equipment Inc. (USARMY)
    P.O. Box 705, Saigon

68. Eurpac Service Inc. (USARMY)
    21 Phan Thanh Gian, Saigon

69. EVCO Sales Co. (USARMY)
    P.O. Box 888, Saigon

70. Everett Steamship Corp.
    20 Nguyen Hue, Saigon

71. Far East Enterprises Inc. (USARMY)
    160 Hien Vuong, Saigon

72. Fischbach & Moore, Inc. (RMK)
    c/o RMK/BRJ, 12 Thong Nhut, Saigon

73. Fisher Radio International Inc. (USARMY)
    P.O. Box 43, Saigon

74. Five Star Photo (USARMY)
    314/3 Phan Thanh Gian, Saigon

75. FMA Inc.
    MAC-V J2, CDEC
    APO 96222

76. Ford Military Sales (USARMY)
    29 Le Loi, Saigon

77. Foremost Dairies
    30 Thong Nhut, Saigon

78. Frederic R. Harris, Inc. (OICC)
    77 Ly Tran Quan, Saigon

79. Fridden Inc. (USARV)
    c/o L.U.C.I.A.
    35 Le Loi, Saigon

80. General Dynamics/Convair (USARMY)
    1st RR Co. (AUN)
    APO 96312

81. General Electric Co. (USARMY)
    370 Tran Quy Cap, Saigon

82. General Electric Services Co. (USARMY)
    Hqs., MAC-V, Tan Son Nhut

83. General Motors (USARMY)
    131 Nguyen Hue, Saigon

84. General Services Co. (USARMY)
    36/7 Lam Son, Gia Dinh

85. Goodyear Aerospace Corp. (USARMY)
    Hq Pacific Air Forces
    APO 96553

86. Greenich International (USARMY)
    OSD/ARPA RDFV/V
    4A Ben Bach Dang, Saigon

87. Grumman Aircraft Engineering Corp. (RMK)
    c/o 73rd Aviation Co. (AS)
    APO 96291

88. Gustav Hirsch Organization (USARMY)
    P.O. Box 87, Saigon

89. Hallmark Card Co. (USARMY)
    400/6 Truong Minh Giang, Saigon

90. Han Jin Transportation Co. (USARMY)
    97-A Nguyen Du, Saigon

91. Harent Inc. (USARMY-USAF)
    38 Tran Khanh Du, Dakao
    Saigon

92. Harilela's (USARMY)
c/o Cholon Main Exchange
APO 96243

93. Hawaiian Dredging Co. (USAID)
56 Duy Tan, Saigon

94. Hay & Son (USARMY)
123 Phan Thanh Gian, Saigon

95. Holmes & S. Narver, Inc. (USAID)
2-B Nguyen Hhuy tu, Dakao
Saigon

96. House of Adler, Inc. (USARMY)
c/o Cholon Main Exchange
APO 96243

97. Hughes Tool Co. (USAF)
Hqs., 34th Gen Spt. Gp (AMS)
APO 96307

98. HRB-Singer Inc. (USAF)
Hq 7AF, 6470 RTS, Compass/Eagle
(Attn: HRB-Singer)
Tan Son Nhut, AB

99. Hughes Aircraft Co. (USARMY)
Phu Lam Sig Bns,
SATCOM Station

100. Hugo Neu Corp. (USARMY)
c/o Caravelle Hotel
Saigon

101. Hycon Mfg. Co. (USAF)
OL-20-96227
Bien Hoa

102. Hydrotecnic Corp. (USAID)
35 Le Loi, Saigon

103. Hyun Dai Construction Co. (OICC)
11 Dang Duc Sieu, Saigon

104. Information System Co (OICC)
126-A Truong Minh Giang, Saigon

105. Intermarine Co., Ltd. (RMK)
B.P. M-17, Saigon

106. International Air Services (USAID)
87 Le Van Duyet, Saigon

107. International Business Machine Corp. (USAF)
7AF, Box J-37 (IDHS)
APO 96307

108. International Dairy Engineering Company of
Asia (OICC)
176 Hai Da Trung, Saigon

109. International Drilling, Inc.
231/D Truong Minh Ky, Phu Nhuan
Saigon

110. International Industrial Co. (USAID)
52 Doan Nhu Hai, Saigon

111. International Recreation Assoc. (USAID)
32 Nguyen Hue, Saigon

112. International Rescue Committee, Inc. (USAID)
c/o USAID, Saigon

113. International Voluntary Services (USAID)
348 Le Van Duyet Noi Dai
Saigon

114. James S. Lee & Co. (USARMY)
290 Pestrus Ky, Cholon

115. John I. Thompson Co. (OICC)
176 Hai Ba Trung, Saigon

116. Joint Commission on Rural Reconstruction
(USAID)
87 Le Van Duyet, Saigon

117. K.B. Kim & Co. (USARMY)
61 Yen Do, Saigon

118. Keang Nam Ent., Ltd. (OICC)
Room 222, Tax Building
135 Nguyen Hue, Saigon

119. Kentron Hawaii, Ltd. (USAF)
6468th AB Wing (BIM/B)
APO 96553

120. Kim Yong Protrait (USARMY)
19 Doan Thi Diem, Saigon

121. Kokusai Kogyo., Ltd. (OICC)
P.O. Box 328, Saigon

122. Kong Fong Ent. Co., Ltd. (OICC)
212 Cong Ly, Saigon

123. Korea Development Corp. (USAID)
314/3 Phan Thanh Gian, Saigon

124. Korea Express - Keangnam Co., Ltd.
(USNAVY)
47 Bui Thi Xuan, Saigon

125. Korean Medical Team (USAID)
87 Le Van Duyet, Saigon

126. Kuk-Dong Enterprise Corp. (USARMY)
611/2 Phan Thanh Gian, Saigon

127. Kukje-Kunyang Co., Ltd. (USARMY)
407/22 Truong Minh Giang. Saigon

128. Kwang Hak Optical Co., Ltd. (USARMY)
57 Tran Nhat Duat, Saigon

129. Lam Brothers Corp. (USARMY)
92 Chi Lang, Gia Dinh

130. R. B. Landis Brothers & Co. Inc.
216 Hien Vuong, Saigon

131. Lear Siegler Service, Inc (OICC)
170 Gia Long, Saigon

132. Lee's Leatherware Corp. (USARMY)
290 Nguyen Hoang, Cholon

133. Leo A. Daly Co. (OICC)
251/10 Cach Mang, Saigon

134. Ling Temco Vought Electrosystems Inc.
(USARMY)
224th Avn. Bn. (RR)s
APO 96307

135. Lockheed Aircraft Corp. (USARMY)
Tan Son Nhut,
APO 96307

136. Lockheed Electronic Co. (USARMY)
Metuchen, New Jersey 08804

137. Lockheed Missiles & Space Co. (USAF)
OSD/ARPA
4-A Ben Bach Dang. Saigon

138. Luzon Stevedoring Co. (USARMY)
c/o Transmar
12 Cong Ly, Saigon

139. Lyon Associates Inc. (OICC)
207 Hien Vuong, Saigon

140. Manning Corp. (USARMY)
33 Le Loi, Saigon

141. McDonnell Douglas Corp. (USAF)
460th TRW
APO 96307

142. Metcalf & Eddy Inc. (OICC)
176 Hai Ba Trung, Saigon

143. M.W.K. International (USAID)
22 Nguyen Hue, Saigon

144. Modern Service Co. (USARMY)
358/5 Phan Thanh Gian, Saigon

145. Motorola Communications International
(USAF)
Bldg. 1123, Tan Son Nhut AB

146. Nambang Jinheung Co., Ltd. (USARMY)]
145/6 Hien Vuong, Saigon

147. National Rural Electric Cooperative Assoc.
(USAID)
87 Le Van Duyet, Saigon

148. Nishimure Shokai Co. Inc. (USARMY)
92 Chi Lang, Gia Dinh

149. Noor's Plaque & Engraving (USAF)
2nd Bde Task Force P.X.
1st Inf. Div.
APO Di An, Vietnam

150. Northwest Airlines Inc. (USAF)
616th Mil. Airlift Spt. Sqdn
APO 96307

151. Ocedan Science & Engineer (OICC)
195 Nguyen Thai Hoc, Saigon

152. Ohio University (USAID)
97 Hong Thap Tu, Saigon

153. Pacific Aircon, Inc. (USARMY)
269/1C Truong Minh Ky, Phu Nhuan

154. Pacific Architects & Engineers, Inc. (USARMY)
135 Nguyen Hue, Saigon

155. Pacific News Agency (USARMY)
P.O. Box 1525, Saigon

156. Pacific Technical Analysts, Inc. (USARMY)
153 Hai Ba Trung, Saigon

157. Pan American World Airways (MAC) (USAF)
23 Ngo Duc Ke, Saigon

158. Page Communications Engineering, Inc.
(USARMY)
98 Tran Quang Khai, Saigon

159. Peril Triumph (OICC)
179 Truong Minh Giang, Saigon

160. Philco Ford Corp. (USAID)
96 Nguyen Huynh Duc, Saigon

161. Planning Research Corp. (USAF)
OSD/ARPA
4-A Ben Bach Dang, Saigon

162. Pope Evens & Robbins International, Ltd.
(OICC)
179 Truong Minh Giang, Saigon

163. Quinton Engineers, Ltd. (OICC)
251/1 Cach Mang, Saigon

164. Rank Xerox Ltd. (OICC)
85B Cao Thang, Saigon

165. Raymond, Morrison, & Knudsen-
Brown, Root & Jones. (RMK-BRJ) (OICC)
2 Duy Tan, Saigon (Joint Venture)

166. Raytheon Co. (USARMY)
USAECOM, APO 96375

167. RCA Service Co. (USARMY)
Data Service Center
Hq USARV 96384

168. R.M. Towill Corp. (OICC)
30 Nguyen Cu Trinh, Saigon

169. Research Analysis Corp. (USAID)
OSD/ARPA
4-A Ben Bach Dang, Saigon

170. Retired Servicemen Engineering Agency
(USAID)
20 Bui Thi Xuan, Saigon

171. Rosa M. Sigua Engineering Corp. (OICC)
94 Le Dai Hanh, Phu Tho, Cholon

172. Roscoe Moss Company (OICC)
104 Bui Thi Xuan, Saigon

173. Rusty's Florist (USARMY)
c/o Cholon Main Exchange
APO 96243

174. Saehan Laboratories (USARMY)
33 Yersin, Saigon

175. Sam Whan Enterprise Co., Ltd. (OICC)
81 Nguyen Cu Trinh, Saigon

176. Sanders Associates (USAF)
Box 5342
APO 96307

177. Sang Woo Tailor (USARMY)
2 Tan Thanh, Saigon

178. Sarl Elwectronics (USARMY)
P.O.Box 957, Saigon

179. Sarvis-Webco Company (USARMY)
96 Hong Thap Tu, Saigon

180. SAX Overseas (E.K.) Ltd. (USARMY)
193 Dong Khanh, Cholon

181. Seabe Inc. (USARMY)
274 Le Van Duyet, Saigon

182. Sea Land Services, Inc. (USNAVY)
181 Tran Hung Dao, Saigon

183. Seatrain Lines Inc. (USNAVY)
30-32 Pasteur, Saigon

184. Siberian Fur Store (USARMY)
313 Nguyen Trai, Cholon

185. Sikorsky Aircraft (USAF)
Air Force Adv. Gp. (MME)
APO 96307

186. Stromberg Carlson Corp. (USARMY)
36/235/1 Cach Mang, Saigon

187. Southern Illinois University/ETT (USAID)
87 Le Van Duyet, Saigon

188. Southern Air Transport, Inc. (USAF)
c/o 616th MASS (MAC)
APO 96307

189. Space Age Engineering, Inc.
32 Ngo Thoi Nhiem, Saigon

190. Stainless Processing Co. (USARMY)
65 Cong Ly, Saigon

191. Standard Dredging Co. (OICC)
c/o Dredge "JAMICA BAY", RVN

192. Star Distributing (USARMY)
203/3 Vo Tanh, Gia Dinh

193. Star Laundry, Inc. (USARMY)
106/108 Hung Vuong, Saigon

194. Suk Kwang Photo Service (USARMY)
P.O. Box 1575, Saigon

195. Summit Industrial Corp. (USAF)
c/o Motorola Corp.
USAF, APO 96307

196. Summer Institute of Linguistics (USAID)
5 Suong Nguyet Anh, Saigon

197. Swager Tower Corp. (USARMY - USAF)
AFVN - Swager Tower Corp.
APO 96309

198. Systems Development Corp. (USAF)
CSD/ARPA
4- Ben Bach Dang, Saigon

199. Taiwan Power Company (USAID)
87 Le Van Duyet, Saigon

200. Techdata, Ltd. (OICC)
P.O. Box 970, Saigon

201. Tectonics Asia A & E Inc. (OICC)
70 Cach Mang, Saigon

202. Texas Instruments (USAF)
Tan Son Nhut, APO 96307

203. The Autometrics-Raytheon Co. (USAF)
Hq. 7AF, 6470 RTS, Compass/Eagle
(Attn: Autometrics-Raytheon)
Tan Son Nhut AB

204. The Boeing Company (USARMY)
2 Hoang Hoa Tham, Gia Dinh

205. The Bunker Ramo Corp. (USAF)
7th AF (DOS)
CMR Box 8176
APO 96307

206. The Flying Tiger Line Inc. (USAF)
Room 22, Terminal Building
Tan Son Nhut Airport, Saigon

207. The Ralph M. Parsons Co. (OICC)
30 Nguyen Cu Trinh, Saigon

208. The Rand Corp. (USAF)
176 Pasteur, Saigon

209. The Simulmatics Corp. (USAF)
1 Tran Qui Khoach, Tan Dinh, Saigon

210. The United Seamen's Services, Inc.
c/o Military Sea Transportation Service Office
(MSTS)
APO 96243

211. Three Eagles Company (USARMY)
414 Minh Mang, Cholon

212. Ticort Enterprises, Inc. (USAF)
590-A Vo Di Nguy, Phu Nhuan

213. Tippetts, Abbett, McCarthy, Stratton (OICC)
Hq. MAC-V (Directorate of Construction)
APO 96222

214. Tong Jin Enterprises (USARMY)
P.O. 1481, Saigon

215. Trans Asia Engineering Assoc., Inc. (OICC)
196 Cong Ly, Saigon

216. Trans World Airlines (MAC) (USAF)
c/o Civil Air Transport
Tan Son Nhut Airport

217. Triumph Development Corp. (OICC)
112-114 Hai Ba Trung, Saigon

218. Univac Div., Sperry Rand Corp. (USAF)
Hq 7th AF (DMSM, Box J-36)
APO 96307

219. University of Maryland/Far East Division
(USAF)
c/o Army Education Center
53rd GS Gp.
APO 96291

220. Vidihome International (USARMY
c/o Caravelle Hotel, Saigon

221. Viet Han Trading Co., Ltd. (USARMY)
74 Cong Ly, Saigon

222. Vietnam Regional Exchange (PACEXs)
APO 96243

223. Vinnel Corp. (USARMY)
23 Gia Long, Saigon

224. Western Electric Co., Inc. (USARMY)
P.O. Box 5495
APO 96307

225. Western Truck & Equipment Co. (USARMY)
c/o Foreign Excess Sales Office, Vietnam
APO 96307

226. Western Union (USARMY)
70 Tu Do, Saigon

227. Westinghouse Electric Corp. (USARMY)
336th Armed Hel. Co.
APO 96227

228. World Airways, Inc. (USAF)
Hanger B,
Tan Son Nhut Airport

229. World Rehabilitation Fund (USAID)
70 Ba Huyen Thanh Quan, Saigon

230. World Wide Consultants Inc. (OICC)
35 Han Thuyen, Saigon

231. World Wide Travel (USARMY)
Phat Hanh Building
66 Nguyen Hue, Saigon